Rethinking Globalism

GLOBALIZATION
Series Editors
Manfred B. Steger
Illinois State University and University of Hawai'i, Manoa
and
Terrell Carver
University of Bristol

"Globalization" has become *the* buzzword of our time. But what does it mean? Rather than forcing a complicated social phenomenon into a single analytical framework, this series seeks to present globalization as a multidimensional process constituted by complex, often contradictory interactions of global, regional, and local aspects of social life. Since conventional disciplinary borders and lines of demarcation are losing their old rationales in a globalizing world, authors in this series apply an interdisciplinary framework to the study of globalization. In short, the main purpose and objective of this series is to support subject-specific inquiries into the dynamics and effects of contemporary globalization and its varying impacts across, between, and within societies.

Globalization and Culture
Jan Nederveen Pieterse

Rethinking Globalism
Edited by Manfred B. Steger

Forthcoming in the Series

Globalization and American Empire
Kiichi Fujiwara

Globalization and Terrorism
Jamal R. Nassar

Globalizational and International Political Economy
Mark Rupert and M. Scott Solomon

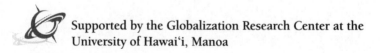 Supported by the Globalization Research Center at the University of Hawai'i, Manoa

RETHINKING GLOBALISM

Edited By
MANFRED B. STEGER

ROWMAN & LITTLEFIELD PUBLISHERS, INC.
Lanham • Boulder • New York • Toronto • Oxford

ROWMAN & LITTLEFIELD PUBLISHERS, INC.

Published in the United States of America
by Rowman & Littlefield Publishers, Inc.
A wholly owned subsidiary of The Rowman & Littlefield Publishing Group, Inc.
4501 Forbes Boulevard, Suite 200, Lanham, MD 20706
www.rowmanlittlefield.com

P.O. Box 317, Oxford OX2 9RU, UK

British Library Cataloguing in Publication Information Available

Library of Congress Cataloging-in-Publication Data Available

ISBN 0-7425-2544-9 (cloth : alk. paper)
ISBN 0-7425-2545-7 (pbk. alk. paper)

Printed in the United States of America

∞ ™ The paper used in this publication meets the minimum requirements of
American National Standard for Information Sciences—Permanence of Paper
for Printed Library Materials, ANSI/NISO Z39.48-1992.

CONTENTS

ACKNOWLEDGMENTS

This volume was handcrafted to outline the major lines of inquiry for Rowman & Littlefield's new *Globalization* series, edited by myself and Terrell Carver. *Globalization* is designed as a highly accessible, reader-friendly collection of books aimed at introducing a large readership to the emerging field of globalization studies. This series would have never seen the light of day without the persistent and generous support of the Globalization Research Center (GRC) at the University of Hawai'i–Manoa. Established in 1998, the GRC is a member of the Globalization Research Network (GRN), a consortium of four research centers, including the University of South Florida, the University of California, Los Angeles, and George Washington University. The GRN seeks to promote interdisciplinary, international, and global studies of pressing problems facing humanity and investigate causes, arguments, and alternatives to present trends and relationships within the phenomena of globalization.

I want to thank the staff members of the GRC, particularly James White, its associate director, and Barry Gills, its former director, for their kind assistance. Special thanks go to Deane Neubauer, the executive director of the GRN, whose support was crucial for getting the series off the ground. Yvonne Yamashita, director of the Conference Center at the University of Hawai'i–Manoa, did a superb job as the principal budget administrator of various international conferences and lectures organized by the GRC that stimulated the development of this series. My dear friend Franz Broswimmer, a research specialist at the GRC and author of *Ecocide*, an insightful study of globalization and ecology, deserves much credit for his constant words of encouragement and his competent professional advice.

I also want to express my gratitude to the contributors to this anchor volume for their genuine engagement and brilliant insights. Writing in accessible, engaging prose, these scholars consider themselves critical globalization theorists who seek to provide readers with a better understanding of discrepancies between globalist claims and actually existing material conditions. It has been a pleasure working with them on this project. Furthermore, I appreciate the consistent support I have received from Illinois State University in pursuit of my research agenda. In particular, I am much indebted to Jamal Nassar, chair of the Department of Politics and Government, and my colleagues Lane Crothers, Carlos Parodi, and Ali Riaz for their unwavering academic and emotional support. Ken Panfilio, my graduate assistant, deserves special thanks for his many contributions to this project, particularly his intellectual creativity and technical expertise.

Both this anchor volume and the entire series have been truly blessed with the involvement of Jennifer Knerr, executive editor at The Rowman & Littlefield Publishing Group, and Renee Legatt, Jennifer's gifted assistant editor. Jennifer is one of those rare intellects who, in a seemingly effortless way, manages to solve even the most difficult problems. Finally, as always, I want to thank my wife, Perle Besserman, for her constant feedback as well as her shared enthusiasm for this project.

INTRODUCTION: RETHINKING THE IDEOLOGICAL DIMENSIONS OF GLOBALIZATION

Manfred B. Steger

After more than a decade of intense scholarly scrutiny, "globalization" remains a hotly contested and surprisingly slippery concept. In spite of the remarkable proliferation of research programs for the study of globalization, academics are still divided on the utility of various methodological approaches, the value of available empirical evidence for gauging the extent, impact, and direction of globalization, and, of course, its normative implications. The failure to arrive at a broad scholarly consensus on the subject not only attests to the contentious nature of academic inquiry in general but also reflects the uneven, contradictory, and ambiguous nature of the phenomenon itself. As Fredric Jameson astutely points out, there seems to be little utility in forcing such a complex social force as globalization into a single analytic framework.[1]

The persistence of academic divisions on these issues notwithstanding, it would be intellectually dishonest not to acknowledge some emerging points of agreement. In particular, the last few years have witnessed a noticeable convergence of scholarly views on the following five views: (1) globalization is actually occurring, (2) globalization can be defined in terms of certain characteristics, (3) globalization is a long-term historical process that, over many centuries, has crossed distinct qualitative thresholds, (4) representations of

1

the "global" require multiple geographical scales, (5) currently dominant economic and technological approaches must be complemented by sustained explorations of the political, cultural, and ideological dimensions of globalization. Let me offer a few brief comments on each of these common themes.

With regard to the first point, it has become increasingly evident in recent years that neither so-called hyperglobalizers nor globalization skeptics have offered convincing arguments for their respective views. While the skeptics' insistence on a more careful and precise usage of the term has forced the participants in the globalization debates to hone their analytic skills, their wholesale rejection of globalization as a "vacuous concept" has often served as a convenient excuse (usually offered in the name of "analytic precision") to avoid dealing with the actual phenomenon itself. Today many scholars acknowledge the existence of significant worldwide social processes that can be appropriately subsumed under the general term "globalization." Rather than construct overarching "grand narratives" of globalization, however, many researchers have instead wisely opted for modest methodological middle-range approaches designed to provide specific explanations of particular manifestations of globalization.

Moreover, as a number of contributors to this volume emphasize, the skeptical claim that globalization does not constitute a truly global dynamic appears to be wedded too rigidly to a narrow economistic understanding of the phenomenon. While it may be true that intense networks of economic globalization and integration have emerged only in particular geographic regions, it is nonetheless important to point out that certain political and cultural aspects of globalization appear to be truly "global" in their reach and impact.

As for the second point of agreement, most influential definitions of globalization foreground certain characteristics that are said to constitute the core of the phenomenon. These common elements are expressed in the following assertions: (1) globalization is not a single monolithic process but a *complex set* of often *conflicting* and *contradictory* social processes; (2) globalization involves the *creation* of new networks of social interconnections as well as the *multiplication, expansion, intensification,* and *acceleration* of existing social exchanges and activities; (3) the resulting "compression of time and space" is not merely an objective phenomenon but manifests itself on the subjective level of individual consciousness.

My own definition of globalization reflects this general consensus on the constitutive elements of the phenomenon: globalization refers to a multidimensional set of social processes that create, multiply, stretch, and intensify worldwide social interdependencies and exchanges while at the same time fostering in people a growing awareness of deepening connections between the local and the distant.[2] It must be emphasized, however, that many researchers also believe that the identification of these general characteristics is a necessary but not sufficient step in developing a better understanding of the nature and direction of globalization.

Third, globalization researchers have increasingly turned toward historical issues, raising, in particular, the question of whether globalization is primarily a modern phenomenon or a process that has been unfolding for millennia. Globalization research in the early 1990s tended to emphasize the novelty of the phenomenon, often dating its origins to the 1960s and 1970s.[3] In recent years, however, the prevailing view on this question has shifted in a direction more weighted toward the longevity of these processes while at the same time recognizing that globalization has undergone dramatic changes and qualitative leaps at certain points in history. As a result, new periodization efforts have yielded revised chronologies that tend to eschew conventional Eurocentric historical narratives and instead present globalization not merely as a linear, diffusionist process starting in the West in the 1970s (or the late nineteenth century or the early sixteenth century) but as a multinodal, multidirectional dynamic full of unanticipated surprises, violent twists, sudden punctuations, and dramatic reversals.[4]

Fourth, scholars increasingly realize the dangers of conceptualizing globalization processes according to rigidly nested geographical scales that separate the "global" from the "national" or the "local." Led by political geographers like Kevin Cox and sociologists like Roland Robertson, this crucial process of rethinking historically contingent categories of spatiality has begun to yield new insights into the partial embeddedness of the global in the national and local, and vice-versa. Saskia Sassen, for instance, has argued that the emerging discipline of globalization studies requires methodologies and theorizations that engage not only global scalings but also national and sub-national scalings as components of global processes, thereby destabilizing conventional hierarchies of scale. As an example for the multiscalar character of various globalization processes, Sassen points to multiple cross-border networks of social activists engaged in specific localized struggles with an explicit or implicit global agenda mediated by global information technologies. The methodological implications of this growing recognition that structurations of the global exist inside the national and local are truly stunning: if the national and local are neither the opposite nor the equivalent of the global, then globalization researchers face the complex task of describing and analyzing interdependent geographies of power that defy old spatial hierarchies focused on the "nation" as *the* container category for social and political analysis.[5]

A fifth emerging point of loose agreement concerns the importance of presenting globalization as a multidimensional process. This implies, first, that an increasing number of globalization researchers recognize that conventional disciplinary borders and thematic lines of demarcation are losing their old rationales in a globalizing world. Hence, the application of various inter- and multidisciplinary frameworks to the study of globalization has become more common. Second, this strong emphasis on multidimensionality has led to a "cultural turn" in globalization studies. From its beginnings in the late 1980s, the fledgling field of globalization studies has been dominated by accounts focusing on economic and technological aspects of the phenomenon. To be sure, a proper recognition of the crucial role of economics and technology should be part of any comprehensive interpretation of globalization, but it is equally important to avoid the trap of technological and economic determinism. Fortunately, the burgeoning literature on various non-structural aspects of globalization attests to the growing recognition of the centrality of ideas, subjectivity, and symbolic exchanges in the current acceleration of globalization processes. As Malcolm Waters observes, the increasingly symbolically mediated and reflexive character of today's economic exchanges suggests that both the cultural and political arenas are becoming more activated and energetic.[6]

It is particularly with regard to this fourth issue that the present volume seeks to make its contribution. The anchor volume of a new series on globalization, this anthology presents globalization as a multidimensional process constituted by complex, often contradictory interactions of global, regional, and local aspects of social life. In particular, the chapters in this anthology provide a much needed analysis of the *global* production and *global* circulation of neoliberal market ideology and its ideological challengers. This focus on the global framework of such discursive formations is sorely missing in most existing studies of the ideological dimensions of globalization. The authors of this volume are united in their strong support of the following premise: globalization contains important discursive aspects in the form of ideologically charged narratives that put before the public a particular agenda of topics for discussion, questions to ask, and claims to make. The existence of these narratives suggests that globalization is not merely a set of material processes anchored in economics and technology, but also constitutes a plethora of stories that define, describe, and analyze these very processes.

Elsewhere, I have referred to the dominant rhetorical package of our time as "globalism"—a market ideology that endows current globalization processes with neoliberal norms, values, and meanings.[7] Given that this ideological talk about globalization in itself contributes to the development of a particular (neoliberal) form of the phenomenon, globalism demands critical analysis in its own right.

Globalism in the 1990s

During most of the last decade, the public interpretation of the origin, direction, and meaning of the profound social changes that go by the name "glob-

4

alization" fell disproportionately to a powerful phalanx of social forces sympathetic to the philosophical principles of the neoliberal Thatcher–Reagan revolution of the 1980s. Located mainly in the global north, these market ideologists consisted of corporate managers, executives of large transnational corporations, corporate lobbyists, journalists and public relations specialists, intellectuals writing to a large public audience, state bureaucrats, and politicians. Saturating the public with idealized images of a consumerist, free market world, these globalists simultaneously distorted social reality, legitimated and advanced their power interests, and shaped collective and personal identities. They marshaled their considerable resources to sell to the public the alleged benefits of market liberalization: rising global living standards, economic efficiency, individual freedom and democracy, and unprecedented technological progress. Globalists promised to "liberate" the economy from social constraints by such neoliberal policies as privatizing public enterprises, deregulating trade and industry, providing massive tax cuts, reducing public expenditures, and maintaining strict control of organized labor. Inspired by the liberal utopia of the "self-regulating market," globalists linked their quaint nineteenth-century ideals to fashionable "globalization talk." Thus globalism represented an impressive repackaging enterprise—the pouring of old philosophical wine into new ideological bottles.

During the 1990s, dozens of magazines, journals, newspapers, and electronic media fed their readers a steady diet of globalist claims. Indeed, the neoliberal discourse of globalization itself turned into an extremely important commodity destined for public consumption. Neoliberal decision makers became expert designers of an attractive ideological container for their political agenda. After all, their desired realization of a global market order depends on the construction of arguments and images that portray market globalization in a positive light. Analyzing countless utterances, speeches, and writings of globalism's most influential advocates, I identified five ideological claims that recur with great regularity throughout the globalist discourse.[8]

Globalization Is about the Liberalization and Global Integration of Markets

This claim is anchored in the neoliberal ideal of the self-regulating market as the normative basis for a future global order. Major newspapers and magazines disseminate countless statements that celebrate the "liberalization" of markets. Globalist voices present the liberalization and integration of global markets as "natural" phenomena that further individual liberty and material progress in the world. Presenting as "fact" what is actually a contingent political initiative, globalists seek to persuade the public that their neoliberal account of global-

5

ization represents an objective, or at least a neutral, diagnosis. To be sure, neoliberals offer some empirical evidence for the occurring liberalization of markets. But it is also the case that their globalist discourse contributes to the emergence of the very conditions it purports to analyze.

Globalization Is Inevitable and Irreversible

At first glance, the idea of the historical inevitability of globalization seems to be a poor fit for an ideology based on neoliberal principles. After all, throughout the twentieth century, liberals and conservatives consistently criticized Marxists for their determinist claims that devalue human free agency and downplay the ability of noneconomic factors to shape social reality. Yet globalists rely on a similar monocausal, economistic narrative of historical inevitability. According to the globalist interpretation, globalization reflects the spread of irreversible market forces driven by technological innovations that make the integration of national economies inevitable. The portrayal of globalization as some sort of natural force, like the weather or gravity, makes it easier for globalists to convince people that they must adapt to the discipline of the market if they are to survive and prosper. Hence the claim of its inevitability depoliticizes the public discourse about globalization. Neoliberal policies appear to be above politics because they simply carry out what is ordained by nature. This implies that, instead of acting according to a set of choices, people merely fulfill world-market laws that demand the elimination of government controls. Since nothing can be done about the natural movement of economic and technological forces, political groups ought to acquiesce and make the best of an unalterable situation. Resistance would be unnatural, irrational, and dangerous.

The claim that globalization is inevitable and irresistible is inscribed within a larger evolutionary discourse that assigns a privileged position to certain countries at the forefront of "liberating" markets from political control. Political scientist Francis Fukuyama, for example, insists that globalization is a euphemism that stands for the irreversible Americanization of the world.[9] And so it appears that globalist forces have been resurrecting the nineteenth-century paradigm of Anglo-American vanguardism propagated by the likes of Herbert Spencer and William Graham Sumner. The main ingredients of classical market liberalism are all present in globalism. We find inexorable laws of nature favoring Western civilization, the self-regulating economic model of perfect competition, the virtues of free enterprise, the vices of state interference, the principle of laissez faire, and the irreversible, evolutionary process leading up to the survival of the fittest.

6

Nobody Is in Charge of Globalization

Globalism's deterministic language offers yet another rhetorical advantage. If the natural laws of the market have indeed preordained a neoliberal course of history, then globalization does not reflect the arbitrary agenda of a particular social class or group. Globalists merely carry out the unalterable imperatives of a transcendental force. People aren't in charge of globalization; markets and technology are.

But globalists are right only in a formal sense. While there is no conscious conspiracy orchestrated by a single, evil force, it does not mean that nobody is in charge of globalization. The liberalization and integration of global markets does not proceed outside the realm of human choice. The globalist initiative to integrate and deregulate markets around the world both creates and sustains asymmetrical power relations. Backed by the powerful countries of the Northern Hemisphere, international institutions like the World Trade Organization (WTO), the International Monetary Fund (IMF), and the World Bank enjoy the privileged position of making and enforcing the rules of the global economy. In return for supplying much needed loans to developing countries, the IMF and the World Bank demand from their creditors the implementation of neoliberal policies that further the material interests of the First World.

Like the rhetoric of historical inevitability, the idea that nobody is in charge seeks to depoliticize the public debate on the subject and thus demobilize antiglobalist movements. The deterministic language of a technological progress driven by uncontrollable market laws turns political issues into scientific problems of mere administration. Once large segments of the population have accepted the globalist image of a self-directed juggernaut that simply runs its course, it becomes extremely difficult to challenge neoliberal policies. As ordinary people cease to believe in the possibility of choosing alternative social arrangements, globalism gains even more strength in its ability to construct passive consumer identities.

Globalization Benefits Everyone

This claim lies at the very core of globalism because it provides an affirmative answer to the crucial normative question of whether globalization should be considered a "good" or a "bad" thing. Globalists frequently connect their arguments to the alleged benefits resulting from market liberalization: rising global living standards, economic efficiency, individual freedom, and unprecedented technological progress. But what about mounting evidence suggesting that income disparities between nations are actually widening at a quicker pace than ever before in recent history? While globalists typically acknowledge the existence of unequal global distribution patterns, they nonetheless insist that the market itself will eventually correct these "irregularities." According to this narrative, such "episodic dislocations" are necessary "in the short run," but they will eventually give way to "quantum leaps in productivity." However, globalists offer no concrete pointers as to when these leaps might actually occur.

Globalization Furthers the Spread of Democracy in the World

This globalist claim is rooted in the neoliberal assertion that free markets and democracy are synonymous terms. Persistently affirmed as "common sense," the actual compatibility of these concepts often goes unchallenged in the public discourse. Indeed this claim hinges on a conception of democracy that emphasizes formal procedures such as voting at the expense of the direct participation of broad majorities in political and economic decision making. This thin understanding of democracy reflects an elitist and regimented model of low-intensity market democracy that typically limits democratic participation to voting in elections. This ensures that those elected remain insulated from popular pressures and thus can govern "effectively."

In addition, the globalist claim that globalization furthers the spread of democracy in the world must contend with evidence that points in the opposite direction. Large transnational corporations (TNCs) often invest in developing countries that are not considered "free" according to generally accepted political rights and civil liberties standards. Why are powerful investors in the global north making these business decisions? For one, wages tend to be lower in authoritarian regimes than in democracies, giving businesses in dictatorships a monetary advantage in selling exports abroad. In addition, lower wages, bans on labor unions, and relaxed environmental laws give authoritarian regimes an edge in attracting foreign investment.

Rethinking Globalism

Throughout the 1990s, these five central claims of globalism constituted the foundation of the dominant discursive regime that bestowed public meaning on the process of globalization. Yet no single ideology ever enjoys absolute dominance. Widening gaps between ideological claims and people's actual experience ushered in a crisis for the dominant paradigm, and dissenting social groups found it easier to convey their countervision to the public. As the twentieth century drew to a close, massive antiglobalist demonstrations erupted in Seattle, Davos, Salzburg, Bangkok, Melbourne, Prague, Quebec City, Gothenburg and many other cities around the world. In August 2001, one of over 100,000 antiglobalist protestors taking to the streets of Genoa was shot to death by a young *carabinieri* belonging to the contingent of over 16,000 police and military troops employed to "guarantee the safety" of the G8 summit delegates. More antiglobalist protesters were killed that summer under similar circumstances in Ecuador and Papua New Guinea.

While still reigning supreme, globalism was nonetheless coming under sustained attack by social forces on both the political left and right. Previously marginalized or ignored, discourses on globalization circulating in the global south were beginning to penetrate the hegemonic northern debates. As a result, the ideological struggle over the meaning and the direction of globalization intensified even further. Then came the terrorist attacks of 9/11. Soon a seemingly perpetual War on Terror took center stage, and the globalists' anticipated *joys* of a borderless world turned into dark *fears* of a borderless world. The sudden confluence of these three factors—the cumulative impact of the antiglobalist movements, the importance of the debates on globalization occurring outside the "West," and the global ramifications of 9/11—produced a backlash scenario that was subjected to intense scrutiny by public commentators and academics alike.[10] The ideological dimensions of globalization, in particular, received special reconsideration.

In a celebrated address to a joint session of Congress nine days after the 9/11 terrorist attacks, U.S. President George W. Bush made it abundantly clear that the deep sources of the new conflict between the "the civilized world" and terrorism were to be found neither in religion nor culture, but in political ideology. By referring to the radical networks of terrorists and governments that support them as "heirs of all the murderous ideologies of the twentieth century,"[11] Bush rejected the idea of a "deideologized world" that had dominated the post-Soviet intellectual landscape. Advanced by Francis Fukuyama more than a decade ago, the "end of ideology" thesis postulated that the passing of Marxism-Leninism marked nothing less than the "end point of mankind's ideological evolution," evident in the total exhaustion of viable ideological alternatives to Western liberalism. Fukuyama explicitly downplayed the significance of rising religious fundamentalism and ethnic nationalism, predicting that the global triumph of the "Western idea" would be irreversible and unstoppable.[12]

History had proven Fukuyama wrong. The first decade of the twenty-first century was quickly becoming a teeming battlefield of clashing perspectives on the meaning and direction of globalization. Today globalism and its challengers are locked in a protracted struggle, in the process adjusting some ideological claims that no longer seem to fit the altered political landscape. While retaining some of its prominent features, free market globalism is currently being transformed into a new ideological formation in which central concepts like globalization, liberty, free markets, and free trade are being increasingly subordinated to and lumped together with the War on Terror led by a single hyperpower—the United States of America and its "allies," or satellite states. Tied to this global empire, the post-9/11 manifestation of globalism is more openly imperialistic and militaristic than its economistic predecessor. To sustain what I call "imperial globalism," military operations and ideological propaganda maneuvers have become as important as, or perhaps even more important than, global trade initiatives. Hence the post-9/11 framework contains a major ideological contradiction: social forces otherwise profiting from expanded global mobility and interchange must come to grips with necessary limitations on certain aspects of globalization.[13]

What does all this mean for the ideological dimensions of globalization? How are globalist (and antiglobalist) ideas and values being disseminated, received, and contested in the global north and south? What are the regional differences? What is the relationship between (anti)globalist ideology and material interests, socioeconomic structures, public policies, and various forms of cultural and religious expression? What are the likely future trajectories of the ideological confrontation between globalism and its challengers? Is there a viable antiglobalist camp? What strategies should antiglobalist dissenters opt for? How can antiglobalist forces develop a viable political vocabulary that articulates more egalitarian alternatives to globalism?

These are but a few of the questions that are raised by the contributors in this volume. For analytical purposes, I have divided the chapters into three parts. Part I is composed of chapters that explore various features and elements of the changing globalist discourse. Part II features contributions that examine central antiglobalist narratives and their evolving political projects. The chapters composing Part III introduce and evaluate perspectives on and critiques of the ideological dimensions of globalization that have emerged in regions of the world other than the hegemonic global north. To reiterate, Part III is particularly important because it presents a range of viewpoints on the subject that are often neglected in the Anglo-American literature on globalization.

Toward a Critical Theory of Globalization

The contributors to this volume are united in their conviction that globalization is an incipient process, slowly giving rise to new forms of globality whose eventual qualities and properties are far from being determined. Globalization is neither inevitable nor irreversible; it does not necessarily have to mean or to be what globalists say it means or is. However, such a skeptical posture toward the claims of globalism should not be interpreted as a blanket rejection of globalization. The central task for scholars committed to a study of the ideological dimensions of globalization lies in offering both the general public and the academic community thoughtful analyses and critiques of globalism, the dominant ideology of our time. In my view, such a project can hardly be sustained by a rigid adherence to an ethos of scientific detachment rooted in notions of "objectivity" and "value neutrality." It is one thing to acknowledge the obvious importance of academic integrity, careful scholarship, and empirical references, but it is quite another to consider the researcher's own values and beliefs solely as a hindrance to a proper "uncontaminated" understanding of social processes.

Hence, a "critical theory of globalization" is explicitly guided by a normative vision—the ideal of a more egalitarian and less violent global order. Critical globalization theorists seek to provide people with a better understanding of how dominant beliefs about globalization fashion their realities and how these ideas can be changed to bring about more equitable social arrangements. A critical theory of globalization interrogates ideological valorizations of asymmetrical power relations that benefit the few and increase the suffering of the many. As Douglas Kellner emphasizes, critical globalization theorists affirm choice, diversity, and democratic self-determination against forms of global domination and subordination.[14] Celebrating the noble human impulse to reflect on the validity and desirability of social institutions and their normative foundations, the contributors to this volume follow, in their own unique ways, in the intellectual footsteps of thinkers loosely associated with the famous Frankfurt Institute of Social Research, who, more than seven decades ago, developed "ideology critique" as a distinct form of social analysis and criticism dedicated to the exposure of the historical roots, assumptions, and interests of the various social forces served by ideology.

Notes

1. Fredric Jameson, preface to *The Cultures of Globalization,* ed. Fredric Jameson and Masao Miyoshi (Durham, N.C.: Duke University Press, 1998), xi–xii.

2. For a representative selection of influential definitions highlighting the same constitutive elements, see Manfred Steger, *Globalization: A Very Short Introduction* (Oxford: Oxford University Press, 2003), 10.

3. Perhaps the most extreme version of this view can be found in Kenichi Ohmae, *The Borderless World: Power and Strategy in the Interlinked World Economy* (New York: Harper Business, 1990).

4. See, for example, Steger, *Globalization,* chap. 2; David Held and Anthony McGrew, *Globalization/Anti-Globalization* (Cambridge: Polity, 2002), 6–7; Mohammed Bamyeh, *The Ends of Globalization* (Minneapolis: University of Minnesota Press, 2000); James H. Mittelman, *The Globalization Syndrome: Transformation and Resistance* (Princeton: Princeton University Press, 2000), 18–19; Andre Gunder Frank, *ReORIENT: Global Economy in the Asian Age* (Berkeley:

University of California Press, 1998); and Jared Diamond, *Guns, Germs, and Steel: The Fate of Human Societies* (New York: Norton, 1997).

5. See Saskia Sassen, "Globalization or Denationalization?," *Review of International Political Economy* 10, no. 1 (2003): 1–22. I am grateful to Saskia for pointing out to me the growing importance of the "scaling question" in globalization studies. For further discussions of this topic, see, for example, A. Amin, "Spatialities of Globalisation," *Environment and Planning* A34, no. 3 (2002): 385-99; and Kevin R. Cox, "Spaces of Dependence, Spaces of Engagement, and the Politics of Scale, or: Looking for Local Politics," *Political Geography* 17, no. 1 (1998): 1–23.

6. Malcolm Waters, *Globalization*, 2d ed. (London: Routledge, 2001), 24.

7. Manfred B. Steger, *Globalism: The New Market Ideology* (Lanham, Md.: Rowman & Littlefield Publishers, 2002).

8. For a detailed discussion of these claims, see Steger, *Globalism*, chap. 3.

9. Merrill Lynch, "Economic Globalization and Culture: A Discussion with Dr. Francis Fukuyama," *Globalization Forum*, www.ml.com/woml/forum/global2.htm (April 12, 2003).

10. For some such responses, see Ken Booth and Tim Dunne, eds., *Worlds in Collision: Terror and the Future of Global Order* (New York: Palgrave, 2002); Craig Calhoun, Paul Price, and Ashley Timmer, eds., *Understanding September11* (New York: Free Press, 2002); Fred Halliday, *Two Hours That Shook the World: September 11, 2001: Causes and Consequences* (London: Saqi, 2002); Peter Marcuse, "Really Existing Globalization after September 11," *Antipode*, September 2002, 633–41; Walter LaFeber, "The Post September 11 Debate over Empire, Globalization, and Fragmentation," *Political Science Quarterly* 117, no. 1 (2002): 1–17; Duncan Green and Matthew Griffith, "Globalization and Its Discontents," *International Affairs* 78, no. 1 (2002): 49–68; and Michael Mann, "Globalization and September 11," *New Left Review*, November-December 2001, 51–72.

11. George W. Bush, "Address to a Joint Session of Congress and the American People" [September 20, 2001], in J. W. Edwards and Louise DeRose, eds., *United We Stand: A Message for All Americans* (Ann Arbor, Mich.: Mundus, 2001), 13.

12. Francis Fukuyama, "The End of History?" *National Interest*, Summer 1989, 3–18.

13. See Marcuse, "Really Existing Globalization after September 11," 636.

14. Douglas Kellner, "Theorizing Globalization," *Sociological Theory*, November 2002, 301.

PART I
GLOBALISM

IDEOLOGIES AND THE
GLOBALIZATION AGENDA

James H. Mittelman

If ideology is a way of looking at the world that justifies or undermines an existing order, then contemporary globalization must be viewed from different observation points. For those who hold power and possess wealth, globalization is an *ideology of freedom* for expanding not only the world's bounty but also human potential. Those at the other end of the social hierarchy experience globalization as an *ideology of domination*, widening the divisions among humankind.

To varying degrees, these perspectives embrace a common element: recognition of a dynamic of inclusion and exclusion. For example, James Wolfensohn, president of the World Bank, presents a vision shared by diverse observers who are rethinking the core ideas of globalization: "Our challenge is to make globalization an instrument of opportunity and inclusion."[1] However, there is a tension between maintaining the dominant ideology and constructing counterideologies of globalization. Each current of ideology sets a different agenda—a broad program, not a detailed blueprint—for future world order. The objectives of this chapter are to identify these ideological clusters, delimit their varied globalization agendas, and critically evaluate them. It will be shown that complex ideologies of globalization are being reworked to fit a changing world order.

15

Approach

This chapter offers close textual analysis but does not explore the extent to which the evolved ideology and emergent counterideologies are actually embraced by the public in different contexts. Gauging latent ideologies of globalization would require empirical research—polling, interviewing, and surveys. In contrast, the emphasis here is on the transcripts of intellectual innovators. The focus is on ideological leadership in the sense that select ideas generated by intellectual visionaries are embodied in powerful institutions and transmitted through policy instruments. The ideas selected are never freestanding but are intimately related to political and material interests. When the outcome is an assertion of ideological hegemony, certain ideas become centerpieces of consensus, and consensus is more cost-effective than coercion. Reworking hegemony allows new ideas to gain salience.

The ideas inscribed in globalizing processes are implicated in the exercise of power. Thought and action—theory and practice—are bound together so as to constrain and facilitate the possibilities for social transformation. That said, ideological analysis helps decipher codes of domination, identify the fault lines of power, and disclose efforts to form representations of counterpower. An ideological approach is useful insofar as it offers insight into the contested agendas for globalization.

As indicated, there is no monolithic doctrine of globalization. Uncertainties abound, there are ambiguities within ambiguities, and domination exists within domination. The consensual aspects—the ideological tonic—of hegemony are uneven, in flux, and in need of constant maintenance. With contemporary globalization, organic intellectuals not only produce new ideas but also make or contest policy. In fact, intellectual participants in this process are linked in myriad formal and informal networks. These arrangements have a material dimension and may facilitate a broad, albeit uneven consensus.[2] Thus, in their respective and sometimes intersecting networks, organic intellectuals are not univocal but share basic values.

Within this range, a main axis is between the ideas framed at the center in North America and Europe and those at the margins. A heuristic that facilitates the examination of fluid blends, not a dichotomy, this distinction is only partly place based and may be grasped in terms of the social relations of power. There are varied axes within the center and at the margins. While making allowance for these entanglements, it is clear that the view of globalization from the top substantially differs from the perspectives at the bottom. The late Claude Ake, one of Africa's leading intellectuals, presented a view from below: "Marginalization is in reality the dynamics of globalization."[3] Indeed, the ideological thrust of globalization is begetting counterthrusts, albeit in embryonic forms. To explore these tendencies, I will first examine the core ideas embedded in the dynamics of neoliberal globalization and the extent to which they are implicated in public discourses.

The Core Ideas

A promiscuous concept, globalization may be best understood as a historical transformation marked by an increasing loss of control in the economic, political, and cultural spheres, especially at the national and local levels. There are, of course, major differences in regard to the structural positions of diverse actors in regard to the extent of this erosion. In all instances, however, a loss of control does not in any sense mean that there are no mechanisms of control.[4]

Contemporary globalization is also about neoliberalism—heightened integration in the world economy. As the *Financial Times* put it: "[Neoliberal] globalisation is merely the free market system on an international scale." Further, "the key is competition. . . . [Neoliberal globalisation] remains perhaps the most effective tool we have to make the world not just more prosperous, but also a freer and more peaceful place."[5] In another formulation, Robert Gilpin, a political economist, weighs the views of the proponents of a neoliberal world economy and their critics who fear the consequences of market domination, and then he advances his own position: "American political and security interests as well as economic interests are served by a united world economy."[6]

Rooted in classical political economy, neoliberalism may be traced to Adam Smith and others in this tradition. In the twentieth century, the free market theories pioneered by philosopher-economist Friedrich von Hayek and his students, including Milton Friedman at the University of Chicago, provided the intellectual underpinnings for the radical agendas of Margaret Thatcher and Ronald Reagan. These leaders propagated the neoliberal values of free markets, individualism, consumerism, competitiveness, efficiency, and self-aggrandizement. They engineered the ideological shift from national Keynesianism to neoliberal globalization, and presented neoliberalism as the generator of material well-being and rising productivity as the solution to social ills.[7] Emphasis was accorded to opening the market, not protecting society. Since the public sector does not compete for profits or market share, its scope, especially social spending, had to be downsized. A policy framework emerged to institute neoliberal ideas, with deregulation, liberalization, and privatization as its bedrock features.

A set of organizing institutions bundles neoliberalism and globalization, and seeks to universalize the core ideas. Among these diverse institutions are the media, the lecture circuit, schools, and universities, with business faculties being key to developing and disseminating neoliberal ideas. MBA programs serve as vital mechanisms in the transnational spread of a distinctive combination of values and hence for the emergence of a common ideological framework among policymakers in divers countries. Indeed, many MBA-toting ministers and senior bureaucrats around the world have been trained in neoclassical economics at leading universities in the United States.

Also important in promoting a single dominant way of thinking about the world are bilateral and multilateral agencies, especially the World Trade Organization (WTO), the World Bank, and the International Monetary Fund (IMF). Testimony to the interests served by international financial institutions is provided by Zbigniew Brzezinski, national security adviser to former President Jimmy Carter:

> one must consider as part of the American system of the global web of specialized organizations, especially the "international" financial institutions. The International Monetary Fund (IMF) and the World Bank can be said to represent "global" interests, and their constituency may be construed as the world. In reality, however, they are heavily American dominated and their origins are traceable to American initiative, particularly the Bretton Woods Conference of 1944.[8]

Brzezinski adds that "global cooperation institutions" (i.e., the WTO, the World Bank, and the IMF) have established abroad major features of "American supremacy."[9] Through policy mechanisms such as structural adjustment programs, international institutions have implemented the free trade model and helped forge the "Washington consensus"—a framework for reorganizing economies and societies around neoliberal principles.

An initial incongruity in this ideology was the ascendance of state-led economies in Asia that did not adopt the path prescribed by neoliberal enthusiasts. Other anomalies, which appeared in rapid succession, were the debacle of "shock therapy" of market reforms in the former Soviet Union and parts of Eastern Europe, spectacularly the 1997–1998 Asian economic crisis in which IMF advice contributed to the descending spiral, and the 2001 Argentine collapse, as the neoliberal formula clearly accelerated the downturn. The cumulative impact of these experiences meant a loss of confidence in the "Washington consensus."

There have been various attempts to refurbish this consensus, such as the 2002 United Nations Conference on Financing for Development in Monterrey, Mexico. But the September 11 attack on the World Trade Center and the Pentagon, icons of globalizing capitalism and U.S. military might, brought into sharp relief the magnitude of perceived problems associated with neoliberal globalization. One element of resurgent Islam powerfully challenged the ethical dimension of this framework and condemned the cultural consequences of the consumerist ethos. Clearly the terrorism crisis is a globalization crisis. The root issues include the neoliberal ideas and heavily American values deemed loathsome by not only the terrorists but also several global justice movements (which, nonetheless, do not endorse the September 11 tactics). The ideas and values associated with neoliberal globalization are nevertheless deeply ingrained in public and policy discourses, which are interwoven. Indeed, the mission of a complex of research institutions and think tanks in Washington, D.C., is to bridge public education and policy formulation. Also, leading public intellectuals who offer policy advice are the propellants for new currents of ideological discourse.[10]

Ideological Discourse

Let us now analyze exemplars of different sets of ideas and values about maintaining or undermining neoliberal globalization. No single exemplar completely typifies an approach, but the ones scrutinized below, to varying degrees, capture key features. The focus here is on four ideological currents: the centrist neoliberal school itself, leading criticism internal to this school (what may be called reformist neoliberal institutionalism), historical-materialist transformism, and development transformism. Although there are significant debates within each of these clusters, shared ideas are evident. The books considered here do not exhaust the range of possible ideologies and counterideologies.[11] In the pages that follow, my major concern is the ways in which these exemplar works frame a globalization agenda.

The Centrist Neoliberal School

Centrist neoliberal thinking is reflected in a World Bank policy research report entitled *Globalization, Growth, and Poverty: Building an Inclusive World Economy*, a team project prepared under the supervision of Nicholas Stern, chief economist and senior vice president at the bank.[12] In this study, the point of departure is that globalization corresponds to increasing integration of economies and societies throughout the world. The main contention is that in most cases, globalization reduces poverty and lessens inequality among countries though, on average, not necessarily within countries. The report emphasizes that globalization produces winners and losers within each society.

To sustain its arguments, this research demarcates three waves of globalization: 1870 to 1914, a period characterized by increasing cross-border flows, when globalization seemed "inevitable"; 1950 to 1980, years marked by greater integration among rich countries; and 1980 to the present, a time of rapid technological advance and a shift of manufactures to developing countries. With the third wave, the "new globalizers"—also termed "successful globalizers"—are beginning to catch up, and the "less globalized" still face rising poverty. The

19

report, rightly in my view, notes that there is no single model of success, thereby recognizing that the policy agendas must be custom fitted. Disavowing nationalism and protectionism, the World Bank forthrightly states that "there are no anti-global victories to report for the postwar Third World. We infer that this is because freer trade stimulates growth in Third World economies."[13] Following a series of chapters focusing on economic phenomena, a penultimate chapter brackets "Power, Culture, and Environment." The "global institutional architecture" is discussed, and an assertion is made that "governments have many degrees of freedom to manage the interaction between trade, capital, and labor flows, on the one hand, and national culture and environment, on the other."[14] Not surprisingly, the prescriptions—the bank's agenda for globalization—give directions for improved market access.

On balance, this study signals a shift from the old orthodoxy. Among the important revisions in neoliberal thinking is a frank recognition of persistent marginalization concomitant to globalization, though, for the bank, marginalization is a descriptive statistical category, not a dynamic concept that turns on competing social forces. There is also an acknowledgment that the state can provide elements of social protection; it is able to play an enabling role, as in the world's two most populous countries, China and India, both of which, in different ways, have sustained large-scale economic growth.

However, the premises of this report are open to challenge. In terms of historiography, are the first two waves really globalization? Or should they be construed as preglobalization? If globalization is tantamount to world history, why employ the concept of globalization at all? And are the World Bank researchers trivializing it? Certainly the noneconomic relationships differ from one period to another (as from colonial rule to the postcolonial order).

While revisionist, is this neoliberal thinking resurrecting discredited modernization theories? In an age of globalization, to what degree is there autonomy for national policy makers, as the modernization thinkers posited? Further, do the neoclassical authors of this study regard the state as an invariant entity from 1870 to the present? More basically, is their basic supposition—globalization may be unidimensionally understood as economic integration—facile?

In light of the material infrastructure of their network, regular access to the world's leading political authorities, and the insinuation of ideas in the exercise of power, there can be little doubt that the 2000 World Bank Report is an important statement—one with great influence. It offers insight into corrections in the lens used by policymakers at the epicenter of globalization.

Reformist Neoliberal Institutionalism

Reformist neoliberals take issue with centrist ideas and the powerful institutions that convey them. These policy intellectuals participate in multiple networks: the lecture circuit, which goes along with quasi-celebrity status; the media industry; venues such as the World Economic Forum, where they interact with the top members of the corporate and political establishment; and research institutes at some of the world's highly endowed universities, which afford material support and are largely U.S. based. A handful of leading economists, technically sophisticated masters of the neoclassical trade, though not uniform in their views (e.g., Joseph Stiglitz, Dani Rodrik, Paul Krugman, and Jeffrey Sachs) have dissented from aspects of orthodox neoliberal globalization. Some of them collaborate in Stiglitz's Initiative for Policy Dialogue, a global network of social scientists established in 2000. Drawing together select experts from around the world, its mission is to explore economic policy alternatives for developing and transition countries and to improve official decision making on economic issues.

Stiglitz was a cabinet member in the Clinton administration (where he was chairman of the Council of Economic Advisers), then senior vice president and chief economist at the World Bank, and winner of the 2001 Nobel Prize in economics. Now a professor at Columbia University, Stiglitz offers an insider's view into core institutions and ideas that drive the globalization agenda.

In his best-selling book *Globalization and Its Discontents,* Stiglitz makes a case and provides evidence (e.g., on rising poverty in the world in the 1990s) somewhat at odds with recent data presented by the World Bank.[15] In explaining why globalization does not work for a multitude of people, particularly in the developing world, Stiglitz constructs a multilevel analysis of globalization that focuses on economic integration, international economic institutions (especially the IMF, described as a "political institution"), the interests of the financial and corporate community, state structures, social stratification, values, and the system of capitalism itself. Melding personal experience and theory in a skillful manner, Stiglitz lambastes the IMF for its hypocrisy and dogmatic adherence to the ideology of market fundamentalism. According to Stiglitz, the agenda should not be just to change the institutions themselves; the mind-sets about globalization and global governance warrant reordering.

Indeed, the case studies are revealing.[16] Stiglitz recounts the advice he personally rendered, the final decisions by political authorities, and the outcome of the heady events. In each instance, Stiglitz feels vindicated. He was right all along, and his ideas are not considered ideology but are elevated to the status of principle. In Stiglitz's mind, ideology takes on a pejorative connotation; it rigidifies thinking. What escapes notice is that ideology may also provide a critical understanding of the way in which a system operates, why it falls short of its goals, and what a just order might look like.

In terms of vision, Stiglitz calls for "debt forgiveness," but why does he adhere to the tired concept of "forgiveness"—after all, who owes what to whom?—

rather than cancellation? His proposal for a "multipronged system of reform" heaps together many different prongs and calls them a "system." In this "system," the task is to *manage* problems. Presto, structural problems are reduced to management issues. Having criticized the market fundamentalists, Stiglitz then expresses his unshaken faith in the redeeming value of competition. At the end of the day, the agenda is to stabilize globalizing capitalism. It is to modify neoliberal globalization without tugging at the roots of its underlying structures.

Historical-Materialist Transformism

Historical-materialist transformers have sought to reinterpret the ideas of capitalism and restructure this globalizing system. Among others in this tradition, William K. Tabb, a professor at the City University of New York and long associated with the Monthly Review network and other circles of socialist scholars, has sought to extend a Marxist understanding.[17]

Pointing out that the media shape consciousness and provide "an ideological context" for globalizing dynamics, his analysis, surprisingly, subscribes to some key representations in the public discourse, such as the notions of a "global village" and an "antiglobalization campaign." In fact, global divisions are quite marked, and villages are being rapidly destroyed by economic globalization and the global AIDS epidemic. Most resistance movements seek to reshape rather than stop globalizing processes. But if resistance is integral to globalization itself, rather than a separate process, then it cannot be antiglobalization. That said, however, Tabb—unlike the exemplar authors cited above—offers a vigorous critique of globalizing capitalism and probes the parameters in which national and international institutions operate.

Like the World Bank researchers and Stiglitz, Tabb is an economist, yet he holds that neoliberal globalization is chiefly a political phenomenon. To develop his argument, Tabb takes a long view, as do Stern and his colleagues at the World Bank. But the authors at the bank historicize neoliberal globalization differently. After situating globalization in the development of capitalism, Tabb submits that there have been fundamental shifts since 1970, especially the end of the postwar era of national Keynesianism, the collapse of the Bretton Woods system of fixed exchange rates that accompanied the rise of the neoliberal regime, and the fall of the Soviet Union.

A historical-materialist perspective is structural in a way that the other worldviews are not. Tabb draws attention to the continuities between "historical imperialism" and contemporary globalization. Further, he emphasizes structural power, that is, imbalances not merely between lenders and borrowers, but the power relations among *both* states, including interstate institutions, and transnational classes. In short, Tabb's rethinking (and Stiglitz's as well) differs from the World Bank's inasmuch as Tabb and Stiglitz are decidedly reflexive on the interactions of ideas and interests.

From Tabb's perspective, the globalization agenda is to bring an end to the "form of indirect rule through global state governance institutions"—the WTO, World Bank, and IMF—and transnational corporations. It is to affect an ideological shift to the priorities of "the emergent movement for global justice." While supporting the importance of reform, the main idea in Tabb's analysis is to establish social control over market forces—a matter of transforming existing social relations.[18]

Development Transformism

Development transformism is presented by Martin Khor, who, like the other exemplar authors, trained as an economist. He directs the Third World Network, a Malaysian-based nongovernmental organization (NGO) that works transnationally with other NGOs to understand and influence policy. His *Rethinking Globalization* focuses on the developing countries, many of them small and fragile actors, that have experienced a reduction in policy latitude and an erosion of sovereignty (including over natural resources) and of local ownership in the national economy.[19]

For Khor, globalization is not a totally new process, but one that has accelerated rapidly in the past few decades. He holds that a hallmark of this period is increasing inequality among and within countries, and these divides are associated with globalizing forces. His data, drawn from United Nations Conference on Trade and Development and United Nations Development Program documents, thus contradict the World Bank's finding that there is no clear evidence for rising inequality among countries. According to Khor, globalization and the whole complex of ideas associated with the neoliberal framework have contributed powerfully to the vulnerabilities of the South. The mechanisms include loan conditionalities, fluctuations in commodity prices and terms of trade, and the volatility of short-term capital flows.

Based on this analysis, the agenda concerns protection against the policies and systemic risks of neoliberal globalization. Khor proposes strategic responses: inter alia, a selective policy of engagement with globalizing processes, a gradual pace, flexibility in choosing a policy mix, the identification of limits on external flows, and strong participation in establishing a regulatory framework. In this regard, he calls for strengthening the United Nations, including its specialized agencies, which have been marginalized in the face of a tilt toward the WTO, World Bank, and IMF. A rebalancing of the state and the market would entail a recognition that they can be mutually reinforcing. Underpinning these ideas is the notion that if social justice and equity were to become a component of globalization, then democratic global governance could be on the agenda.

At the end of the day, the development perspective scrutinized here offers a vision that both converges with and diverges from aspects of the other ideological currents. Like the World Bank researchers and Stiglitz, Khor concentrates on the interactions between states (and interstate institutions) and markets. Unfortunately, in *Rethinking Globalization*, he is mostly silent about problems within the developmental state. The World Bank, Stiglitz, and Tabb, more than Khor, examine internal differences within countries. Unlike the World Bank researchers, Tabb peers into relational, not only gradational, divisions. He explores social relations, which Khor sets aside in favor of global imbalances. Surely these theoretical tools and frames of analysis are basic to the production of new ideas about globalization.

Ideology in Flux

In sum, neoliberal globalization may be grasped in terms of its intersubjective dimensions and transnational networks as they relate to political and material interests. Today, ideological consensus is increasingly contested and weakening. The fissures are widening. For diverse stakeholders, the challenge is to remake globalization into an *ideology of emancipation* for the many, not the few. Requisite to this task are not only new ideas but also countervailing power. Indeed, as demonstrated above, there is a substantial emergence of alternative sets of ideas: very different perspectives of a desirable globalization agenda. Ultimately, this contestation is a question of whose agenda will win out in the political strife. It comes down to a matter of reconciling core ideas and who controls the globalization agenda.

Among the competing agendas, common ground exists, at least on one point: the contemporary era is marked by a bundling of neoliberalism and globalization. However, there is disagreement about what inference to draw from this convergence. Some ideologists clearly favor tightening the bundle, whereas others advocate an unbundling of neoliberalism and globalization. Indeed, what would globalization be like without neoliberalism?

Rethinking the debate over ideas thus shifts the globalization discourse from linking to delinking globalization and the neoliberal framework. Sequentially, delinking would be tied to relinking economic reform and social policy. But this counterideology is partial. The goal worth pursuing is to search for new philosophical principles that could help imagine options, guide policy, and inform strategies tailor-made for distinctive contexts. Even if there is no one best way to harness globalization so that it provides for both economic gains and social equity, surely much greater overall vision is still required.

Notes

1. As quoted in William Pfaff, "Globalization Is Discredited," *Japan Times*, February 29, 2000.
2. Robert W. Cox, "Ideologies and the New International Economic Order: Reflections on Some Recent Literature," *International Organization*, Spring 1979, 257–302; Robert W. Cox, "A Perspective on Globalization," in *Globalization: Critical Reflections*, ed. James H. Mittelman (Boulder: Lynne Rienner, 1996), 21–30.
3. Claude Ake, *Democracy and Development* (Washington, D.C.: Brookings Institution, 1996), 114.
4. James H. Mittelman, *The Globalization Syndrome: Transformation and Resistance* (Princeton: Princeton University Press, 2000), 7; James Mittelman and Norani Othman, eds., *Capturing Globalization* (London: Routledge, 2001).
5. Henry Paulson, "The Gospel of Globalisation," *Financial Times*, November 13, 2001.
6. Robert Gilpin, *The Challenge of Global Capitalism: The World Economy in the 21st Century* (Princeton: Princeton University Press, 2000), 348.
7. Daniel Yergin and Joseph Stanislaw, *The Commanding Heights: The Battle between Government and the Marketplace That Is Remaking the Modern World* (New York: Simon & Schuster, 1998).
8. Zbigniew Brzezinski, *The Grand Chessboard: American Primacy and Its Geostrategic Imperatives* (New York: Basic, 1997), 27.
9. Brzezinski, *Grand Chessboard*, 28.
10. Rewarded with recognition (e.g., on talk shows) and prizes for their contributions, many star policy intellectuals could be named, for example, Princeton economist Paul Krugman is a columnist for the *New York Times*, an organ of power that is sometimes referred to as the fourth branch of the U.S. government.
11. Right-wing populist and anarchist ideologies of globalization are probed in Mark Rupert, *Ideologies of Globalization: Contending Visions of a New World Order* (London: Routledge, 2000); and Manfred B. Steger, *Globalism: The New Market Ideology* (Lanham, Md.: Rowman & Littlefield, 2002).
12. World Bank, *Globalization, Growth, and Poverty: Building an Inclusive World Economy* (Washington, D.C.: World Bank; New York: Oxford University Press, 2000).
13. World Bank, *Globalization, Growth, and Poverty*, 37.
14. World Bank, *Globalization, Growth, and Poverty*, 142.
15. Joseph E. Stiglitz, *Globalization and Its Discontents* (New York: Norton, 2002), 5; cf. Nicholas Stern, *A Strategy for Development* (Washington, D.C.: World Bank, 2000), 20.
16. Stiglitz overextends himself in presenting a vast array of case studies. For him, like the World Bank and IMF, Uganda is a poster child. The Musev-

eni government has brought relative peace after years of dictatorships, helped spur economic growth, extended education without user fees, and improved health care, including a campaign to fight AIDS. Stiglitz waxes enthusiastic about these achievements without noting that while receiving substantial infusions of international funds, Museveni has enforced his idea of a "no party democracy," maintained a huge defense budget, and sent his military to loot the Democratic Republic of the Congo. Similarly, Stiglitz tells half the story when he argues that Malaysian Prime Minister Mahathir's capital controls were an effective response to the 1997–1998 Asian economic crisis (which in fact was a globalization crisis). Stiglitz is right as far as he goes, but either overlooks or does not know that investors and traders maneuvered around the controls and that others negotiated deals with the government. In any event, Mahathir, hardly a practitioner of good governance, lifted the controls after one year and sought to bolster Malaysia's rentier capitalism. The point here is that Stiglitz fails to get his stories right.

17. See William K. Tabb, *The Amoral Elephant: Globalization and the Struggle for Social Justice in the Twenty-First Century* (New York: Monthly Review Press, 2001).

18. Similarly, Stiglitz, *Globalization and Its Discontents*, 76, 242, and 252, calls for "a transformation of society," but the meaning is unspecified.

19. Martin Khor, *Rethinking Globalization: Critical Policy Issues and Policy Choices* (New York: Palgrave/St. Martin's, 2001).

THE MATRIX OF
GLOBAL ENCHANTMENT

Paul James

Contemporary globalization is remarkable creature. It is an agile, blousy Hollywood-style genie that rarely lives up to its promises yet all too often slips relatively unscathed out of the fire of its fiercest critics.[1] It employs many maneuvers to evade critique, but I want to concentrate on two key ways in which the critics inadvertently contribute to capitalist globalization being seen as either inevitable or as a (contested) cultural common sense. First, to the extent that globalization is treated as a process of spatial extension only pertaining to the last two or three decades, we tend to overlook the long-term development of practices and ideas that underpin its contemporary power. Second, to the extent that globalism is reduced to an ideology of capitalist economic expansion, we tend to miss out on the way in which it is now carried by a matrix of ideological assumptions across the whole range of contemporary modes of practice from globalizing capitalism to disembodying techno science.[2] A number of scholars, such John Tomlinson, Arjun Appadurai, Manfred Steger, Roland Robertson, and James Mittelman, have recognized the broader dynamics of globalization, but when it comes to discussing globalism as an ideology-subjectivity, most commentators critically focus on deconstructing ideologies that directly defend the globalizing market. Both of these critical moves contribute to reducing globalism to one of its expressions—neoliberal globalism. To be sure, neoliberalism is one of the dominant philosophies of our time; however, part of the power of neoliberalism is, strangely, that it is at one level so contested. Its glaring prominence blinds us to the breadth and depth of a matrix of associated ideologies that are left relatively uninterrogated. In the process, some of the assumptions associated with globalism in general slip away unnoticed.

The usual approach is to concentrate on ideologies of progress and economic development, of instrumental management and economic rationalism, but this misses out on lots of others. Take, for example, the following ideologies, which are usually uncontested or taken for granted. They are sensibilities that affect different people in uneven ways, but they nevertheless constantly impinge on the various life worlds of modernized, globalized souls.

1. Interconnectivity, the cultural imperative to be always available in a loop of potential communicative connection, preferably electronic. This message is being "benignly" and constantly reinforced by the globalizing mobile phone market.[3] We feel it in our bodies to the extent that most of us are uncomfortable with its opposite—unchosen isolation. Even when we are in the face-to-face presence of others, we feel the need "to know," to be in mediated connection with what is happening in the world.

2. Mobility, the imperative to develop a capacity to move across borders. Here the unease comes from an aversion to being relegated to a projected mire of parochialism. It is easy to see how these ideologies of mobility and interconnectivity intersect with globalism. Electronic interconnectivity, both as practice and idea, helps sustain our sense of viable open mobility largely free of the attendant perceived risks of dealing with strangers face-to-face. As the world globalizes, it simultaneously becomes full of strangers and full of people with whom communication is possible. This further relates to an ideology of security.

3. Security, the imperative to manage one's place in the mobile risk society. This includes an imperative to manage rogue elements or processes that assail that sense of relative comfort. It is indicative that while opposition to the U.S. war on Iraq intensified, it would have taken a brave person in the West to say that Osama bin Laden is philosophically on to something of value. The definition of him as a rogue element, whether evil or merely criminal, has been almost totalizing.

4. Justice and democracy, the imperative to couch any claims to action in the world in terms of human rights discourse. For example, the importance of deposing the Taliban was in part legitimized by the Bush administration in terms of Taliban oppression of Afghani women. In the aftermath of the war in Afghanistan the continuing oppression of women, documented by such groups as Human Rights Watch Report, is either glossed over or passed into irrelevancy

28

by assertions of the importance of "doing something in the first place." In other words, we are drawn into the importance of a doctrine of war making now known in the international relations literature as "humanitarian intervention" in the name of freedom.

5. Freedom, autonomy, and transcendence, the imperative to overcome limits and oppressions. Who in our modern/postmodern world but a few recalcitrants or neotraditionalists would argue that any one of these imperatives could be intrinsically bad?[4] This, I argue, is precisely their power as ideologies. At one level, these ideologies are connected as cross-cutting and often contradictory precepts, shoveled into a grab bag of clichés that can be delivered out of context, out of contestation. At a deeper level, they form the cultural ground on which we walk. While the many critics of corporate globalization have been addressing the problems of globalism as they directly confront us, neoliberal and neoconservative commentators such as Francis Fukuyama[5] have with minimal scrutiny been quietly redefining the ground beneath.

This chapter addresses these tendencies by broadening out the concept of globalism. It does so across three related sections. First, it broadens the definitions of globalization and globalism; second, it sets out a series of methodological arguments about how we might better understand them; and third, it examines one intersection of ideological presuppositions around the concepts of freedom-autonomy-security as it relates to a contemporary example of globalization—the "war on terror."

Defining Globalism

The terms associated with "globalism"[6] appear to be the easiest set of concepts in the world to define. In one way, globalization is simply the spatial extension of social relations across the globe. It is literally evoked in the picture that we have become accustomed to seeing in satellite photographs. However, that definition leaves us concentrating on the past few decades. A working definition of the cluster of terms around "globalism" begins by relating the various intersecting modes of practice, including the modes of communication, production and exchange, to their extension across world space. Across human history, as those practices have at one level become more materially abstract, they have maintained or increased their intensity while becoming more extensive and generalized.

Globalization is thus most simply the name given to the matrix of those practices as they extend across world-space. Exemplary contemporary systems of materially powerful but disembodied extension include the stamping presses of finance capital, electronic warfare, or electronic broadcast culture.

There are, however, earlier or more concrete forms of globalization that need to be incorporated into any definition. There are lines of global connection carried by agents of the early expansionist imperial states, by traders on the silk routes, and by crusading war makers going off to "smash the infidels" simply because they were there, living in the same world.[7] These lines of connection were conducted through a quite different matrix of assumptions than those that sit behind contemporary globalization. The Crusaders did not draw on ideologies of justice or freedom to defend these activities, whereas, by a remarkable reversal of sentiments, George W. Bush began the "War on Terror" by first calling it a crusade.

Thus globalization can be defined as the unevenly structured manifold of social relations, materially enacted through one or more of the various dominant modes of practice—exchange, production, communication, organization, and inquiry—and extended across *world space,* where the notion of "world space" is itself defined in the historically variable terms that it has been practiced and understood phenomenally through changing *world time.* It is thus a process, a matrix of ongoing material practices enacted in the name of historically changing sets of ideological clothing.

The associated concept of "globalism" is defined as the dominant matrix of ideologies and subjectivities associated with different historical formations of global extension. The definition thus implies that there were premodern or traditional forms of globalism and globalization long before the driving force of capitalism sought to colonize every corner of the globe, for example, going back to the Roman Empire in the second century C.E., and perhaps to the Greeks of the fifth century B.C.E.[8] As the Roman Empire drew lines of practical connection across vast expanses of the known world, Claudius Ptolemaeus (c. 90–c. 150 C.E.) revived the Hellenic belief in the Pythagorean theory of a spherical globe. He wrote systematically about a world space stretching from Caledonia and Anglia to what became known as Java Minor. Alongside the secular empire, the Roman Catholic Church, as its name suggests—*katholikos* universal, *kata* in respect of, *holos* the whole—had globalizing pretensions.

This does not mean that globalism was the dominant or even a generalized understanding of the world. Sacred universalism is not necessarily the same as globalism. By contrast to the European clerics of globalization, the Chinese form of universalism was inwardly turned. For example, although the Celestial Kingdom had produced printed atlases that date long before the European Ortelius's supposedly first historical atlas, early maps of China show the world as fading off beyond the "natural extent" of territory.[9] While evidence suggests that the Chinese may have traveled the world, this does not mean that they acted through a subjectivity of globalism. In other words, the Chinese centered their empire, whereas the Romans globally extended theirs. If the Roman Peutinger Table is any indication, the Roman worldview was globalizing to the extent that it traveled in geometric lines that stretched as far as the traveling eyes of the agents of empire could see.[10] In the current context, it does not matter whether or not the United States has the same territorial ambitions as the Romans. Globalizing imperialism, as I will argue in the final section, can in different historical contexts take the territorialized form of extending embodied or institutional power or, in the present period, the territorializing form of making the world safe for globalizing democracy.

Theorizing Globalism

Before moving on to the example of freedom as a totalizing yet contradictory ideology of globalization, I want to make five brief methodological points that carry forward the definitional discussion and help to generalize some starting points for an alternative theory of globalization.

1. Globalization involves extensions of social relations across world-space, defining that world space in terms of the historically variable ways that it has been practiced and socially understood through changing world time. In other words, long before that stunning satellite photograph of the globe hit us in the face with the obviousness of planet earth, there were different practices and conceptions of world space. We may not have previously come close to the current condition of self-conscious globality—an unprecedented development in human history—but processes of globalization and the subjectivities of globalism were occurring, both intended and unintended, to the extent that social relations and subjectivities (together with their ecological consequences) were being given global reach. For example, *subjective* projections of the globe (globalism) emerged with the incipient development of a technical-analytical mode of inquiry by the ancient Greek philosophers. An understanding of the inhabited world-space (the *oecumene*) began to be debated during the sixth and fifth centuries B.C.E., combining information both from phenomenal experience such as oral testimony and from abstract principles such as geometry.[11] Lines of *objective* global spatial extension (globalization) developed in the traditional empires, arguably, for example, with the Roman Empire as it sought to control the known world.

Here I am very sensitive to the critical excursions of Justin Rosenberg in his raunchy polemic, *The Follies of Globalisation Theory*.[12] As he argues, some writers have elevated changes in the nature of time and space into a grand architecture of explanation that tends to dehistoricize the processes of global extension. Notwithstanding Rosenberg's telling methodological injunction that if globalization involves spatial extension it cannot be explained by invoking the claim that world space is now global—the explanation and the thing being explained, he rightly says, are thus reduced into self-confirming circle—it is still, I suggest, legitimate to treat globalization as a *descriptive* category referring to a process of extension across a historically constituted world space. An explanation as to why the dominant modes of practice contribute to the genie of globalization is not contained inside the definition, even if a method for beginning such an inquiry is inferred. With a few refinements that is all that I am doing here.

2. The form of globalization has been, and continues to be, historically changing. This can be analytically understood in terms of globalization taking fundamentally different forms across world history, or even within one historical moment. In any particular period, globalization ranges from embodied extensions of the social, such as through the movements of peoples, to the disembodied extensions, such as through communications on the wings of textual or digital encoding. In terms of the present argument, across human history, the dominant forms of globalization range from the *traditional* (primarily carried by the embodied movement of peoples and the projections of traditional intellectuals) to the *modern* and *postmodern* (primarily carried by disembodied practices of abstracted extension and the projections of a emergent cosmopolitan class of the intellectually trained).[13]

The definition thus is also sensitive to Roland Robertson's argument that globalism is a deep historical and variable process. However, by including the Roman Empire as having both globalizing sensibilities and practices it extends Robertson's chronicle of the "germinal stage" back long before the beginning of *modern* forms of globalism in the fifteenth century with the *revival* of a spherical view of the world.[14] The earlier form of globalism is what might be called "traditional globalism"—with all the attendant issues of social form that the concept of "traditionalism" entails. This means that the present approach fundamentally questions modernists like Anthony Giddens, who suggest that globalism is a consequence of modernity, and utterly rejects theorists such as Martin Albrow who, in a fit of theoretical exuberance, claims that globality is now replacing modernity.[15]

Giddens, in this view, does not have more than a single-layered sense of history, and Albrow makes a stunning category mistake. Albrow overlooks the issue that "modernism" and "globalism" come to us from two categorically different levels of analysis: "globalization" is a descriptive term, an empirical generalization made about various processes of spatial extension, whereas "modernism" is a categorical term that can only be understood in terms of positing either a kind of subjectivity/aesthetic or a general ontological formation. Processes of globalization developed long before modernity (understood provisionally in epoch terms only as a dominant not totalizing formation), and they will probably continue long after its heyday. However, this does not mean that globality is replacing modernity. It means that the dominant form of globalization and globalism is changing, as is the once assumed dominance of modernism. Even as modern forms of globalism and imperialism continue, they are overlaid with postmodern forms: from the globalization of capital as it commodifies future time through speculative hedging, to the globalization of cinematic culture with its postmodern sensibility signaled, for example, in the title of a new magazine of Hollywood gloss—*Empire*.[16] Abstracted from history, the title carries no more than the most obvious superficial irony.

3. The driving structural determinants of contemporary globalization are capitalism (based on an accelerating electronic mode of production and an expanding mode of commodity and financial exchange), mediatism (the systemic interconnectivity of a mass-mediated world, based on a mode of electronically networked communication), and techno-scientism (based on a new intersection between the mode of production and the mode of inquiry). Contemporary globalization has reached its present stage of relative globality under conditions of the intersection of each of these modes of practice. For example, satellite transmission, cable networking, and the Internet were all developed techno scientifically as means of communication in state-supported capitalist markets that rapidly carried globalization to a new dominant level of technological mediation.[17]

4. One of the driving ideological determinants of contemporary globalization is the contested philosophy of neoliberalism. However, the ideological-subjective grounding of globalization also goes much deeper and wider than ideologies of the economic. Globalization is carried forward through the relatively uncontested territory of the taken-for-granted assumptions of our time. Ideologies of economic globalism from notions of market freedom to the joy of a "borderless world" have naturalized the techniques and technologies of global extension as the inevitable outcomes of material progress. However, more than that, globalism partakes of the excitement that surrounds generalized notions of autonomy, mediation, and interconnectivity.

5. Globalization does not inevitably sweep all aside before it. All that is solid does not melt into air. For example, processes of globalization eventually undermine the sovereignty of the nation-state, but there is no inevitability about such an outcome, neither in logic or reality. It is salutary to remember that the institutions and structures of modern globalization and the modern nation-state were born during the same period. They were formed through the concurrent processes, with the tension between these two phenomena occurring over boundary formation and sovereignty and not existing in general. This argument goes directly against those who treat nation formation and global formation as the antithetical outcomes of, respectively, a "first and second modernity," or those who narrowly define globalization as that which undermines the nation-state.[18] In the context of contemporary globalization we have seen both nationalist revivals and reassertions of tribalism. In the present climate, nation-

alism is one of those too easily dismissed ideologies, one that keeps returning from the dead despite the confidence of the obituary writers.

F Is for Freedom, G Is for Globalism, and P Is for Patriotism

Continuing the theme of the relationship between globalism and nationalism, it is important to recognize how certain kinds of postnationalism or civic nationalism are comfortably presented as compatible with the globalization of the market. While critics of corporate globalization rightly point to the contradiction between the homeland emphasis on national integrity and the neoliberal emphasis on "no borders" versions of the capitalist market, such critique has little effect on the proponents of this dual projection. The dominant neoliberal definition of the market as the open flow of commodities, commercial culture, and capital across the world is treated, within this new dominant common sense, as the outward extension of national interest.

For an ideologue such as Lynne Cheney, overt nationalism is a bad thing, but patriotic support of America as the nation that exemplifies the virtue of global freedom, including freedom of the market, cannot be but a good thing. In her recent children's book, *America: A Patriotic Primer*,[19] the market—neoliberal or otherwise—does not get a mention. We travel from "A is for America, the land that we love," to "Z is for the end of the alphabet, but not of America's story. Strong and free we will continue to be an inspiration to the world," without any defense of capitalist globalization. Nevertheless, during that journey the abiding presumption is of *the* globalizing nation reaching out and carrying the possibilities of freedom to others. In this last section of the present chapter, discussing the ideology of freedom as one of the ideologies of globalism is thus intended as a way of showing the breadth of the ideologies that underpin globalization.

The notion of freedom includes a bevy of associated words that flock together, words such as "autonomy," "liberty," "independence," "emancipation," "choice," and "openness." While the meaning of "freedom to choose" has been rewritten by the marketeers with cars named "Freedom" and "Freelander," and with the Ford 2003 advertising slogan, "No Boundaries," the subjectivity of freedom transcends left and right debates. Even neoliberal notions of freedom are much broader than usually portrayed and related to such ideologies as "making the world free for democracy." Ronald Reagan expressed it beautifully as a divine assignment to spread the "sacred fire of human liberty." The only way potentially to enhance our sense of security and democracy is, first, to totalize the freedom of "us," "the good nations" (I cannot think of a better name for "us") and, second, to objectify the others as abstract strangers and a potential threat. It is an apparent paradox because this particular concept of "freedom" entails developing the infrastructure to defend the free movement and operation of some, and to strictly curtail the freedom of others. Examples abound. The Patriot Act of 2001 is a massive document extending powers that were already more than adequate for the purpose. Since September 11, secret hearings and detentions have been held for 1,200 persons in the United States, mostly Muslim persons arrested on immigration charges under the USA Patriot Act. Others have been detained in a military prison in a U.S.-controlled section of Cuba without recourse to legal representation. On June 5, 2002, we first heard the announcement of an intention to revive the long-dormant powers of the 1952 immigration law with tens of thousands of visitors from Islamic countries to be fingerprinted, potentially increasing to five million persons per year by 2005.

The failure of "totalizing control" to ever attain static ascendancy gives us a way of explaining why the culture war over the concept of "freedom" is so important. Whether we are talking about the "freedom/fear" and "freedom/terror" contrasts, or the "global free trade/national closure" polarity, the concept of "freedom" has become paramount. In the United States as the *home* of the *free*, all of those terms have become linked as coextensive. Totalizing security projections have been projected inward as "homeland security." This has involved organizational coordination and breathless announcements of a new single permanent department to secure the American homeland. Led by Secretary Tom Ridge, the Department of Homeland Security will coordinate security matters with the FBI and CIA.. Careful language use is pervasive and extends to the titles of bits of legislation: the term "Patriot Act" acts as a form of cultural closure on the possibility that the intended changes can be criticized as curtailing freedom. Speeches for home consumption continually posit a fight between freedom and fear with the repetitive use of phrases such as "weapons of mass destruction," "rogue states," and the "need for preemptive strikes" with the third figure, preemptive intervention, supposedly combating the second figure, rogue states, in order to make the world safe from "WMD."

At the same time, even when projected externally and globally, much of the rhetoric is for domestic consumption in the West. The "axis of evil" notion deliberately echoes Reagan's "evil empire," and both have their origins in the World War II period. Similarly the concept of global action in the name of humanity has a history going back into the middle of the twentieth century; for example, the use of images of globalism has long been part of national U.S. institutions of war making or space exploration. The official icons for the U.S. Department of Defense, the Navy SEALS, the Joint Special Operations Command, the Strategic Computing Program, and DARPA as a whole take the globe as their symbol of territorial reach.

The war on terrorism is predicated on rhetoric that legitimates attacking the source of evil in distant locations. In George Bush's terms, "We must be ready to strike at a moment's notice in any dark corner of the world" (West Point

35

speech, June 1, 2002). Overlaying that older rhetoric is a newer claim about the legitimacy of preemptive strikes to protect our way of life against totalizing evil. Donald Rumsfeld speaking at NATO headquarters in Brussels (June 6, 2002), opened up this new convergence of the notions of "freedom to act" and "totalizing control." "Absolute proof cannot be a precondition for action," he said. He was supported by the British defense secretary talking about the possibility of using nuclear weapons against the threat of chemical and biological attack. This is part of a postmodern redefinition of the conventions of international law. *Preemption* and *retaliation* become illegal as rationales for action under the conventions of modern international law. It became illegitimate to strike first just in case something might happen or to respond to single act of aggression by retaliating in kind to send a message. The traditional notion of "an eye for an eye" that provided the map for earlier tracks of globalization such as the Crusades was rejected.

However, in these contradictory times retaliation has come back in reconstituted form—this time as a pastiche of floating and ad hoc rationalizations. In the aftermath of September 11, it was claimed that the attack was so massive that it could be taken as, in effect, a declaration of continuous war thus warranting continuous defense.[20] This was despite the fact that no one declared war, no one even took responsibility for the act of terror, and only circumstantial evidence was available to decide on whom the retaliation should be effected. Within no time the terrorists had a name. They were all Islamic, and they were found in every primeval corner of the globe.

The stakes are high. This makes seemingly academic tasks, such as adequately defining globalization and being clear about what it is, extremely important. Defining globalization as the uneven but structured manifold of connections across world space, taking that space in the historically variable terms that it has been *socially understood* through changing world time, arguably helps us recognize both its objective and subjective character. Furthermore, broadening the terms of analysis leads to the suggestion that we are less likely to come to the conclusion that our globalization is good and theirs is bad. Globalization is always ethically ambiguous. Like all social practices, globalization is always structured as relations of power, and these relations of power—both structural and ideological—need to be analyzed in the broadest possible way.

Notes

1. The genie metaphor is not really any different from the metaphor of the juggernaut used by Anthony Giddens, *The Consequences of Modernity* (Cambridge: Polity, 1990); or the Hindu god Shiva used by Manfred B. Steger, *Glob-*

alism: The New Market Ideology (Lanham, Md.: Rowman & Littlefield, 2002). It is used here because it highlights historical tensions of meaning that are relevant to globalization: in this instance between the evil genie of the darker Arabian tales and the rock and roll cowboy-style genie of Hollywood's *Aladdin*.

2. The concept of a matrix carries in its multiple meanings the contradictorily embodied/disembodied nature of abstracted social relations that the present study is attempting to describe. In its most general meaning a matrix is a setting in which something takes form, has its origin, or is enclosed. In obstetrics matrix refers to the body of the womb. By contrast, in mathematics it refers to a regularized array of abstract elements. And in engineering (my personal favorite given the current expressions of globalism) it refers to a bed of perforated metal placed beneath an object in a machine press against which the stamping press operates.

3. George Meyerson, *Heidegger, Habermas, and the Mobile Phone* (Cambridge, U.K.: Icon, 2001).

4. And of course they are not intrinsically bad, but then neither are their opposites: isolation, bounded or immobile placement, insecurity, authority, closure, and lack of choice. It is again indicative that despite, or perhaps because of, the abstract distance that constitutes the modern/postmodern reader as intellectually trained, "we" are likely to find such an alternative list confronting. We may know in our intellects that judgment on what is good or bad depends in all cases on negotiating the ethical principles that undergird human practice; however, in our liberal heart of hearts, social outcomes such as closure or lack of choice appear intrinsically bad.

5. Francis Fukuyama, *The Great Disruption: Human Nature and the Reconstitution of Social Order* (London: Profile Books/Free Press, 1999).

6. "Globalism" is here treated as the inclusive category for associated terms such as "globalization," "globalizing," and "global formation." This is similar to the way the concept of "nationalism" is used in the literature to stand in for the cluster of associated but differently defined terms—"nation," "nation-state," "nation formation," and so on.

7. At this stage "smashing the infidels" meant civilizing them by means of sword and burning oil, not engaging in genocide.

8. William Arthur Heidel, *The Frame of the Ancient Greek Maps* (New York: Arno, 1976).

9. See Jeremy Black, *Maps and History: Constructing Images of the Past* (New Haven: Yale University Press, 1997), 2–3, on Standen's thesis about the ahistorical depiction of the Great Wall, whether or not it had been built.

10. A stylized map of the empire, about twelve-feet long and rolled out like a narrow scroll. It is known from a thirteenth-century copy. In modern cartographical terms it is unrecognizably distorted. Made more than two thousand years earlier is a Mesopotamian clay tablet with a circular Assyro-centric map

showing the Euphrates joining the Persian Gulf and surrounded by the "Earthly Ocean." See Norman J. W. Thrower, *Maps and Man: An Examination of Cartography in Relation to Culture and Civilization* (Englewood Cliffs, N.J.: Prentice-Hall, 1972).

11. Christian Jacob, "Mapping in the Mind: The Earth from Ancient Alexandria," in *Mappings*, ed. Denis Cosgrove (London: Reaktion, 1999).

12. Justin Rosenberg, *The Follies of Globalisation Theory: Polemical Essays* (London: Verso, 2000).

13. This point is influenced by Leslie Sklair, *The Transnational Capitalist Class* (Oxford: Blackwell, 2001), though the emphasis on the "intellectually trained" gives his argument a different slant. (See his chapter in the present volume.)

14. Roland Robertson, *Globalization* (London: Sage, 1992). His historical mapping of the "phases" of globalism is the subject of chapter 3.

15. Giddens, *Consequences of Modernity*; Martin Albrow, *The Global Age* (Cambridge: Polity, 1996).

16. *Empire*, EMAP consumer magazines, first published in the United Kingdom in 1992, began publication in Australia in 2001. Website: www.empire-online.com.au. While it is unlikely that the marketing department of the magazine directly considered the resonance with Antonio Negri and Michael Hardt's wildly popular academic book *Empire* (Cambridge: Harvard University Press, 2000), the overlap of names is, to use a Marxist refrain, probably no coincidence. At the very least it indicates an ideological confluence—"empire" has again become a sexy theme.

17. Asa Briggs and Peter Burke, *A Social History of the Media: From Gutenberg to the Internet* (Cambridge: Polity, 2002).

18. See, for example, Ulrich Beck's presumptive definition of globalization as denoting "the processes through which sovereign national states are crisscrossed and undermined" in *What Is Globalization?* (Cambridge: Polity, 2000), 11. This also put me at odds with Mohammed Bamyeh, *The Ends of Globalization* (Minneapolis: University of Minnesota Press, 2000), and his arguments about the death of the nation-state. (See also his chapter in the present volume.)

19. Lynne Cheney with Robin Preiss Glasser, *America: A Patriotic Primer* (New York: Simon & Schuster, 2002).

20. Jonathan Steele, "The Bush Doctrine Makes a Nonsense of the UN Charter," *Guardian*, June 7, 2002, www.guardian.co.uk.

"*BOREDOM*" ♡-Jessica

THE END OF CAPITALIST GLOBALIZATION

LESLIE SKLAIR

Theory and research on globalization appears to have reached a mature phase in a relatively short period of time.[1] Most attempts to survey the field, while differing radically on their interpretations of the literature, agree that globalization represents a serious challenge to the state-centrist assumptions of most previous social science. Nevertheless, the "natural" quality of societies bounded by their nation-states, the difficulty of generating and working with data that crosses national boundaries, and the lack of specificity in most theories of the global, all conspire to undermine the critique of state centrism. Thus, before the idea of globalization has become firmly established, the skeptics are announcing the limits and, in some extreme cases, the myth of globalization. Globalization, in the words of some populists, is nothing but "globaloney."

Many globalization theorists and researchers, including myself, have a good deal of sympathy with the skeptics. However, I shall argue that globalization is more than an ideology, though various versions of globalization can be and have been promoted as ideologies. Globalization in a generic sense needs to be distinguished from its dominant type—capitalist globalization—and both of these have to be confronted in theory and research if we are to have any grasp of the contemporary world. This can be done in the context of what I have termed global system theory. To illustrate its central themes, I argue that the global system can best be analyzed in terms of transnational practices and, in this way, alternatives to capitalist globalization can be conceptualized. In order to reach this stage in the argument it is necessary to distinguish three competing approaches to globalization—internationalist (state-centrist); transnationalist (globalization as a contested world historical project with capitalist and other variants), and globalist (capitalist globalization as a more or less completed and irreversible neoliberal capitalist project).

The chapter concludes with the argument that capitalist globalization cannot succeed in the long term because it cannot resolve two central crises—class polarization and ecological unsustainability on a global scale. This lays the transnational capitalist class and its institutions open to the attacks of an ever widening antiglobalization movement and makes the search for alternatives to capitalist globalization urgent. I introduce the idea that the best prospect for ending capitalist globalization in the long run lies in the globalization of economic and social human rights, and that this is attainable through the spread of genuine democracy.

Competing Approaches to Globalization

By "competing approaches" I mean ideas about the fundamental unit of analysis used when we discuss globalization.[2] This is basic to all scientific inquiry, and argument around the scientific method and paradigms of science revolve around agreements and disagreements over these basic units of analysis. In this context there are three types of units of analysis that different (competing) groups of globalization theorists and researchers take to define their field of inquiry. First, and most commonly, the internationalist (state-centrist) approach to globalization takes as its unit of analysis the state (often confused with the much more contentious idea of the nation-state). In this approach, globalization is seen as something that powerful states do to less powerful states, and something that is done to less powerful groups of people in all states. It is sometimes difficult to see where this line of argument differs from older theories of imperialism and colonialism and more recent theories of dependency. The theme of globalization as the new imperialism is quite common among radical critics of globalization, by which they invariably mean (but do not always say) capitalist globalization. I reject this view on the grounds of theoretical redundancy and empirical inadequacy. It is theoretically redundant: if globalization is just another name for imperialism, more of the same, then the term is redundant at best and confusing at worst. State-centrist approaches to globalization offer no qualitatively new criteria for globalization and, paradoxically, appear to offer at least nominal support to those who argue that globalization is a myth.

The globalist approach is the antithesis to the state-centrist thesis, for example, in the work of Kenichi Ohmae (formerly McKinsey chief in Japan) and other management gurus (but very few actual researchers). Globalists argue that the state has all but disappeared, that we have already entered a borderless world, and that globalization is a done deal. The global economy is driven by nameless and faceless market forces, the globalist unit of analysis, often referred to as neoliberal globalization. I reject this approach for its failure to theorize correctly the role of the state and the interstate system, for globalists (like state-centrists) are unable to analyze adequately the changing role of the state in sustaining the hegemony of capitalist globalization.

The transnational approach to globalization is the synthesis of the collision of the flawed state-centrist thesis and the globalist antithesis. I consider this to be the most fruitful, facilitating theory and research on the struggle between the dominant but as yet incomplete project of capitalist globalization and its alternatives. My own version of this synthesis proposes "transnational practices" (TNPs) as the most conceptually coherent and most empirically useful unit of analysis. Within the familiar political economy categories—economy, politics, and (somewhat less familiar) culture-ideology—we can construct the categories of economic, political, and cultural-ideological TNPs and conduct empirical research to discover their characteristic institutional forms in the dominant global system (manifestation of globalization). However different they are, these three approaches stem from a real phenomenon: generic globalization.

Generic Globalization

The central feature of all the approaches to globalization current in the social sciences is that many important contemporary problems cannot be adequately studied at the level of nation-states, that is, in terms of national societies or international relations, but need to be theorized (more or less) in terms of globalizing (transnational) processes, beyond the level of the nation-state. Globalization researchers have focused on two new phenomena that have become significant in the last few decades:

1. The electronic revolution, notably transformations in the technological base and global scope of the electronic mass media, and most of the material infrastructure of the world today;[3]
2. The subsequent creation of transnational social spaces in which qualitatively new forms of cosmopolitanism flourish.[4]

I take these two new phenomena—the electronic revolution and transnational social spaces generating cosmopolitanism—to be the defining characteristics of globalization in a generic sense. They are both irreversible in the long run (absent global catastrophe) because the vast majority of the people in the world, rich or poor, men or women, black or white, young or old, able or disabled, educated or uneducated, gay or straight, secular or religious, see that generic globalization could serve their own best interests, even if it is not necessarily serving their best interests at present. This is the world most people live in, big landlords as well as subsistence farmers in villages, corporate executives as well as laborers in sweatshops in major cities, well-paid professionals as well as informal workers in tourist sites, comfortable manual workers as well as desperate migrants in transit in the hope of better lives.

These polarities point to the inescapable fact that we do not live in a world of abstract generic globalization but actually existing capitalist globalization. The dominant global system at the start of the twenty-first century is the capitalist global system, and I argue that the most fruitful way to analyze and research it is in terms of its transnational practices.

Global System Theory

Global system theory is based on the concept of transnational practices, practices that cross state boundaries but do not originate with state agencies or actors (although they are often involved). This conceptual choice offers a working hypothesis for one of the most keenly contested disagreements between globalization theorists and their opponents, namely, that the nation-state is in decline.[5] The concept of transnational practices is an attempt to make more concrete the issues raised by such questions in the debate over globalization. Analytically, transnational practices operate in three spheres, the economic, the political, and the cultural-ideological. The whole is what I mean by the "global system." The global system at the beginning of the twentieth-first century is not synonymous with global capitalism, but the forces of global capitalism dominate the global system. Individuals, groups, institutions, and even whole communities—local, national, or transnational—can exist, perhaps even thrive, as they have always done outside the orbit of the global capitalist system. But this is becoming increasingly more difficult as capitalist globalization penetrates ever more widely and deeply. The building blocks of global system theory are the transnational corporation—the characteristic institutional form of economic transnational practices—a still evolving transnational capitalist class in the political sphere, and the culture-ideology of consumerism in the culture-ideology sphere.

In the economic sphere, the global capitalist system offers a limited place to the wage-earning masses in most countries. The workers, the direct producers of goods and services, have occupational choices that are generally free within the range offered by prevailing class structures. The inclusion of the subordinate classes in the political sphere is very partial. The global capitalist system has little need of the subordinate classes in this sphere. In parliamentary democracies, successful parties must be able to mobilize the masses to vote every so often, but in most countries voting is not compulsory and mass political participation is usually discouraged. In nondemocratic or quasi-democratic capitalist polities even these minimal conditions are absent.

The culture-ideology sphere is entirely different. The aim of global capitalists is total inclusion of all classes, and especially the subordinate classes insofar as the bourgeoisie can be considered already included. The culture-ideology project of global capitalism is to persuade people to consume above their biological needs in order to perpetuate the accumulation of capital for private profit, to ensure that the global capitalist system goes on forever. The culture-ideology of consumerism proclaims, literally, that the meaning of life is found in the things that people possess. To consume is to be fully alive, and to remain fully alive people must continuously consume. The notion of men and women as economic or political beings is discarded by global capitalism, quite logically, as the system does not even pretend to satisfy everyone in the economic or political spheres. People are primarily consumers. The point of economic activity for "ordinary members" of the global capitalist system is to provide the resources for consumption, and the point of political activity is to ensure that the conditions for consuming are maintained. The importance of the transnational corporations and of consumerism are now widely recognized by proponents, opponents, and those who claim to be neutral about globalization, but the idea of the transnational capitalist class is less familiar and much more controversial.

The Transnational Capitalist Class

The transnational capitalist class (TCC) is transnational in the double sense that its members have globalizing rather than, or in addition to, localizing perspectives. It typically includes people from many countries who operate transnationally as a normal part of their working lives. The transnational capitalist class can be conceptualized in terms of the following four fractions:

1. Those who own and control major TNCs and their local affiliates (corporate fraction)
2. Globalizing state and interstate bureaucrats and politicians (state fraction)
3. Globalizing professionals (technical fraction)
4. Merchants and media (consumerist fraction)

This class sees its mission as organizing the conditions under which its interests and the interests of the system can be furthered in the global and local context. The concept of the transnational capitalist class implies that there is one central transnational capitalist class that makes systemwide decisions. It connects with the TCC in each locality, region, and country. While the four fractions are distinguishable analytic categories with different functions for the global capitalist system, the people in them often move from one category to another (sometimes described as the "revolving door" between government and business, *pantouflage* in French).[6]

Together, these groups constitute a global power elite, ruling class, or inner circle in the sense that these terms have been used to characterize the class structures of specific countries.[7] The transnational capitalist class is opposed not only by those who reject capitalism as a way of life and/or an economic system but also by those capitalists who reject globalization. Some localized, domestically oriented businesses share the interests of the global corporations and prosper, but many cannot and perish. Influential business strategists and management theorists commonly argue that to survive, local businesses must globalize. Though most national and local state managers fight for the interests of their constituents, as they define these interests, government bureaucrats, politicians, and professionals who reject globalization and espouse extreme nationalist ideologies are comparatively rare, despite the recent rash of civil wars in economically marginal parts of the world. Although there are anticonsumerist elements in most societies, there are few cases of an anticonsumerist party winning political power anywhere in the world.

The transnational capitalist class is transnational in the following respects.

1. The economic interests of its members are increasingly globally linked rather than exclusively local and national in origin. Their property and shares and the corporations they own and/or control are becoming more globalized. As ideologues, their intellectual products serve the interests of globalizing rather than localizing capital. This follows directly from the shareholder-driven growth imperative that lies behind the globalization of the world economy and the increasing difficulty of enhancing shareholder value in purely domestic firms. While for some practical purposes the world is still organized in terms of discrete national economies, the TCC increasingly conceptualizes its interests in terms of markets, which may or may not coincide with a specific nation-state, and the global market, which clearly does not. I define "domestic firms" as those serving an exclusively sovereign state market, employing only local conationals, whose products consist entirely of domestic services, components, and materials. If you think that this is a ridiculously narrow definition for the realities of contemporary economies, then you are more than halfway to accepting my concept of globalization.

2. The TCC seeks to exert economic control in the workplace, political control in domestic and international politics, and culture-ideology control in everyday life through specific forms of global competitive and consumerist rhetoric and

practice. The focus of workplace control is the threat that jobs will be lost and, in the extreme, the economy will collapse unless workers are prepared to work longer and for less in order to meet foreign competition. This is reflected in local electoral politics in most countries, where the major parties have few substantial strategic (even if many rhetorical and tactical) differences, and in the sphere of culture-ideology, where consumerism is rarely challenged.

3. Members of the TCC have outward-oriented globalizing rather than inward-oriented localizing perspectives on most economic, political, and culture-ideology issues. The growing TNC and international institutional emphasis on free trade and the shift from import substitution to export promotion strategies in most "developing" countries since the 1980s have been driven by alliances of consultancies of various types, indigenous and foreign members of the TCC working through TNCs, government agencies, elite opinion organizations, and the media. Some of the credit for this apparent transformation in the way in which big business works around the world is attached to the tremendous growth in business education since the 1960s, particularly in the United States and Europe, but increasingly all over the world.

4. Members of the TCC tend to share similar lifestyles, particularly patterns of higher education (increasingly in business schools) and consumption of luxury goods and services. Integral to this process are exclusive clubs and restaurants, ultra-expensive resorts on all continents, private as opposed to mass forms of travel and entertainment, and, ominously, increasing residential segregation of the very rich secured by armed guards and electronic surveillance all over the world, from Los Angeles to Moscow, from Manila to Beijing.

5. Finally, members of the TCC seek to project images of themselves as citizens of the world, not just their place of birth. Leading exemplars of this phenomenon include French-born Jacques Maisonrouge, who became in the 1960s the chief executive of IBM World Trade; the Swede Percy Barnevik who created Asea Brown Boverei, often portrayed as spending most of his life in his corporate jet; the German Helmut Maucher, CEO of Nestlé's far-flung global empire; David Rockefeller, said to be one of the most powerful men in the United States; the legendary Akio Morita, founder of Sony; and Rupert Murdoch, who actually changed his nationality to pursue his global media interests. Today major corporate philanthropists, notably Bill Gates and George Soros, embody the new globalizing TCC.

The inner circle of the TCC gives a unity to the diverse economic interests, political organizations, and cultural and ideological formations of those who make up the class as a whole. As in any social class, fundamental long-term unity of interests and purpose does not preclude shorter-term and local conflicts of interests and purpose, both within each of the four fractions and between them. The culture-ideology of consumerism is the fundamental value system that keeps the system intact, but it permits a relatively wide variety of choices, for example, what I term "emergent global nationalisms" as a way of satisfying the needs of the different actors and their constituencies within the global system. The four fractions of the TCC in any region, country, city, society, or community perform complementary functions to integrate the whole. The achievement of these goals is facilitated by the activities of local and national agents and organizations connected in a complex network of global interlocks.

A crucial component of this integration of the TCC as a global class is that virtually all senior members of the TCC will occupy a variety of interlocking positions, not only the interlocking directorates that have been the subject of detailed studies for some time in a variety of countries, but also connections outside the direct ambit of the corporate sector, the civil society as it were servicing the statelike structures of the corporations. Leading corporate executives serve on and chair the boards of think tanks, charities, scientific, sports, arts and culture bodies, universities, medical foundations, and similar organizations. In this sense claims that "the business of society is business" and "the business of our society is global business" become legitimated in the global capitalist system. Business, particularly the transnational corporation sector, then begins to monopolize symbols of modernity and postmodernity like free enterprise, international competitiveness, and the good life and to transform most, if not all, social spheres in its own image.

The End of Capitalist Globalization

The literature on globalization is suffused with a good deal of fatalism. Some progressive academics, popular writers, and political and cultural leaders seem to accept that there is no alternative to capitalist globalization and that all we can do is to try to work for a better world around it.[8] While I cannot fully develop the counterargument to this fatalism here, it seems to me to be both morally indefensible and theoretically shortsighted. Capitalist globalization is failing on two counts, fundamental to the future of most of the people in the world and, indeed, to the future of our planet itself. These are the class polarization crisis and the crisis of ecological unsustainability. There is evidence to suggest that capitalist globalization may be intensifying both crises.[9] Nevertheless, globalization should not be identified with capitalism, though capitalist globalization is its dominant form in the present era. This makes it necessary to think through other forms of globalization, forms that might retain some of the positive consequences of capitalism (insofar as they can exist outside capitalism) while transcending it as a socioeconomic system in the transition to a new stage of world history.[10]

One path out of capitalism, which is clear to some but quite unclear to most, takes us from capitalist globalization (where we are), through what can be termed cooperative democracy (a transitional form of society), to socialist globalization (a convenient label for a form of globalization that ends class polarization and the ecological crisis). One strategy to achieve such a transformation involves the gradual elimination of the culture-ideology of consumerism and its replacement with a culture-ideology of human rights. This means, briefly, that instead of our possessions being the main focus of our culture and the basis of our values, our lives should be lived with regard to a universally agreed system of human rights and the responsibilities to others that these rights entail. This does not imply that we should stop consuming. What it implies is that we should evaluate our consumption in terms of our rights and responsibilities and that this should become a series of interlocking and mutually supportive globalizing transnational practices.

By genuinely expanding the culture-ideology of human rights from the civil and political spheres, in which capitalist globalization has often had a relatively positive influence, to the economic and social spheres, which represents a profound challenge to capitalist globalization, we can begin seriously to tackle the crises of class polarization and ecological unsustainability. But political realism dictates that this change cannot be accomplished directly; it must proceed via a transitional stage. Capitalism and socialism, as can be seen in the case of market socialism in China, are not watertight categories. Capitalist practices can and do occur in socialist societies (e.g., making workers redundant to increase profits) just as socialist practices can exist in capitalist societies (e.g., trying to ensure that everyone in a community enjoys a basic decent standard of living). The issue is hegemony, whose interests prevail, who defends the status quo (even by reforming it), who is pushing for fundamental change, and how this is organized into effective social movements for change globally.

The transition to socialist globalization will eventually create new forms of transnational practices. Transnational economic units will tend to be on a smaller and more sustainable scale than the major TNCs of today; transnational political practices will be democratic coalitions of self-governing and cooperative communities, not the unaccountable, unelected, and individualistic transnational capitalist class. Cultures and ideologies will reflect the finer qualities of human life, not the desperate variety of the culture-ideology of consumerism. These sentiments might appear utopian (indeed they are) and other alternatives are also possible. But in the long term, muddling through with capitalist globalization is not a viable option if the planet and all those who live in it are to survive.

Thus, although the discourse and practice of what I have labeled "capitalist globalization" seem to suggest that it is a force for convergence, the inability of capitalist globalization to solve the crises of class polarization and ecological unsustainability makes it both necessary and urgent to think through alternatives to it. This implies that capitalist globalization contains the seeds of divergence.

The globalization of human rights leading to what can (but need not necessarily) be termed "socialist globalization" is certainly one, if presently rather remote, alternative, and there are many others. Communities, cities, subnational regions, whole countries, multicountry unions, and even transnational cooperative associations could all in principle try to make their own arrangements for checking and reversing class polarization and ecological unsustainability. The twenty-first century will likely bring many new patterns of divergence before a global convergence on full human rights for all is established. This is unlikely to occur in a world dominated by transnational corporations, run by the transnational capitalist class, and inspired by the culture-ideology of consumerism.

Notes

1. There are few ideas in the social sciences that have spawned textbooks of several hundred pages a decade after they were announced. See, for example, Jan A. Scholte, *Globalization: A Critical Introduction* (London: Macmillan, 2000) and dozens of collections, notably Frank Lechner and John Boli, eds., *The Globalization Reader* (Oxford: Blackwell, 2000). There is a useful account of the origin of the term in the social sciences in the first, short textbook, Malcolm Waters, *Globalization* (London: Routledge, 1995), chapter 1. The present chapter borrows from my own contributions, *The Transnational Capitalist Class* (Oxford: Blackwell, 2001) and *Globalization: Capitalism and Its Alternatives* (Oxford: Oxford University Press, 2002), the third and significantly revised edition of a book originally published in 1991.

2. In *Globalization*, chapter 3, I distinguish four competing conceptions of globalization that focus on who or what is driving the processes. The approaches discussed here are at a higher level of generality, at the level of metatheory rather than theoretical concepts.

3. See, for example, M. Costell, *The Rise of the Network Society* (London: Blackwell, 2000); E. Herman and R. McChesney, *The Global Media* (London: Cassell, 1997).

4. Worked out in different ways in Thomas Faist, *The Volume and Dynamics of International Migration and Transnational Social Spaces* (Oxford: Oxford University Press, 2000); Ulrich Beck, *World Risk Society* (Cambridge: Polity, 1999); Peter Smith and Luis Guarnizo, eds., *Transnationalism from Below* (Brunswick, N.J.: Transaction, 1998).

5. For good critical discussions of these issues, see R. Holton, *Globalization and the Nation-State* (London: MacMillan, 1998) and S. Strange, *The Retreat of the State* (Cambridge: Cambridge University Press, 1996).

6. For a constructive critique, see A. R. Embong, "Globalization and Transnational Class Relations: Some Problems of Conceptualization," *Third World Quarterly* 21(2000): 989–1000.

7. Preglobalization capitalist class theory, for which see John Scott, *Corporate Business and Capitalist Class* (Oxford: Oxford University Press, 1997), does not necessarily exclude the globalizing extension proposed here.

8. The most politically important example is the Third Way thesis; see Anthony Giddens: *The Third Way and Its Critics* (Cambridge: Polity Press, 2000).

9. These two crises of capitalist globalization are elaborated in Sklair, *Globalization*, 47–58 and passim.

10. The following paragraphs are based on Sklair, *Globalization*, chap. 11.

GLOBAL CONTAINMENT: THE PRODUCTION OF FEMINIST INVISIBILITY AND THE VANISHING HORIZON OF JUSTICE

Mary Hawkesworth

It requires a great deal of strength to be able to live and to forget the extent to which to live and to be unjust is one and the same thing.

—Nietzsche[1]

The human struggle against power is the struggle of memory against forgetting.

—Kundera[2]

State-Prescribed Subordination of Women

The Filipina domestic worker is an emblem of globalization. Produced by an "export-led development strategy of the Philippines, the feminization of the international labor force, and the demand for migrant women to fill low-wage service work in many cities throughout the world,"[3] the Filipina labor diaspora now encompasses 130 nations.[4] The flow of Filipina labor has been facilitated by contracts negotiated by the Philippine government with the governments of receiving states in Asia, the Americas, Europe, and the Middle East. Among the provisions of these labor contracts are a number of significant violations of women's rights,[5] including extensive curtailment of reproductive freedom,[6] the freedom to marry and engage in sexual relationships of one's own choosing,[7] freedom of movement,[8] and freedom of domicile.[9] The contracts also violate a number of fair labor practices.[10]

Rather than enforce the rights of Filipina citizens under the law of the Philippines,[11] implement the rights afforded women under the Convention to Eliminate All Forms of Discrimination Against Women (CEDAW), or enforce the rights of migrant workers under the international Covenant on the Protection of the Rights of All Migrant Workers,[12] in negotiating, monitoring, and enforcing these overseas employment contracts, the Philippine government actively subordinates Filipinas. Contrary to the assumptions of many Westerners, the majority of Filipina overseas domestic workers are college-educated women. In negotiating contracts that consign middle-class women professionals to domestic labor in foreign households, the Philippine government prescribes gender subordination along multiple axes. By actively promoting the marketization of "care work," the Philippine government transforms highly educated Filipinas into their most marketable product.[13]

The government-negotiated contracts transform Filipina overseas domestic workers from autonomous adults into dependents of their employers. Denied control over the conditions of their lives and work, over decisions concerning love, marriage, reproduction, and physical mobility during the terms set by their contracts, Filipina domestic workers must request their employer's permission to leave the house and to leave the country. They have no recourse when reasonable requests are denied or when they are subjected to physical and sexual abuse by their employers. In transforming Filipina citizens from rights-bearing individuals in their home nations to dependents in their host nations, the Philippine government's overseas labor contracts reverse the historic trajectory of the bourgeois state's struggle against feudalism. Instead of emancipating subjects from feudal ties, the Philippine government reinscribes the serf's dependence on the feudal lord in the relation between Filipina domestic worker and her employer. Within the confines of globalization, the Philippine government is inscribing a new gendered form of serfdom at the heart of productive relations in the global service economy. In the midst of multiple campaigns for women's rights as human rights, one might ask why this new mode of state-sponsored indentured service is not on the international social justice agenda.[14]

If the foreign domestication of college-educated Filipinas is one gendered sign of globalization, the "de-domestication" of poor women in the United States is another. While the Philippine government enacts gender subordination in a frame that constructs Filipinas as heroes performing extraordinary service to the state, the U.S. Congress deployed a rhetoric of deviance to construct poor women as welfare cheats who threaten to subvert the American work ethic. As the culmination of a series of "workfare" programs that required welfare recipients to work outside the home as a condition for receipt of benefits, the Personal Responsibility and Work Opportunity Reconciliation Act of 1996 (PRWORA) abolished the "right" to social provision, imposed mandatory work requirements on recipients of Temporary Aid to Needy Families (TANF), and enabled states to impose a variety of intrusive regulations on the lives of poor women, including restrictions on poor women's privacy rights, reproductive choices, and bodily integrity.[15] Under TANF, poor single mothers are subjected to sexual regulation by the state that severely infringes their constitutional rights to privacy. "They are required to submit to interrogations about their sexual histories, to undergo genetic tests to establish paternity, and to assist the state to collect support payments from the absent fathers of their children even if they do not want to be dependent upon them—and in many cases, even if they are fleeing from the absent father's violent conduct."[16] For poor women in the United States, the state has not been rolled back.

Thus it would appear that under globalization, as in earlier capitalist formations, opposites embrace. The heroization and vilification of women produce common effects. Whether deploying promises of higher pay and civic patriotism or castigations of dependency accompanied by threats of benefit termination, some states are moving women out of their homes, away from their families, and into the paid labor force. State policies are actively promoting menial jobs and severe restrictions on women's liberty, effectively supplanting caring for kin outside of the cash nexus. While the nation-state may be weakening or hollowing out in relation to the financial architecture of global capital, the case of Filipina overseas domestic workers and the case of TANF recipients in the United States suggest that certain "democratic" regimes are intensifying their regulation of women's lives in ways that undercut individual freedom and privacy. In both instances, the state is thoroughly complicit in constricting women's rights, diminishing women's status, and subjecting women to the arbitrary power of others. Yet this ongoing state-prescribed subordination of women seldom reaches the threshold of visibility. And feminist efforts to publicize such issues and to devise political strategies to redress them are repeatedly erased from public awareness.

In focusing on state policies that subordinate women as emblematic of globalization, my goal is to demonstrate that globalization is a gendered phenomenon, while simultaneously asking why the gendered dimensions of globalization seldom surface in public and academic debates, despite ongoing feminist efforts to "engender" these globalization debates. How is the invisibility of women produced and sustained? How is feminist activism around gendered inequities constitutive of globalization rendered invisible? Despite extensive evidence of growing gender inequity,[17] what ideological and material practices help produce the belief that women have no need for feminism and the world has no need for feminist conceptions of social justice?

53

Producing Invisibility

Nietzsche suggests that it takes great strength *not* to live with the recognition of injustice, but to forget the injustice constitutive of life. How is that strength produced in the age of globalization? Are there mechanisms that assist such forgetting, strategies that foster unknowing? Reflection on the means by which women's state-sponsored subordination and feminist activism to redress that subordination are kept below the threshold of visibility may afford some insight into the production of sanctioned ignorance, forms of unknowing actively produced and legitimated by dominant discourses.

The emergence of second wave feminism as a global phenomenon coincided with waning of the Cold War and the resurgence of capitalism under the sign of globalization. At the same time that the West was declaring victory over the Soviet system and equating democratization with neoliberal economic reforms and liberal democratic political reforms, feminists were documenting pervasive and growing inequality within capitalist states and between the North and South. The "feminization of poverty," which feminists have demonstrated to be a growing global phenomenon, bears potent witness to the limitations of neoliberal prescriptions for sustainable development. The vibrant activism of feminists against structural adjustment policies and around the politics of subsistence makes a mockery of claims that capitalism remedies poverty. The ongoing struggle of feminists for gender balance in governance, for women's equal participation in public and private decision making, constitutes a formidable challenge to liberal democratic regimes in which women are woefully underrepresented across all leadership terrains. Global campaigns for women's rights as human rights, for an end to violence against women, and for an end to sex trafficking and sex slavery, for the implementation of CEDAW and the Beijing Platform for Action have brought women from all parts of the world together in coalition to eliminate all vestiges of male domination.

Despite unprecedented levels of feminist activism around the globe,[18] feminism is pronounced "dead," "obsolete," "outmoded" with remarkable frequency by pundits and the Western press.[19] Stories of successful feminist campaigns seldom make the news. As Melissa Deem pointed out, "feminists do not control the timing of their appearance or the content of their message"[20] in print or visual media. Accounts of women's oppression surface not when feminists sound the alarm, but when they are useful to legitimate military or police operations of questionable legality, as the recent U.S. invasion of Afghanistan makes painfully clear. Within this global frame, "powerless women" need to be saved by powerful men, not to be empowered in their own right by their own activism.

How, then, are so many diverse forms of feminist activism that challenge capitalist strategies for the emancipation of women, erased or contained?

Discursive Tactics: Gender Displacement

The mechanisms that produce feminist invisibility are multiple and complex. Some tactics, however, are easier to trace than others. Consider, for example, a recent article in the *New York Times Magazine*, "Globalization: The Free Trade Fix," by Tina Rosenberg. While Rosenberg explicitly notes that "almost all sweatshop workers are young women [who] endure starvation wages, forced overtime, and dangerous working conditions,"[21] the two global workers she describes in detail in the article are both men. Thus any fledgling recognition of the gendered dimensions of globalization is quickly displaced by identification with and concern for the plight of male workers. Rhacel Salazar Parrenas has pointed out a similar strategy of gender displacement in the Philippine government's discursive construction of the heroic overseas contract worker. Although government statistics indicate that Filipinas constitute 60 percent of the migrant labor force, the government intentionally promotes the image of a male migrant as the

> iconic figure of the modern-day heroes. . . . The Philippine government prefers to project a representative male instead of a female image so as to downplay the reality that more women than men are leaving the Philippines. The government does so in order to downplay one of the greatest costs of exportation, which is the vulnerability of female migrant workers. Concentrated in domestic and entertainment work, Filipina migrants—77.8% of whom could be found in service occupations in 1996—enter more vulnerable occupations than do their male counterparts.[22]

Whether a journalist's unintentional slip or a government's intentional strategy to divert public attention, gender displacement is quite successful as a tactic to remove women from the global frame. Such gender displacement surfaces regularly in academic texts on globalization as well as in the popular press and in government policy.

Let us consider another example: the gendered rhetoric structuring the abstract categories of analysis within Hardt and Negri's massive tome, *Empire*.[23] Although Hardt and Negri cite several feminist texts and embrace Donna Harraway's cyborg imagery, women's work in the production of subsistence, on the global assembly line, as migrant service workers, in physical and social reproduction, and as transformative agents is thoroughly occluded in this massive account of globalization. Indeed, unless "affective labor" is read as a synonym for women's work (a move that feminists would find deeply problematic), women play virtually no role in the deterritorialized politics and economics of *Empire*. Allegedly gender-neutral nouns such as "proletariat" or "multitude" engulf and subsume women, while reproduction, a process in which women figure prominently in past and present worlds, is miraculously taken over by men.

The production of life figures prominently in Hardt and Negri's critique of global capital, and in their prophetic vision of social change. But these modes of reproduction are homosocial at best. Thus in criticizing the reduction of all relations to the cash nexus, Hardt and Negri note:

> production and reproduction are dressed in monetary clothing. . . . The great industrial and financial powers thus produce not only commodities but also subjectivities. They produce agentic subjectivities within the bio-political context: they produce needs, social relations, bodies, and minds— which is to say, they produce producers.[24]

By conflating social reproduction with all modes of reproduction, Hardt and Negri can dispense with women and attribute pride of place in the generation of life to "the great industrial and financial powers," a cohort in which women are markedly underrepresented.[25]

Like many Marxists before them, Hardt and Negri identify the manipulation and management of difference as part of the "current ideology of corporate capital."[26] Thus feminist activists/theorists who foreground gender difference, like postcolonial and critical race theorists who foreground national, racial, or ethnic differences, are simply (albeit unwittingly) playing on a terrain that serves the interests of capital.[27] According to Hardt and Negri, far from being liberating, such difference-based strategies are futile and destructive, for they continue to undermine the solidarity of the "emerging multitude," which constitutes the universal and revolutionary global class.[28] Thus not only are women displaced in Hardt and Negri's account of globalization, but some feminist activism is roundly rejected as reactionary.

Neoliberal Tactics

While Hardt and Negri afford a powerful example of the means by which women are displaced from contemporary academic accounts of globalization, proponents of neoliberalism have their own repertoire for rendering women, women's issues, and feminist activism invisible. Chief among these are invocations of individual choice and privatization. Tina Rosenberg's essay again provides a helpful point of departure. After providing a gruesome account of the physically harmful and financially exploitive working conditions of a Chilean man employed in a chicken processing plant whose products are exported to Europe, Asia, and other countries in Latin America, Rosenberg asks, "Is this man a victim of globalization?" Rosenberg's response to the question is telling. Although she notes that at one time she might have thought him a victim, she now realizes that such a stance is mistaken. Exploitation of the sort experienced by the Chilean worker is a mistaken focus for antiglobalization protests because the global assembly-line worker chose to take this job and is benefiting from it.

> But today if I were to picket globalization, I would protest other inequities. In a way, the chicken worker, who came to the factory when driving a taxi ceased to be profitable, is a beneficiary of globalization. So are the millions of young women who have left rural villages to be exploited gluing tennis shoes or assembling computer keyboards. The losers are those who get laid off when companies move to low-wage countries, or those forced off their land when imports undercut their crop prices, or those who can no longer afford life-saving medicine—people whose choices in life diminish because of global trade. Globalization has offered this man a hellish job, but it is a choice he did not have before, and he took it; I don't name him because he is afraid of being fired. When this chicken company is hiring, the lines go around the block.[29]

A number of neoliberal stock arguments are packed into this brief paragraph, first and foremost, the appeal to individual choice. A contract voluntarily entered into by a worker, who is a rational economic maximizer, is an inappropriate target for those interested in social justice. The agency manifested by the individual who consents to exploitive working conditions negates efforts to categorize the worker as oppressed. The Chilean man, a rational calculator of his economic interests by virtue of his conscious decision to opt for the global assembly line over the entrepreneurial venture of taxi driving, circulates as the sign under which millions of women workers are subsumed. Nothing need be said about the options that structured their "choices" of work. The familiar prejudices that pit modernization unequivocally against tradition carry additional argumentative weight. The global factory rescues the Chilean man (and the millions of women who trail in his wake) from "the idiocy of rural life."[30] Global capitalism affords opportunities, wage labor, which make individuals better off. Proof of the benefits that global capital affords: individuals compete for the opportunity to be exploited.

Such an account of the generic worker masks the unique vulnerabilities that women workers face in global factories. Invasive pregnancy tests to which women employees are regularly subjected as a condition of work and sexual harassment on the job disappear behind the mask of the self-interested maximizer. Local mobilizations by women workers against abusive working conditions are rendered invisible by depictions of jobs freely taken. Moreover, international feminist mobilizations against gender-specific abuses are repudiated as a mode of Western hegemony that fails to comprehend the agency of women workers in export processing zones.

The neoliberal depiction of globalization is unquestionably the dominant view circulating in the United States. Thus it is not surprising that those who take their news exclusively from dominant media outlets may not know anything about the gendered inequities of globalization or "glocal" feminist mobilizations to address them. Their social amnesia is produced and accredited by mainstream politicians, journalists, economists, and political scientists.

The effects of neoliberalism are not restricted to popular understandings of globalization, however. They are also apparent in a form of "restructuring" that significantly transforms the conditions under which feminist activists attempt to engage gender-based injustices. Over the past decade, feminist activism has undergone "NGOization."[31] Operating as nonprofit entities within neoliberal definitions of the "private" sphere, NGOs provide services that the state is unwilling or unable to provide. Once consigned to the scope of NGO activity, what had previously been considered a matter of public policy is redefined as a project of a private organization. Thus the context of feminist political activism subtly changes. What social movement feminists understood as a political struggle for social justice, the rights of women citizens or for women's rights as human rights can be construed by neoliberals as a dispute over private resources. In changing the framing assumptions from a movement for social justice to the private pursuit of economic resources, feminist goals are depoliticized and resignified as "private" endeavors.

Thus in working as NGOs on projects vital to women's physical safety and economic survival, feminists are privatized. Feminists (as well as gay and lesbian activists and antiracist activists) are characterized by neoliberals as proponents of "special interests," who unfairly demand "special rights." Within the neoliberal frame, appeals to social justice are reduced to claims for "special treatment" and readily dismissed as violations of individual (i.e., white male) rights, as well as universal norms. The moral suasion afforded by demands to remedy injustice is effectively neutralized as neoliberalism transforms feminist activism to one more mode of the pursuit of self-interest and depicts the state as a neutral arbiter, which simply provides an equal playing field on which private interests compete.

Depoliticizing the State

Neoliberalism's transformative power extends beyond the reclassification of feminist activism from a struggle for social justice to a pursuit of private interests. It subtly transforms perceptions of the state itself. With the rise of social democracy in the aftermath of World War II, social justice activists understood the state as a viable site of political contestation. Through political party platforms as well as the politics of direct action, proponents of social justice engaged the nation-state as the primary means by which to struggle against the enormous power of the capitalist market. Many feminists, like other progressive activists, perceived the state as a unique vehicle in the struggle for social justice because the state had the capacity to bestow equal rights, to legislate policies to redress historic exclusions and inequities, to use its tax revenues toward redistributive ends, to provide all citizens with a decent quality of life, and to change exploitive conditions of labor. In forging their political agenda, feminists intentionally sought to expand the notion of a "public" issue. Thus they suggested that an issue is public "1) if it is treated as politically important; 2) if it is understood as causally related to societal structures in which all citizens are implicated; and 3) if its solution is viewed as requiring a collective effort to bring about relief for victims and reform to prevent further occurrence."[32]

Those feminists who made the state the target of their political efforts sought to force the official institutions of government to treat women and women's concerns as matters of political importance. Through court cases and legislative battles, they fought to demonstrate exactly how the law constructs and sustains public/private spheres and the relations of gender inequality that pervade them. By illuminating state complicity in the subordination of women, some feminists tried to foster public awareness of the depths of collective responsibility for centuries of women's exclusion, marginalization, and exploitation in the hope that public knowledge of injustice would trigger collective action to change the laws, the social structures, and the personal relations shaped by them.[33]

Neoliberalism privatizes these feminist endeavors by subsuming them under interest group politics at the same time that it redefines the role of the state. Over the past few decades, neoliberalism has profoundly altered perceptions of the kinds of contestations possible within the nation-state.[34] Resurrecting the classical view that inequality among people is natural rather than politically constituted and maintained, neoliberals insist that state efforts to reduce inequality are futile, wrong-headed, and necessarily oppressive. Rather than indulge utopian fantasies, the role of the state, on this view, is to promote individual freedom, understood as the individual's pursuit of material self-interest. The state can best advance this end by facilitating economic development, which in turn will resolve social problems. State strategies to foster economic development include deregulation of the corporate sector, provision of special incentives for economic development in free enterprise zones, reductions of income, estate, and corporate taxes, and elimination of welfare "dependency." Within the parameters set by neoliberalism, the political agenda should be winnowed down to the provision of essential business services and security (domestic and global). There is no space on this streamlined neoliberal agenda for feminist politics. At best, feminist efforts to expand the public agenda appear oddly anachronistic, a remnant of the misguided but buoyant politics of the 1960s. At worst, feminist discourses are construed as petulant groveling in "victimization," which dupes women into practices that worsen their condition.[35]

The Politics of Resignation

While neoliberals advocate the cultivation of the corporate-friendly "night watchman" state as a matter of intentional public policy, many voices participating in contemporary globalization debates suggest that the retrenchment of the welfare state is less a matter of willful political design and more a consequence of the relentless forces of globalization. Discussions of the "hollowing out" of the state, the "erosion of sovereignty," and the "demise of welfare state" concur in the neoliberal conclusion that there is no scope for social justice politics on the contemporary political horizon.[36]

While such pessimistic assessments are understandable given capitalism's resurgence since 1990, the politics of resignation incorporated in such assessments erase one of the most vibrant decades of feminist activism on record. In contrast to neoliberal strategies that acknowledge feminism's existence even as they denigrate it as private interest pleading, naive utopianism, or oppressive interventionism, the grim analyses of the contemporary political scene advanced by some scholars of the left write feminism out of existence altogether. Nigerian women's courageous activism against multinational oil corporations, Mexican women's activism to bring to justice those who raped and murdered some three hundred young women working in maquiladora factories, Somali women's brilliant strategy to constitute themselves as a "tribe" in order to be included in nation building when the law organized participation on a tribal basis, the redistributive work of women serving on village councils in India, the subsistence farming collectives organized by Russian women to sustain their villages while the transition to capitalism leaves them without jobs (or with jobs without wages), the mobilization of women in Senegal to preserve collective fishing rights essential to the survival of their people after their government transferred exclusive fishing rights to European companies, vibrant and successful efforts to organize Filipina overseas domestic workers into unions offering collective strategies to create sustainable economic alternatives to circular and recurrent labor migration, to mention just a few ongoing feminist projects,[37] are all erased, rendered invisible, impossible, or foolish by the accounts of some leading scholars on the left. Profound pessimism thus can also serve as a powerful mechanism in the production of feminist invisibility.

Conclusion

Feminist invisibility can be produced by manifold means advanced for radically different reasons by people espousing markedly different ideological commitments. Not seeing, not acknowledging, not knowing, ignoring, declaring impossible or futile are various technologies of invisibility. Used by those on the right as well as some on the left, these tactics, singly and jointly, eliminate feminist activism from public awareness and from the horizon of social justice. Rather than acknowledge the contingency of a world in which feminist struggle can produce change and open new possibilities, voices on the left and the right converge in depicting a world in which male domination seems peculiarly fixed and unchanging. That such an appearance of fixity is illusory does not mitigate the power of the image. When feminist activism is forgotten, erased from the past and present, or caricatured as impossibility for the future, male domination is shored up as the horizon of social justice continues to recede. Forgetting of this magnitude has a decidedly misogynous edge.

Rather than acquiesce in this forgetting, I would like to suggest that the production of invisibility be understood as a form of sanctioned ignorance or social amnesia, as an active mode of unknowing or forgetting that facilitates the perpetuation of injustice. Like other ideological formations, this privileged mode of unknowing distorts reality, justifies the status quo, and protects the self-images of those in positions of power.[38] In erasing feminist activism from public awareness and women's issues from the political agenda, social amnesia fosters the perpetuation of sexism, racism, androcentrism, and heterosexism on the spurious ground that nothing can be done. Power and privilege remain undisturbed as those who possess them rest in a "twilight condition" characterized by the surrender of hope, the loss of hope in the future, and a general waning of historical consciousness.[39] Fortunately for those concerned about social justice, feminist activism continues while the unknowing thrash about in their sleep.

Notes

I would like to thank Manfred Steger and the participants in the Conference on the Ideological Dimensions of Globalization for their helpful suggestions for the revision of an earlier version of this chapter.

1. Friedrich Nietzsche, "The Uses and Disadvantages of History," in *Untimely Meditations*, ed. Daniel Breazeale, trans. R. J. Hollingdale (Cambridge: Cambridge University Press, 1983).

2. Milan Kundera, *The Book of Laughter and Forgetting* (New York: Penguin, 1980).

3. Rhacel Salazar Parrenas, "Transgressing the Nation-State: The Partial Citizenship and 'Imagined Community' of Migrant Filipina Domestic Workers," *Signs* 26, no. 4 (2001): 1129–54.

4. It is estimated that 3.8 million Filipinas are currently working overseas. They constitute 60 percent of the migrant labor force of their nation. Economists have estimated that remittances from overseas migrant workers provide the Philippines with its largest source of foreign currency, an estimated $8 bil-

lion per year (Margaret Magot, "Rome: A Magnet for Tourists, Filipina Domes-
tics," *Women's ENews*, www.womenenews.org (April 22, 2003). Among other
things, these remittances are used by the Philippine government to cover the
$1.8 billion of annual interest on loans accumulated from the World Bank and
the IMF; Ninotchka Rosca, "The Philippines' Shameful Export," *The Nation*
260 (15): 522–27, 1995. In the absence of migrant labor, unemployment in
the Philippines would increase by 40 percent; Stephen Castles and Mark Miller,
The Age of Migration (New York: Guilford, 1998).

 5. For detailed discussions of the specific provisions of these contracts in var-
ious nations, see Abigail Bakan and Daiva Stasiulis, *Not One of the Family: Foreign
Domestic Workers in Canada* (Toronto: University of Toronto Press, 1997); Kim-
berly Chang Campani and L. H. M. Ling, "Globalization and Its Intimate Other:
Filipina Domestic Workers in Hong Kong," in Marianne Marchand and Anne Run-
yon, eds., *Gender and Global Restructuring* (London: Routledge, 2000), 27–58;
Nicole Constable, *Maid to Order in Hong Kong* (Ithaca, N.Y.: Cornell University
Press, 1997); Patricia Daenzer, "An Affair between Nations: International Relations
and the Movement of Household Service Workers," in Bakan and Stasiulis, *Not
One of the Family*; Joaquin Gonzalez and Ronald Holmes, "The Philippine Labour
Diaspora," *Southeast Asian Affairs* (1996): 300–317; Mongaya Filomenita
Hogsholm, "Philippine International Migration," *Forum on Philippine International
Migration,* www.philsol.nl/fora/FFON97-editorial.htm (April 22, 2003); Rhacel
Salazar Parrenas, "Migrant Filipina Domestic Workers and the International Divi-
sion of Reproductive Labor," *Gender and Society* 14, no. 4 (2000): 560–81;
Rhacel Salazar Parrenas, *Servants of Globalization: Women, Migration and Domes-
tic Work* (Stanford: Stanford University Press, 2001); Rhacel Salazar Parrenas,
"Transgressing the Nation-State: The Partial Citizenship and Imagined Global
Community of Migrant Filipina Domestic Workers," *Signs* 26, no. 4 (2001):
1129–53.

 6. The Singapore contract, for example, stipulates that Filipina domestic
workers must submit to pregnancy checks every six months and be deported
if they become pregnant.

 7. The Singapore contract, for example, forbids marriage or cohabitation
with Singaporean citizens or permanent residents.

 8. The Singapore contract, for example, specifies that Filipina domestic
workers may not leave the country during the two-year term specified in work
contract without their employer's written permission.

 9. Contracts with Middle Eastern and Asian states stipulate that Filipina
domestic workers must live with their employers. Even the contract with
Canada, which is far more benign in certain respects, mandates that Filipina
domestic workers must live with their employers for first two years, unless
given explicit permission by the employer.

 10. According to the Singapore contract, for example, Filipina domestic work-

ers are allowed one day off per month, only after completing a three-month probationary period.

11. Parrenas, "Transgressing the Nation-State," 1151.

12. Wendy Sarvasy and Patrizia Longo, "Cosmopolitanism and Feminism: A Democratic Partnership beyond Borders" (paper presented at the 2002 annual meeting of the Western Political Science Association in Long Beach, California), 22. Sarvasy and Longo point out that the Philippines ratified this international agreement, which had been adopted by the United Nations in 1990 and passed implementing legislation, the Migrant Workers and Overseas Filipinos Act of 1995, even as it continued to monitor and enforce these exploitative overseas worker contracts. The Philippine Department of Labor and Employment maintains jurisdiction over the overseas contract workers through the Philippines Overseas Employment Agency.

13. The remittances from overseas contract workers provides the Philippine government more revenue than the export of electronic goods.

14. Although Filipina feminists working in migrant organizations are mobilizing around this issue, state-prescribed gender subordination through overseas labor contracts does not seem to have surfaced on the international social justice agenda. On the contrary, some activists have hailed the Philippine government's contracts for creating "basic rights" for Filipina domestic workers and some scholars have interpreted these contracts as laying the foundation for a new form of Kantian "cosmopolitan citizenship." See, for example, Meera Samantha and Rozana Isa, "Malaysia: Foreign Domestic Workers—The Obstacles," in Rita Raj, ed., *Women at the Intersection: Indivisible Rights, Identities, and Oppressions* (New Brunswick, N.J.: Center for Women's Global Leadership, 2002), 42.

15. In 1977 Congress passed a series of amendments to the Food Stamp Act, establishing the first workfare demonstration projects that required food stamp recipients "to work at public service jobs in return for their household's food stamp benefits." The Omnibus Budget Reconciliation Act of 1981 extended the concept of workfare to additional social welfare programs including Aid to Families with Dependent Children, the primary federal welfare program. By 1987, thirty-seven states had initiated workfare programs applicable to some portion of their welfare recipients. With the passage of PRWORA, workfare became mandatory throughout the fifty states. For detailed discussion of these programs, see Michael Katz, "From the War on Poverty to the War on Welfare," in *In the Shadow of the Poorhouse: A Social History of Welfare in America* (New York: Basic, 1989); Joel Handler and Yeheskel Hasenfeld, *The Moral Construction of Poverty: Welfare Reform in America* (Newbury Park, Calif.: Sage, 1991); Mimi Abramovitz, *Regulating the Lives of Women: Social Welfare from Colonial Times to the Present* (Boston: South End 1996); Gwendolyn Mink, *Welfare's End* (Ithaca, N.Y.: Cornell University Press, 1998); Jill Quadagno, *The Color of Welfare: How*

Racism Undermined the War on Poverty (New York: Oxford University Press, 1994).

16. Anna Marie Smith, "The Sexual Regulation Dimension of Contemporary Welfare Law," *Michigan Journal of Gender and Law* 8, no. 2 (2002): 121–218.

17. According to UNIFEM women constitute nearly 70 percent of the world's 1.2–1.3 billion poor. The 564 million rural women living in poverty in 1990 represented a 47 percent increase above the number of poor women in 1970. The poorest quintile of the world's population (1 billion people) earn only 1.4 percent of the world's wealth. In the twenty-first century, the poorest working women in the global south still earn less than $1 per day.

18. For overviews of contemporary feminist activism, see Margaret Kirk and Kathryn Sikkink, *Activists beyond Borders: Advocacy Networks in International Politics* (Ithaca, N.Y.: Cornell University Press, 1998); and Amrita Basu, ed., *Women's Movements in Global Perspective* (New Delhi: Kali for Women, 1999).

19. For an analysis of the recurrent proclamations of feminism's death, see Mary Hawkesworth, "On the Semiotics of Premature Burial," Peg Zeglin Brand Lecture in Gender Studies, Indiana University, April 18, 2002.

20. Melissa Deem, "Scandal, Heteronormative Culture, and the Disciplining of Feminism," *Critical Studies in Mass Communication*, March 1999, 86–94.

21. Tina Rosenberg, "Globalization: The Free Market Fix," *New York Times Magazine*, August 18, 2002, 28–33, 50, 74–75.

22. Parrenas, "Transgressing the Nation-State," 1137.

23. Michael Hardt and Antonio Negri, *Empire* (Cambridge: Harvard University Press, 2000).

24. Hardt and Negri, *Empire*, 32.

25. Examining the contributions of women across classes, Anne McClintock notes that women do two-thirds of the world's work, earn 10 percent of the world's income, and own less than 1 percent of the world's property. McClintock, *Imperial Leather: Race, Gender, and Sexuality in Colonial Context* (New York: Routledge, 1995), 13.

26. Hardt and Negri, *Empire*, 150.

27. Hardt and Negri, *Empire*, 150–55.

28. Hardt and Negri, *Empire*, 395–408.

29. Rosenberg, "Globalization," 32.

30. Marx and Engels were only two of many who succumbed to the allure of modernization theory. *The Communist Manifesto* (1848; New York: Meredith Corporation, 1955), 14.

31. See Sabine Lang, "The NGOization of Feminism," in *Transitions, Environments, Translation*, ed. Joan Scott, Cora Kaplan, and D. Keates (New York: Routledge, 1997), 101–20.

32. Kristen Kelly, *Domestic Violence and the Politics of Privacy* (Ithaca, N.Y.: Cornell University Press), 77.

33. In sketching this brief account of state-centered strategies advanced by feminists, I do not mean to suggest that all feminists shared the same state-centric focus nor that all feminists agreed on particular legislative and litigious tactics. I am simply trying to capture particular assumptions about the state as a site of political contestation that informs state-centric feminist activism. For discussions of debates within feminism about tactics of political mobilization and the role of the state, see Mary Hawkesworth, "Feminist Rhetoric: Models of Politicization" and "Re/Vision: Feminist Theory Confronts the Polis," in *Beyond Oppression: Feminist Theory and Political Strategy* (New York: Continuum, 1990).

34. For a thoughtful discussion of this transformation in Britain and the United States, see Kenneth Hoover and R. Plant, *Conservative Capitalism in Great Britain and the United States: A Critical Appraisal* (New York: Routledge, 1989).

35. For recurrent examples of this view, see Christine Hoff Sommers, *Who Stole Feminism?* (New York: Touchstone/Simon & Schuster, 1995); and the newsletters and website of the Independent Women's Forum (www.IWF.org).

36. See, for example, Barry Hindess, "Class and Politics," in *The Routledge Encyclopedia of Government and Politics,* ed. Mary Hawkesworth and Maurice Kogan, 2d rev. ed. (London: Routledge, 2003); Anthony Giddens, *The Third Way* (Cambridge: Polity Press, 2000), 43; and Peter Evans, "The Eclipse of the State? Reflections on Stateness in an Era of Globalization," *World Politics* 50, no. 1 (1998): 62–87.

37. For an overview of women's mobilizations around the globe, see Sheila Rowbotham and Stephanie Linkogle, *Women Resist Globalization: Mobilizing for Livelihoods and Rights* (London: Zed, 2001).

38. For a discussion of these dimensions of ideology, see Manfred B. Steger, *Globalism: The New Market Ideology* (Lanham, Md.: Rowman & Littlefield, 2002), 7–8.

39. Andreas Huyssen, *Twilight Memories: Marking Time in a Culture of Amnesia* (New York: Routledge, 1995).

IDEOLOGY AND GLOBALIZATION: FROM GLOBALISM AND ENVIRONMENTALISM TO ECOGLOBALISM

Timothy W. Luke

This chapter explores the ideological dimensions of globalization by considering how the Earth's ecologies are being transformed into sites for globalist intervention. By fusing environmentalism with globalism, many scientific experts, some major corporations, and a few far-sighted governments are generating new theories and practices, which, they believe, are required for managing "the environment" on local, regional, national, and global levels of operation. Indeed, many existing procedures of ecomanagerialism are being readied for a world-scale "ecoglobalism."[1] Such developments warrant further consideration, and this chapter begins that investigation.

To untangle these influences, it helps, as Ulrich Beck and Manfred Steger have argued, to draw distinctions between globalism, globality, and globalization. "Globalization" denotes "the processes through which sovereign national actors are criss-crossed and undermined by transnational actors with varying prospects for power, orientations, identities, and networks."[2] "Globality" marks the unique existential conditions of what is regarded as a world society. While the ideological roots of this globality have varied over the past few centuries, we have been living for quite some time in a world where "the totality of social relationships" to a significant degree "are not integrated into or determined (or determinable) by national-state politics."[3]

Finally "globalism," because it is an ideology, seems to be what is most distinctive about the present moment. A market ideology that endows globalization with neoliberal beliefs, claims, ideas, and values, globalism is usually propounded by the managerial, professional-technical, and intellectual classes.[4] It proceeds monocausally and economistically, reducing the multidimensionality of globalization to a single economic dimension that is itself conceived in a linear fashion. If it mentions the other dimensions of globalization—ecology, culture, politics, civil society—it does so only by placing them under the sway of the world market system.[5] Understood in this sense, globalism implies a cohesive set of beliefs and practices that requires all states, societies, and cultures to be managed like a corporate capitalist enterprise.

Having become militant proponents for the ideologies of globalism, corporations often turn their goods and services into an integral part of the market's globalization. These corporate practices serve as an implicit sign of their clients' globality, and a marker, if only complicitly and for now, of their consumers' and suppliers' submission to globalism. To manage the anarchy emerging from today's "globally disorganized capitalism," it now appears that ecoglobalism might serve useful purposes by engineering different varieties of ecological constraint as the operational means of a loose, but still nonetheless effective, system of green market regulation.

Globalism and Environmentalism

Whether one denies its reality or celebrates its advent, the ideas that interweave globalism and environmentalism into the management of a "natural capitalism"[6] are similar to Edward Said's concept of "orientalism." Such a body of theory and practice" in which "there has been a considerable material investment," these ideas serving as "an accepted grid for filtering" statements out of, and into, general discursive culture.[7] To some extent, globalism and environmentalism must be recognized as an unfolding project, or "a *distribution* of geopolitical awareness." Thus various ecoglobalist voices express a wide array of interests which, "by such means of scholarly discovery, philological reconstruction, psychological analysis, landscape and sociological description . . . not only create but also maintain . . . a certain *will* or *intention* to understand, in some cases to control, manipulate, even to incorporate, what is a manifestly different" as well as tied to "an uneven exchange with various kinds of power."[8] Thus entering in the arena of globalism—as well as antiglobalism—often amounts to nothing short of "a career."

Globality and the environment are sites that anchor efforts to apprehend domains of economic and political action, which are becoming caught up in their own ongoing expression in new spatial formations. Conceptualized as a "globe," the planet Earth and its many "environments" have been recognized as material realities for centuries.[9] Yet their recent discovery as spatial formations belies the workings of new economic, political, and social forces that are staking out and then digging into these formations of spatiality to serve as their own vital formative spaces.[10] The Earth as a site for political projects such as globalism and environmentalism is being put into play as something "new." The social formations that are spinning up these formative spatialities must be examined more carefully to ascertain their discontinuities with what has come before as well as the continuities with what has always taken place.

Globality now evolves as a wholly ambiguous development. It uneasily brings liberation with domination, freedom with control, openness with inaccessibility.[11] Globalism can appear, on one hand, as a celebration of the Earth's potential for anchoring a truly transnational civil society—at once highly cosmopolitan, Creole, and contextualized. On the other hand, globalism can appear as the consolidation of a conscious corporate strategy—at root aimed at implementing neoliberal modes of political economy on a planetary, continental, and regional level in a fashion that remakes the places with locality into spaces of globality.[12] This strategy for pursuing economic growth sparks its own antagonistic opposition among new rainbow coalitions of antigrowth, anticonsumption, antitechnology, or anticorporate activists.[13]

Concern about economic activity, however, easily can morph into equally intense concerns about ecology. Environmentalism in this register often is little more than a bundle of anxieties about the Earth's degradation under incessant economic pressure to exceed the renewable carrying capacities of the planet's ecologies. Frequently this stance represents genuine professional-technical reservations about sustaining today's transnational civil society and economy at any levels that can balance equity against efficiency with some measure of ethical integrity. Big science can push a variety of projects rooted in environmentalism, but these disciplines typically follow managerialist approaches to ecosystem preservation.[14] Such tactics in turn trigger their own conflicts as progrowth, proconsumption, protechnology, or procorporate agendas for environmental protection rise in opposition against other scientists and technicians by mobilizing their own scientific and technical readings of the same ambiguous testimony of nature.[15]

Concrete manifestations of these convergent projects are found in many quarters. Prestigious private universities, whose business schools, engineering schools, and natural resource schools are coaligning to offer degrees in sustainability studies, green engineering, and management of renewables, are only some of the most obvious venues. A $20 million project at Princeton University, launched by British Petroleum and Ford for a ten-year energy research program in 2000, has been eclipsed by a new $175 million energy and climate research project anchored at Stanford University. Dubbed the Global Climate and Energy Project, bankrolled mostly by ExxonMobil and dedicated to reaching the two billion humans now living on Earth without access to transnational energy commodity chains, this program will integrate studies of alternative energy sources, hydrocarbon energy use, and mass transportation systems to find "Earth-friendly" energy systems.[16]

Apparently the transnational capitalist class has recognized that ecological sustainability is a vital choke point in its new world order.[17] Some of these interests are more than willing to begin "creating the next industrial revolution" in the form of what is already being labeled as "natural capitalism."[18] Once again, the alliance of globalism and environmentalism provide productive paths for a "career." "Society" will not produce "economy" against "Nature," so the work of producing a new "ecology" goes hand in hand with the project of reproducing society around as new "economies of Nature."

In this context, it is crucial that students of globalism recognize how globalization directly promotes the transnational proliferation of certain environments over others. Today's globality is a world process that represents the propagation of a few agro-industrial monocultures (rice, corn, wheat, potato, beef, sheep, pig, chicken production), several particular urban landscapes (automobile suburbs, concentrated high-rise inner cities, massive sprawl driven by auto, train, tram commuting), and profusions of hybridized biotic imperialisms (exotic plant and animal species migrating in planned and unplanned expansions from continent to continent and hemisphere to hemisphere). Looked at from afar, worrying about these changes can appear to be "environmentalist," but, up close and personal, it also is quite "globalist."

Henri Lefebvre has argued that "every society produces a space, its own space," and "this will have other consequences."[19] Indeed, many societies have come and gone on the Earth, and a globality of sorts has existed in other times.[20] Today, however, the transnational corporate capitalist economy and society produce their own peculiar places in the sites and structures of contemporary globalist and environmentalist spatiality. The generation of these social spaces has resulted in the rapid proliferation of commodified social labor and its abstract space. The production of globality and ecology in the particular forms taken by contemporary globalism and environmentalism also represents, as Lefebvre notes, "the dissolution of old relations on the one hand and the generation of new relations on the other."[21] In many ways, the agendas of neoliberal globalization seem to be intent on effacing absolute spaces of locally consecrated sites for Nature as well as the historical spaces of regionally territorialized national places.[22]

The Roots of Ecoglobalism

Contemporary urban formations, industrial ecologies, and public infrastructures are vast clusters of artifacts that have been created in particular times and places to carry the ideological forms and functions of specific cultural, economic, and political values. Within the matrix of ecoglobalism, the tacit consent of the client, consumer, and citizen given to the expert, producer, and bureaucrat is tantamount to the granting of life-extending, life-enhancing, and life-enlarging benefits in exchange for bearing costs and acceding to authority. These contracts of convenience also underpin the careers required by ecoglobalist systems of governmentality, which propound structures of population, territory, and sovereignty in a manner that ensures the most convenient disposition of people and things in the environmental regulation of the conduct. As a result, Nature is transmogrified by discursive processes into "natural resources," thus rendered into fungible material used to legitimize many political projects.[23]

The modern research university is one of the main sites for generating, accumulating, and then circulating such knowledge about Nature, as well as determining which human beings will be empowered to interpret nature to society.[24] As the primary structure for issuing credentials to individual learners and legitimating collective teachings, universities help construct our understanding of the natural world.[25] Over the past generation, advanced study in environmental science on many university campuses and in most corporations has become a key source of new representations for "the environment" as well as the home base for the scientific disciplines that generate analyses of Nature's meanings.[26] These educational practices produce ecomanagers, or professional-technical workers with specific knowledge (which has been scientifically validated), together with the operational powers (as they have been institutionally constructed) to cope with "environmental problems" on what are believed to be sound scientific and technical grounds.

Here the dominant globalist discourse spawns many professional careers. Technical experts working on and off campus create disciplinary articulations of various kinds of "knowledge" to generate performative techniques of "power" over, but also within and through, what is worked up as Nature in the managerial structures of modern economies and societies. These institutionalized attempts to capture and contain the forces of Nature underpin the strategies of ecomanagerialism—as, for example, the Global Climate and Energy Project at Stanford University suggests.[27] Techno-scientific knowledge about the environment is, and always has been, changing with interpretive fashions, shifting political agendas, developing scientific advances, and meandering occupational trends.[28]

Schools of environmental studies and colleges of natural resources, therefore, provide networks for an ecoglobalism in which the relations of this productive power can set the categories of knowledge and fix the limits of professional practice through the training of ecomanagers. In accord with the regimes of truth prevailing in instrumental techno science, academic centers of environmental studies ideologically reproduce bodies of practice and types of discourse, which the executive personnel managing contemporary state and social institutions regard as "objective," "valid," or "useful" to facilitate economic growth.[29] This network links together techno-scientific activity, the simulation of spaces, the intensification of resources, the incitement of discoveries, the formation of special kinds of knowledge, the strengthening of controls, and the provocation of resistance— activities understood by many experts in the environmental sciences and studies as "the empiricities" of Nature.[30]

The new empiricities behind the ideology of ecoglobalism presume a place for Nature that promotes its rough and ready "resourcification" for the global economy and national society. The Earth must be reimagined to be little more than a standing reserve, a resource supply center, and a waste reception site. Once presented in this fashion, Nature then provides human markets with many different environmental sites for the productive use of resourcified flows of energy, information, and matter as well as the sinks, dumps, and wastelands for all the by-products that commercial products leave behind. Nature is always a political asset. Still, its fungibilization, liquidification, and capitalization in ecomanagerialism cannot occur without expert intellectual labor whose resourcifying activities prep it, produce it, and then provide it for the global marketplace.[31] The trick in natural resources or environmental affairs education for ecoglobalists is to appear conservationist, while moving very fast to fungibilize, liquefy, and capitalize natural resources for more thorough, rapid, and intensive utilization.

With the rise of ecoglobalism, older sustained metaphors of Nature as a static and depletable storehouse shift toward Nature as a dynamic and renewable system.[32] Seeing these possibilities, and then mastering their management for optimal performance—both as producers of raw materials and conservers of systemic services—is the decisive engagement for ecoglobalism. These commitments have pushed the thoughts and actions of many people away from "sustained yield" and toward "sustainability" in the overall management of natural resources. Ecoglobalists activate their managerial command over the Earth's spaces and places as well as operationalize a measure of operational discipline over environmental resources, risks, restorations, renewables, and recreations.

These disciplinary articulations of ecoglobalism center on establishing and enforcing the right disposition of things by policing humanity's conduct in Nature and society. Nature loses transcendent qualities as its material stuff appears preprocessed by science as mere "environments" full of exploitable, but also protectable, "natural resources," which the right managers can manipulate as they buckle down to the business of administering Earth's "natural resource systems." Ecoglobalist careers emerge where and whenever these relations of power permeate and shape the social body around the environment, but these relations of power cannot be invented or implemented without the production and circulation of globalist and environmentalist discourses.[33] Multiple traces of these conceptual cogeneration cycles, through which power charges truthful knowledges and mediates productive power, can then be tracked into the world's schools of business management and colleges of natural resources.

Conclusion

Practices like ecomanagerialism come into being because virtually everyone desires the goods and services made possible by the global economy's burgeoning productivity—even though these performative outcomes are getting more difficult to realize because of either mass resistance to many industries' by-products or actual physical scarcities caused by resource depletion. At this point, new dangers emerge. In my view, one of the most dangerous developments is the common failure on the part of many environmentalists to recognize how ecomanagerialism can actually work in impure, subjective, and mediated ways to degrade, displace, or destroy Nature as such.

But since there is no pure, objective, unmediated Nature, it appears reasonable to ask why human beings should not coevolve with an artificialized Nature driven by market forces. Indeed, ecoglobalists routinely engage in highly self-interested efforts to reconstruct Nature so that its heavily marketized moments of degradation, displacement, and destruction always benefit them as producers and consumers.[34] Critical environmentalists must not stand by idly as these dangerous claims are being made. One of their chief tasks should be to disclose the political maneuvers underlying the longstanding project of preserving, protecting, and managing "Nature" for the good of "humanity." After all, "humanity" almost never meant "all human beings." In truth, it refers to a minority, or those "we's" with the capital, technology, expertise, and power to efficiently use—and thereby effectively threaten—Nature. Indeed, to bring everyone now alive up to U.S. standards of living would require four more Earths.[35]

Moreover, critics need to point out that ecoglobalist concerns are usually raised in liberal democratic societies in relation to "careers," especially in discussions of corporate regulation, licensing, patenting, and chartering or professional accreditation, certification, licensing, and retraining. These veils of expertise and ownership are very rarely pierced because the oversight activities required by the state often are ironically used to prevent a public questioning of experts and owners to ensure communal codetermination in expert decisions and ownership issues are avoided.[36] Critical discussions, then, should probe the structural conditions and limits that prevent such interventions, while hinting at the benefits of broader community engagement in what professional-technical experts and corporate owners/managers do behind the veils of expertise and ownership.

The opposition to globalism expressed by many environmentalist citizen movements—in different ways and on diverse levels—often centers on problems of rationality in ecology.[37] Many democratic movements have embarked on a quest to renew a communal politics around these issues.[38] Locally, antiglobalist groups immediately ask "Who, whom?" when they learn, for example, that ExxonMobil is underwriting a new global climate project. Additional questions point to the multidimensionality of the problem: Who says we need so much energy? For what purposes are they saying this? Who are the "we" who decides, and then why choose this way of producing energy? Who are the "we" that will benefit? How will the relevant indicators of energy output be defined—as kilowatt hours, radiation leaks, less hydrocarbon pollutants, more jobs, extra cancer deaths, more electrified conveniences, more tons of poisonous wastes that remain dangerous for centuries? What happens to wastes? Who pays unanticipated costs? Are the benefits truly beneficial? Can these costs and benefits be accurately documented or fully accounted? And who decides which criteria or discourses will define what is rational, reasonable, fair, efficient, hazardous, or safe?

Local activists are correct in arguing that business-biased, far-away forces too often have imposed bad decisions, arrived at through faulty means, on millions of citizens/clients/consumers who had little democratic input or legal recourse to their unfair or harmful outcome. This kind of anonymous authoritarianism, and the illegitimate rationalization without representation that ecoglobalism implies, constitute the main targets of many circles of democratic, antiglobalist resistance.[39] But critics must also offer constructive arguments. After all, alternatives exist. By turning to shareholder rights groups, social responsibility activism, environmental justice organizing, citizens' technological juries, and deliberative design panels, one can push antiglobalization movements to undertake more democratic, egalitarian forms of action.

Notes

1. Timothy W. Luke, "Training Eco-Managerialists: Academic Environmental Studies as a Power/Knowledge Formation," in *Living with Nature: Environmental Discourse as Cultural Politics*, ed. Frank Fischer and Maarten Hajer (Oxford: Oxford University Press, 1999), 103–20.

2. Urlich Beck, *What Is Globalization?* (Cambridge: Polity, 2000), 11; and Manfred B. Steger, *Globalism: The New Market Ideology* (Lanham, Md.: Rowman & Littlefield, 2002), 47–54.

3. Beck, *What Is Globalization?* 10.
4. Steger, *Globalism*.
5. Beck, *What Is Globalization*, 9; and, Steger, *Globalism*, 47–54.
6. Paul Hawken, Amory Lovins, and L. Hunter Lovins, *Natural Capitalism: Creating the Next Industrial Revolution* (Boston: Little, Brown, 1999).
7. Edward W. Said, *Orientalism* (New York: Vintage, 1979), 6.
8. Said, *Orientalism*, 12.
9. Today "globalization" is taken as the ultimate background condition of world affairs. Globalization is neither a new nor a stable phenomenon, and it has always led to the pursuit of various careers. A century ago in 1902, another cultural, ideological, and spatial project for a different sort of globalization was being generated by the transnational empires, anchoring a European colonialism tied to England, France, Germany, Italy, Spain, Portugal, Russia, or the Netherlands. These empires vied with each other as well as the non-European, but still Western(izing), empires of Japan, Ottoman Turkey, and the United States to create one kind of globalized economy and society whose modernity rested on aristocratic myths, haute bourgeois culture, and racial formulas of authority.

Five decades ago in 1952, yet another cultural and spatial order for globalization was being cemented together by two opposing ideological zone regimes. The Cold War's contest between a Western liberal democratic capitalism, centered on NATO countries and the United States, faced off against an Eastern European state-planned communism, tied to the Warsaw Pact countries and the Soviet Union. Those two competing visions of modernity offered the world antithetical alternatives for globality centered on either individualist or collectivist notions of organizational efficiency, technological prowess, and personal consumption.

In 1937—the midpoint of 1902 and 1952—another globalizing project for reimagining the culture and economy of the world was contained in the fascist polities of Germany, Italy, Japan, Portugal, and Spain. The aggressive racialist, nationalistic, and military cast of fascist globality, however, led to its defeat in war. The few fascist regimes that survived World War II never regained respect, and their example is now ignored. In fact, almost all of these divergent representations of cultural identity, national place, and global power have crumbled to ruins after 1914, 1945, and 1989. Today's world is built on those ruins, but the current sites of its globalization all have their own new emergent properties—most of which give globality an increasingly private, domestic, or personal cast.

Globalization can be a powerful framework for analyzing new developmental trends for this new century. While this point is too easily granted in the twenty-first century, the exact nature of globalization is still only vaguely specified in most accounts of its impact on contemporary economies and societies. Major measures of globalizing change have been evident throughout the last six centuries. European capitalist states, enterprises, and cities have been building markets around first the Old World and then the New World in pursuit of greater power and profit. Those projects all have remade public culture, urban life, and national identity in the so-called "West" and "East" from the days of Henry the Navigator to the present, although often in ways much different than today's globalism.

10. Nigel Thrift, *Spatial Formations* (London: Sage, 1996).

11. Pierre Bourdieu, *Acts of Resistance: Against the Tyranny of the Market* (New York: New Press, 1998).

12. During the nineteenth and twentieth centuries, one type of "globalization" unfolded as part of the project of modernization. It pitted the promise of democracy, affluence, equality, and reason against the traditional injustices of rural poverty, aristocratic privilege, and oppressive religion. Evincing individual choice against collective predestination was a heroic struggle. Yet those battles arguably had been won in many places around the world by the end of the twentieth century. Defining the risks or determining the costs and benefits that rational choices should be made over and above other rational choices is much more difficult; as early as 1959, C. Wright Mills saw these more indefinite ambiguities of permanent risk and incommensurable metrics of value as the stuff of the postmodern. See *The Sociological Imagination* (Oxford: Oxford University Press, 1959), 178–94.

13. John Young, *Sustaining the Earth* (Cambridge: Harvard University Press, 1990).

14. R. E. Gumbine, "What Is Ecosystem Management?" *Conservation Biology* 8 (1994): 27–38.

15. David Rothenberg, *Hand's End: Technology and the Limits of Nature* (Berkeley: University of California Press, 1993).

16. Andrew Revkin, "Exxon-Led Group Is Giving a Climate Grant to Stanford," *New York Times,* November 21, 2002, A26.

17. Leslie Sklair, *Globalization: Capitalism and Its Alternatives* (Oxford: Oxford University Press, 2002).

18. See Hawken, Lovins, and Lovins, *Natural Capitalism.*

19. Henri Lefebvre, *The Production of Space* (Oxford: Blackwell, 1991), 53.

20. As John Wills effectively demonstrates in *1688: A Global History* (New York: Norton, 2001) there were few inhabited places on the planet in 1688 that were entirely free from foreigners, world trade, or other globalizing cultural influences. On foot, horseback, or wooden ships, the currents of world commerce carried goods, people, and ideas in a fashion that already was developing a global imaginary. Even three centuries ago, there were confrontations between "the West" and "the Rest."

21. Lefebvre, *Production of Space*, 52.

22. David Harvey, *The Condition of Postmodernity* (Oxford: Blackwell, 1989).

23. Edmund Husserl, *The Crisis of European Science and Transcendental Phenomenology* (Evanston: Northwestern University Press, 1970).

24. Frank Fischer, *Technocracy and the Politics of Expertise* (London: Sage, 1990); John Meyer, *Political Nature* (Cambridge: MIT Press, 2001).

25. Michael Gibbons et al., *The New Production of Knowledge: The Dynamics of Science and Research in Contemporary Societies* (London: Sage, 1994).

26. Hanna J. Cortner and Margaret A. Moote, *The Politics of Ecosystem Management* (Washington, D.C.: Island, 1999).

27. Revkin, "Exxon-Led Group," A26.

28. Michel Foucault, *The Order of Things: An Archaeology of the Human Sciences* (New York: Vintage, 1970); Frank Fischer, *Technocracy and the Politics of Expertise* (Newbury Park, Calif.: Sage Publications, 1990).

29. Timothy W. Luke, "Environmentality as Green Governmentality," in *Discourses of the Environment*, ed. Eric Darier (Oxford: Blackwell, 1999), 121–51.

30. Foucault, *Order of Things*, 362–63.

31. Luke, "Environmentality as Green Governmentality."

32. Gumbine, "What Is Ecosystem Management?" 27–38.

33. Klaus Eder, *The Social Construction of Nature: A Sociology of Ecological Enlightenment* (London: Sage, 1996); Edward O. Wilson, *The Future of Life* (New York: Knopf, 2001).

34. John Barry, *Rethinking Green Politics: Nature, Virtue, and Progress* (London: Sage/Sandilands, 1999); Meyer, *Political Nature*.

35. Wilson, *The Future of Life*, 23.

36. Fikret Berkes and Carol Folke, eds., *Linking Social and Ecological Systems: Management Practices and Social Mechanisms for Building Resilience* (Cambridge: Cambridge University Press, 2000).

37. Barry Commoner, *Making Peace with the Planet* (New York: Pantheon, 1990).

38. Catriona Sandilands, *The Good-Natured Feminist: Ecofeminism and the Quest for Democracy* (Minneapolis: University of Minnesota Press, 1999).

39. Ulrich Beck, "Risk Society and Provident State," in *Risk, Environment, and Modernity*, ed. Scott Lash, Bronislaw Szerszynski, and Bryant Wynne (London: Sage, 1996); Timothy W. Luke, "Moving at the Speed of Life? A Cultural Kinematics of Telematic Times and Corporate Values," *Cultural Values* 2, no. 2–3 (1998): 320–39.

GLOBALIZING MILITARIES

Kathy E. Ferguson and
Phyllis Turnbull

In his farewell address to the nation at the end of his presidency in 1961, Dwight Eisenhower warned Americans to beware of the military-industrial complex:

> This conjunction of an immense military establishment and a large arms industry is new in the American experience. The total influence—economic, political, even spiritual—is felt in every city, every Statehouse, every office of the Federal government. We recognize the imperative need for this development. Yet we must not fail to comprehend its grave implications. Our toil, resources and livelihood are all involved; so is the very structure of our society.[1]

Eisenhower, of course, set these warnings in a conventional U.S.-centered understanding of political life. Yet two opportunities for further thought issue from the former president's—and former general's—reflections. The first, clearly present in his speech, is his profound ambivalence about both the military-industrial complex and the technological revolutions of his day. Compelled, he believed, to create "a permanent armaments industry of vast proportions," he urged the citizens and leaders of the United States to guard against this "unwarranted influence" on "liberties and democratic processes." Compared to his successors, he heeded the "downside" of empire. Government contracts, he feared, would become "a substitute for intellectual curiosity"; public policy might be held hostage by "a scientific-technological elite"; military research could gobble up federal funds; and the vast power of the military establishment and arms industry posed "the potential for the disastrous rise of misplaced power."[2] Ike, at least in this speech, was not simply a cheerleader for power, a posture that has since become the presidential norm; of subsequent presidents, only Jimmy Carter was willing to be anything less than 100 percent in favor of expanding hegemony.

The second opportunity for further thought is absent from Eisenhower's reflections, but increasingly available to ours. Ike thought he could tell war from peace. Eisenhower's wars were, to at least some extent, separable from the pre-war and postwar periods and from the stories that could be told about them. While the state's ways of thinking about war have always played a constitutive role in producing war, today's "new wars" have taken a quantum leap toward seamlessness between planning/executing and narrating/conducting operations. As James Der Derian makes clear in *Virtuous War*, the remarkable speed and commensurate collapse of distance made possible by today's electronic technologies and "you are there" simulations produce indistinctness between the two dimensions. Planning and execution—the conduct of planning-training-conducting-mopping up-covering up-dissimulating—occur by means of digital mergings of infospace and battle space. The same mimetic practices collapse the representation of war and its conduct. As Der Derian explains:

> The new wars are fought in the same manner as they are represented, by military simulations and public dissimulations, by real-time surveillance and TV live-feeds. Virtuality collapses distance, between here and there, near and far, fact and fiction. It widens the distance between those who have and those who have not. Representing the most penetrating and sharpest (to the point of invisibility) edge of globalization, it disappears the local and the particular. It leaves little space for the detached observer.[3]

To Eisenhower's military-industrial complex, Der Derian adds new virtual allies, the media-entertainment network. Hollywood's easy access to military hardware (including aircraft carriers and fighter planes), ready mergers of kids' video games and the gaming of military training, corporate partnerships with universities to produce simulation laboratories—these produce a new militarized cultural landscape. The indistinctness of relations between planning and conduct, between narrative and operations, both expands militarized power and disperses it.

Both the changing technologies of war and the condensed representations of war have altered the context for receiving the former president's remarks, making them sound both accurate and quaint. It was not simply that no one was listening, since Ike's warnings have been widely quoted in the past fifty years. Rather, global political processes may explain the nation's deafness; the changing security practices in processes of globalization may have contributed to muting Eisenhower's reservations about the military-industrial complex.[4]

What Happens to Militaries As Things Globalize?

The globalization of militaries takes places at both the organizational and the operational level. Organizationally, globalization brings changes in the sites of militaries, their command structures, bases of support, and relations to sovereign states. This level is about "where" militaries are. Operationally, globalization refigures the practices of recruitment, training, conduct, and representation of war. This level is about "how" militaries are. Militaries globalize at both levels, sometimes independently of each other.

There are two main directions of change in large national institutions as global capitalism does its work. In one direction, institutions "go international," that is, they follow the example of global markets, expanding beyond state or organizational boundaries. In the second direction, institutions "go private," moving out of the domain of public claims and into that of private ownership. These two directions are clearly connected, since both the internationalizing and the privatizing moves take institutions into more thorough immersion in global markets.

Locating militaries within this complex process seems odd, at first, because militaries are conventionally attached to states. The prevailing definition of a state, going back at least to Max Weber, is the monopoly on the legitimate use of force. Sovereignty has largely meant, in practice, the state's ability to use its military to maintain control over its territory. Given this tight connection of militaries to sovereign states, how do militaries fit into the globalizing processes that connect activities and events across or under state boundaries?

How Militaries Internationalize

United Nations peacekeeping forces seem good examples of things to come— multinational militaries donning internationally coded blue helmets and working together to keep warring factions apart. The number of U.N. peacekeeping operations and the range of tasks performed have both expanded in the 1990s. U.N. troops now deliver aid, protect (or attempt to protect or fail to protect) civilians, disarm and demobilize combatants, support elections, and report violations of international law as well as monitor and maintain ceasefires.[5] In addition, regional organizations like NATO or the Economic Community of West African States (ECOWAS) also field peacekeeping missions.[6] However, while troops from many nations contribute to peacekeeping forces, the sovereign state's hand in these maneuvers remains strong. There is no direct U.N. recruitment or training; troops are still enlisted and trained by states, and, in the case of the United States, nearly always commanded by a U.S. officer. In the case of Europe, the transnationalization of militaries is more advanced. Mary Kaldor, for example, argues that after World War II,

> the rigidification of the alliances in Europe and the establishment of integrated command systems, together with a global network of military connections through military assistance, arms sales and training, effectively meant that most countries, apart from the superpowers, abandoned the unilateral capacity to wage wars. Although there as been some renationalization of armed forces in the aftermath of the Cold War, there has also been a whole set of new arrangements—multinational peace-keeping, arms-control agreements involving mutual inspection teams, joint exercises, new or renewed organizations like the WEU, Partnership for Peace, NATO Coordination Council (NACC) which constitute an intensification of transnationalization in the military sphere.[7]

While these globalizing shifts are clearly significant in Europe, and may presage future developments, at this point in history the United States is primarily giving lip service to multinational military activities. It spends more on its armed forces than any nation in history and is soon likely to outdistance the next nine states combined.[8] While there are important questions to ask about how peacekeeping service may differ from conventional national deployments,[9] international peacekeeping missions are not at the heart of the U.S. military's self-definition nor at the center of its resource investments. The real action is elsewhere.

How Militaries Privatize

One direction for the privatization of security lies in the creation of mercenary and private paramilitary armies. Once the province of science fiction writers such as William Gibson and Neal Stephenson, highly trained soldiers for hire play an emergent role in altering the traditional makeup of armies and the sources of manpower for organized violence.[10] Another face of military privatization manifests in the host of "contractors" who are employed by privately owned corporations but located in military bases and paid out of military coffers.[11] Contractors such as DynCorp and MPRI—often referred to as private military companies—supplement the state in politically expedient ways, taking on the tasks of feeding and training soldiers, constructing facilities, gathering intelligence, policing borders, managing base facilities, and so forth.[12] The activities of these private military companies reconfigure security around a market model or, more rarely, an ideological one. Such directions are echoed in private practices of domestic and organizational security that reframe the concept of secure space through, for example, gated communities, private security forces made up of former military personnel, or the privatization of prisons. Robert Mandel argues that private security organizations "have expanded to a degree that they outnumber most national armies."[13]

While mercenary armies or private contractors can extend and complicate state military technologies, they are, at least in the United States, subordinate to the primacy of the state. Yet state militaries have long been privatized in another way, bound to particular private interests in the name of generic national security. Looking at the long, intense history of military intervention to protect the interests of capital, we believe that the U.S. military is already privatized. It has historically been engaged in the process of winding state sovereignty around the spindle of corporate interests.

The interactive trio of national, corporate, and military interests has a long and cozy history. In "A Century of Military Interventions: From Wounded Knee to Yugoslavia," Zoltan Grossman compiles a list of 128 U.S. military interventions from 1890 to 1999. The patterns look something like this:[14]

Outright wars, occupations, and military blockades: 33
Interventions in other nation's revolutions or elections: 29
Bombing and threats of military or nuclear action: 24
Political overthrows, coups, attempted coups, or invasions: 12
Protection of business interests (mines, banana fields, banks): 11
Strike breaking, domestic and foreign: 7
Land disputes involving Native Americans: 6
Domestic race riots: 4

This list suggests that the U.S. military is seldom used, for example, to uphold the rights of striking workers or secure the entitlements of displaced peoples. Corporate holdings, not popular aspirations, define national interests.

Contemporary spokespersons for U.S. military presence in the world are frequently quite forthcoming about the links between global economic ventures and national military might. Speaking to the Senate in 2000 about the U.S. naval presence in the world, Admiral J. P. Reason, commander in chief of the U.S. Atlantic fleet, made the following statement:

A key part of the global economy's growth has been the proliferation of multinational corporations, many U.S.-owned or partnered. They have improved the profitability and efficiency through the free exchange of goods and services around the entire world. And this was made possible by

83

freedom of the seas, guaranteed by your United States Navy. In short, the navy has been and continues to be a sine qua non, a necessary precondition, of global economic prosperity and U.S. national security.[15]

Admiral Reason's candid remarks were reinforced by those of Admiral Vern Clark, chief of naval operations for the U.S. Navy. Addressing the Defense Subcommittee of the House Appropriations Committee, Admiral Clark goes beyond Reason in his appeal to U.S. sovereignty:

> In 2002 and beyond, our Navy's posture, programs, and character will be shaped by the mission of projecting sovereign American power in support of national interests while forward-deployed to the far corners of the earth. . . . A premier instrument of American power, your Navy operates around the globe, demonstrating command of the seas, ensuring the free flow of trade and resources, providing combat-ready presence, and assuring access for joint forces.[16]

Global corporate interests, U.S. global military presence, and American national identity are wound tightly together in these remarks. Sovereignty, instead of staying home as Weber suggested, travels with the military, a mobile claim on legitimacy. "Stability" and "aggression" take their meaning in relation to corporate interests, which are said to correspond with national interests. Ike's national military-industrial complex has become a global "military-corporate complex."[17] Where Eisenhower both promoted and warned against the power of a national military-industrial establishment, Admirals Reason and Clark have no trouble connecting multinational corporations with American economic prosperity and national security.

The happy marriage between global economic prosperity and American national security both depends on and disguises the complex combination of "free trade" and protectionism that enables the two to cohabit, a combination mediated by the magical phrase "national security." Military contractors need unimpeded access to the markets of the less developed countries, where weapons developed and tested by the United States and other industrial nations are sold. Yet these same industries need protectionist policies at home in order to undercut or absorb competitors, subsidize mergers, advertise and sell weapons, conduct research, and in other ways benefit from the enormous public wealth poured into corporate military interests. "National security" functions as the durable loophole through which corporate military subsidies can pass, keeping markets "free" when it comes to selling the stuff and protected when it comes to making and marketing it.

As globalization intensifies oligopolies, including aerospace, defense, information technology, real estate, food, banking, telecommunications, and media, exclusive national ownership becomes illusory; yet American interests often predominate. This helps explain why the rest of the world often experiences globalization as Americanization: not only sources of capital and soldiers but also hegemonic cultural codes and consumer patterns merge American commodity capitalism with global economies.

National Security Oligopolies

Three prominent national security oligopolies cementing military/industrial/ financial linkages are the Carlyle Group, the Cohen Group, and Halliburton Company. The first of these made the news briefly when Carlyle's connections to the bin Laden family of Saudi Arabia came to light. This outfit doesn't bother to lobby Congress because it is composed of persons, including presidents and prime ministers, cabinet members and other top-level government officials, whose access to current decision makers is already guaranteed. They act as financial advisers to foreign governments, bringing government and corporate officials together, smoothing the relations among men in power.[18] By the mid-1990s, Carlyle had become "the nation's eleventh largest defense contractor, owning companies that make tanks, aircraft wings, and a broad array of other military equipment. It also owns health care companies, real estate, internet companies, a bottling company, and even *Le Figaro*, the well-known French newspaper."[19] Between 1997 and 2002, the Carlyle Group raised $14 billion from investors and pegs their average rate of return at 36 percent.[20] Their investment strategy focuses on particular industries such as communications and defense, where government policies and spending play big roles in defining markets.

Out-of-work Democrats have also gotten their feet in the revolving door of opportunity. Two days after leaving his post as secretary of defense for President Bill Clinton, William Cohen formed the Cohen Group, an "international strategic consulting" organization that helps corporate executives to "get doors opened and deals moving."[21] These wheeler-dealers transmute their political contacts into know-how for orchestrating what Toni Morrison has called the "unholy trinity" of "political interests, corporate interests, military interests."[22] A high-level cabinet position with the federal government is apparently the right sort of on-the-job training for selling global political access.

While the Cohen Group is new to the high-level access game, the Halliburton Company—a mammoth Dallas-based oil services, energy, and construction company—is a long-time player. It builds camps, bases, and roads for military and commercial customers, installs equipment, sells spare parts, and so on. This corporate defense nexus was headed by Vice President Richard Cheney after he left his earlier position as U.S. defense secretary until just before he was elected to his current office. Cheney's career gives new meaning to the speed of the revolving door. It is alleged that Halliburton was partial owner in two firms that signed contracts to sell more than $73 million in oil production equipment and spare parts to Iraq while Cheney was CEO at Halliburton.[23] During Cheney's watch, Halliburton's stock price sank, energy prices dropped, and the SEC began an investigation into its accounting practices as managed by Arthur Andersen. But President Bush's declaration of war on terror gave new life to Halliburton. According to Jeff Gerth and Don Van Natta Jr., Halliburton subsidiary Kellogg Brown and Root recently became the "exclusive logistics supplier for both the Navy and the Army, providing services like cooking, construction, power generation, and fuel transportation."[24] This ten-year contract has no lid on costs and is only the logistical one with the army lacking an estimated cost.

As number one in the world in the oil field services company, Halliburton wears its roustabout reputation openly. "They drop these boys in and they construct a town," relates Special Forces operative Stan Goff.[25] Musing on the company's ability to construct facilities and explore for oil under hostile conditions, Vice President Cheney is said to have observed, "The Good Lord didn't see fit to put oil and gas only where there are democratic regimes friendly to the United States."[26] Perhaps Brown and Root will get the contract to build some of the new base-in-a-box units designed by army labs. These off-the-shelf modules can accommodate 550 soldiers "in comfort, with satellite televisions, chapels, showers, laundry rooms, complete kitchens as well as climate-controlled tents."[27] Among the pieces of the box is a containerized chapel with sufficient accoutrements to take care of the spirits of Christians, Jews, and Muslims. Making war a better way of life, promoters allege, "'These kits benefit soldiers. . . . they've got just about everything you've got at home except a wife.'"[28]

In the ethereal world of militarized corporate capitalism, shell games abound. Our earlier distinction between organizational and operational dimensions of militaries—the "where" and the "how"—applies as well to their corporate brethren. Units of oligopolies are deemed to have a separate governing board, which creates an area of deniability to the larger units such as Halliburton. Unsurprisingly, the management ranks of Halliburton are filled with civilians and military men who know their way around the Pentagon and the bid process. Cheney lustily denies any attempts to influence Pentagon awards of contracts to Halliburton, and perhaps he did not. Before he became vice president, he says that he sold $20 million of Halliburton stock, and he gave the rest of his stock to charity after taking the new office. No doubt he did. These superficial divestments miss the point of oligopolistic power: it works outside of both the petty world of bribes and the formal mechanisms for regulating conflicts of interest. Cheney's protestations focus on the organizational site of his memberships: he used to be head of Halliburton, but now he is not. He appeals to the change of organizational hats to convince us that he now serves the public interest. But the real action is in the realm of operations, the processes, links, connections, the exchanges that pass information, transfer knowledge, establish relations, maintain interactions. This realm is hard to pin down, difficult to empirically establish. In this realm global capitalism and militarism do a great deal of their work.

Conclusion

Returning to President Eisenhower's oft quoted midcentury warnings about the military-industrial complex, what happened to the field of audibility concerning the military's relation to the nation and the world? What produced the nation's hearing loss with regard to the costs and dangers of militarism?

We suggest that it is not a question of listening harder, but rather a question of what is hearable. Hegemonic sets of interests and ways of thinking have lodged the military-industrial complex firmly at the heart of what counts as the national interest. Political language practices produce and reflect this naturalization of militarism. "Winning wars" has been replaced by "defending national security." "Merchants of death" have become respectable defense contractors. These euphemisms do more than conceal violence, they enable it, by both what they do not say and their open-ended promise. "National security," like "development" and "globalization," are limitless concepts. There is no boundary against which they push, no opposite against which their debts to otherness might come due. "War" is not just more frank than "national security"; "war" suggests the possibility of peace. Similarly, "industrialization" or "capitalism" suggest other possibilities, such as agriculture or socialism, while "development" and "globalization" go on forever, offering no articulation of a desirable end. There is never enough national security, never enough development, never enough globalization. Critiques of militarism and global capitalism must develop a political vocabulary that articulates desirable alternatives in order to displace the infinite promise of the hegemonic claims.[29]

President Eisenhower thought that national boundaries were a secure aspect of military power, in retrospect a very undynamic view. The U.S. military pursues "sovereignty" aggressively, on a worldwide scale, with a global sense of entitlement. Referring to security plans for U.S. warships in foreign ports, Admiral Clark assured reporters that "this is about taking our sovereignty to places where there are nations and peoples out there who don't like what we represent."[30]

The current direction of U.S. military policy seems to be toward an unholy mix of privatization and internationalization on American terms. Perhaps the "distinctly national internationalism" for which President Bush calls in his foreign policy doctrine[31] is not such a contradiction after all. Empire is, one might say, one form of globalization. Arguably globalization is not the same as Americanization in important cultural and social realms—music, film, literature, resistance politics, for example. But global militarism is largely made in America. Unilateralism + advanced weapons design and sales + nearly unlimited military budgets = globalization of American militarism on American terms.

We began with the question, What happens to militaries as the world globalizes? The answer seems to be that the U.S. military emerges as the world bully, cajoling allied militaries and international support when possible, overriding it when necessary.

While President Eisenhower both promoted and regretted the creation of a "permanent armaments industry of vast proportions," in the subsequent half century the vastness of these proportions dwarfs anything Ike could have foreseen. The current arms race entails an astonishing permeability between military and corporate worlds. Since 1993 the United States has boasted the lion's share of the market in worldwide arms sales.[32] These arms are frequently sold to countries with dismal human rights records, to both sides in regional conflicts, to countries that U.S. soldiers are sent to fight, and to countries that received not just the weapons but also the jobs producing those weapons. In addition to the direct cost of the arms, U.S. taxpayers subsidize mergers among arms producers and even guarantee the loans to economically unstable foreign nations so they can buy some of these weapons.[33]

Beyond these massive increases in the quantity of this military-industrial complex are the qualitative shifts in both its constitutive participants and its discursive range. The enthusiastic participation of media and entertainment industries in the military/corporate nexus knits militarization into culture at the level of daily life; kids' video games, Internet use, and blockbuster movies merge with military training programs, battlefield tactics, and recruitment schemes. These dissolve distinctions between planning, execution, and recovery, between conducting war and representing it, into a "zone of indistinction" in which we are always in the interwar.[34]

During the first half of the 1990s there were about 5.5 million war deaths. Three-fourths of them were civilians, including a million children.[35] Under current circumstances it becomes difficult to imagine a sitting president even noticing the sacrifices exacted by militarism, much less warning the nation about these costs in the way that Eisenhower did:

> Every gun that is fired, every warship launched, every rocket fired signifies, in the final sense, a theft from those who hunger and are not fed, those who are cold and not clothed. The world in arms is not spending money alone. It is spending the sweat of its laborers, the genius of its scientists, the hopes of its children.[36]

Notes

1. Dwight Eisenhower, "Eisenhower's Farewell Address to the Nation," *Readings Online for the Department of Political Science at Marquette University*, http://mcadams.posc.mu.edu/ike.htm (April 22, 2003).

2. Eisenhower, "Farewell Address."

3. James Der Derian, *Virtuous War: Mapping the Military-Industrial-Media-Entertainment Network* (Boulder: Westview, 2001), xviii.

4. By "globalization" we refer to predatory global capitalism. The sometimes bland language of global "movements" or "flows" conceals the violence and the inequalities distinguishing, say, voluntary from involuntary movements, commodities traded from those stolen, or people seeking pleasure or profit from those escaping death. We want to both unroll the claims of progress toward global economic well-being made by globalization's advocates and contest the dominance of the economic dimensions in our understanding of globalization. The broad enthusiasm for global "progress" hides global violence, a constituent partner rather than an unfortunate and easily correctable side effect. Progress and violence are indivisible at two levels: historically, modernity's expansion eliminates prior ways of life or labor; discursively, alternative imaginaries are undermined by the unending restoration of the narrative of universal betterment.

5. Mary Kaldor, *New and Old Wars: Organized Violence in a Global Era* (Stanford: Stanford University Press, 1999), 112.

6. Kaldor, *New and Old Wars*, 113.

7. Kaldor, *New and Old Wars*, 139.

8. Tony Judt, "Its Own Worst Enemy," *New York Review of Books*, August 15, 2002, 12.

9. Cynthia Enloe, *The Morning After: Sexual Politics at the End of the Cold War* (Berkeley: University of California Press, 1993), 260.

10. Martin Van Creveld, *The Transformation of War* (New York: Free Press, 1991); Van Creveld, *The Rise and Decline of the State* (Cambridge: Cambridge University Press, 1999).

11. William Arkin, "The Underground Military," *Washington Post*, May 7, 2001.

12. "Procuring" could also be added to the list. "In Bosnia, employees of DynCorp were found to be operating a sex-slave ring of young women who were held for prostitution after their passports were confiscated." Leslie Wayne, "America's For-Profit Secret Army," *New York Times*, October 13, 2002, sec. 3, p. 1.

13. Robert Mandel, *Armies without States: The Privatization of Security* (Boulder: Lynne Rienner, 2002), 8.

14. Zoltan Grossman, "A Century of US Military Interventions: From Wounded Knee to Yugoslavia," SWANS Commentary, www.swans.com/library/art6/zig055.html (April 22, 2003).

15. Miro Cernetig, "The Tip of the Spear," Globe and Mail, October 20, 2000, 5.

16. Vernon E. Clark, "The United States Navy: On Watch for America's Security," statement before the House Appropriations Committee, Subcommittee on Defense, Washington, D.C., July 23, 2001.

17. Steven Staples, "Confronting the Military-Corporate Complex" (address to the Hague Appeal for Peace, The Hague, May 12, 1999), 2.

18. Some of the Carlyle Group's luminaries include former president George H. W. Bush, former secretary of state James A. Baker, former budget director Richard Darman, former secretary of defense Frank Carlucci, former prime minister John Major, former president of the German Bundesbank Karl Otto Poehl, former Philippine president Fidel V. Ramos, former South Korean president Park Tae Joon, past or present chairmen of BMW, Hoffman-LaRoche, Nestlé, LVMH-Moet Hennessy, Louis Vuitton, and Aerospatiale, the French Airbus partner. Leslie Wayne, "For the Old Bush Team, a Whole New Ballgame," International Herald Tribune, March 6, 2001, reproduced on Bill Totten's home page: www.billtotten.com/english/ow1/00460.html.

19. As of this writing, Louis Verstner Jr. from IBM is slotted to replace former defense secretary Frank Carlucci as chairman. "Carlyle has diversified considerably. The arms business represents about 10 percent of the firm's current investments, down from 60 percent at the peak in the 90's." Steve Lohr, "Gerstner to Be Chairman of Carlyle Group," New York Times, November 22, 2002, C3.

20. Melanie Warner, "The Big Guys Work for the Carlyle Group," Fortune, March 18, 2002, 1.

21. Honolulu Star Bulletin, May 27, 2001, B14.

22. Commencement address at Smith College, New York Times, May 26, 2001, A10. Other Clinton appointees quickly followed suit, including Sandy Berger, former national security adviser; Thomas F. McLarty III, former chief of staff; Richard C. Holbrooke, former ambassador to the United Nations; and William E. Kennard, former chairman of the Federal Communications Commission. Cohen modestly pointed out that his government service has given him access to "major, major" business leaders who "need advice." Honolulu Star Bulletin, May 27, 2001, B14.

23. Colum Lynch, "Halliburton's Iraq Deals Greater Than Cheney Has Said: Affiliates Had $73 Million in Contracts," Washington Post, June 23, 2001, A01.

24. Jeff Gerth and Don Van Natta, "In Tough Times, a Company Finds Profits in Terror War," New York Times, July 13, 2002, A1.

25. Jordan Green, "USA: Halliburton—To the Victors Go the Markets,"

CorpWatch, February 1, 2002, www.corpwatch.org/news/PND.jsp?articleid=1752.

26. Green, "USA: Halliburton."

27. Pratap Chatterjee, "Force Provider: The Base in a Box," *CorpWatch*, May 2, 2002, www.corpwatch.org/issues/PID.jsp?articleid=2468.

28. William Oliver, supervisor, quoted in Chatterjee, "Force Provider."

29. For further discussion of the language of militarism, see Kathy E. Ferguson and Phyllis Turnbull, *Oh, Say, Can You See? The Semiotics of the Military in Hawai'i* (Minneapolis: University of Minnesota Press, 1999).

30. Steven Lee Myers, "America to Press Security in Distant Ports," *New York Times*, December 6, 2000, A14.

31. See Kathy Ferguson and Phyllis Turnbull, "Fruitful Oxymorons in the Bush Security Doctrine" (forthcoming).

32. Ferguson and Turnbull, "Fruitful Oxymorons," 2.

33. Ferguson and Turnbull, "Fruitful Oxymorons," 3.

34. Giorgio Agamben, *Homo Sacer: Sovereign Power and Bare Life* (Stanford: Stanford University Press, 1998).

35. Dan Smith, *State of War and Peace Atlas* (Oslo: International Peace Research Institute, 1997), 25.

36. Mike Moore, "More Security for Less Money," *Bulletin of Atomic Scientists*, September-October 1995, 37.

PART II
ANTIGLOBALISM

IDEOLOGY IN THE AGE OF
DIGITAL REPRODUCTION

Terrell Carver

Globalism as neoliberal ideology invokes illusions and erasures that promote class interests. To do this, it draws on foundational ideologies of nature, civilization, science, progress, and consumption. It uses ideology to produce ideology, commodifying digital media in a realm of specious commercial "democracy." Antiglobalism must of necessity counteract the political efficacy of globalism by circulating signs that challenge the foundational ideologies as well as the neoliberal doctrines of globalism. The political potential and actual efficacy of this depends on contrary symbols and narratives that promote action.

This chapter contrasts the so-called Marx and Engels of the Internet age, Michael Hardt and Antonio Negri (in their book *Empire*) with the vision and politics of the *Communist Manifesto*, interpreted as a political intervention of its time. Reading Marx and Engels outside the hindsight and teleologies of "traditional Marxism" (which came later) presents a critique of Hardt and Negri's philosophical idealism and political nullity. Their antiglobalism thus resembles the "critical criticism" to which Marx and Engels were politically and intellectually opposed because it addressed an audience of intellectuals with conceptual sleight of hand.

Marx, Engels, and Globalization

In terms of a global outlook on the thrust and effect of capitalist development, it is hard to do better than the *Communist Manifesto* (1848). In vivid language Marx and Engels sketched a time when capitalism wasn't, and then narrated its history up to their own present. The terms in which they did this were scathingly critical yet objectively analytical. Their critical theory of capitalism was not an anachronistic and moralizing one that said it should have never been, yet their political tone was one of resistance and transformation to a post-capitalist future. Their textual dramaturgy was one of struggle, specifically class struggle, ending in the victory of the exploited class over the exploiters or, alternatively, their "common ruin."[1]

Analytically Marx and Engels took the view that human history arises dynamically when surplus production kicks in, and some people then work for the benefit of others through regulatory mechanisms of power and punishment. Precapitalist regimes, as they are considered in Marx and Engels's work, are thus ways of licensing their view that capitalism is neither "natural" (i.e., primeval and unchanging), nor nondevelopmental (i.e., a view that "history is over"). On their account the tension between humans that requires politics, in particular the formation and maintenance of property systems, arises from the organization of production on an unequal basis with respect to human needs and talents as distributed among individuals. Patterns of unequal distribution consequently follow, however ameliorated by political ("bread and circuses") or "private" (family and charitable) patterns of "redistribution."

Marx and Engels have a theory of globalization in the *Communist Manifesto*, namely, that capitalism has arisen alongside of, in preparation for, and in the service of the mechanized production of goods and services. Not all of these things and activities are in their view especially useful for humanity in general or for individuals in particular, nor are these systems carefully managed in terms of resourcing, conservation, and waste disposal. While the vastly increased productivity, vastly increased array of goods, and vast transformations of landscape and society are in a sense celebrated in the *Communist Manifesto*, the downside is made excruciatingly clear. This is spectacular immiseration and impoverishment cruelly below the level of previous systems of production, tantalizingly institutionalized amid obvious evidence of wealth, security, and leisure. The global dynamic arises through conquest (Marx specifically mentions "the Spanish discovery of gold in the Americas"), its impact in stimulating production and new productive systems in Europe, and the onward march of colonization and imperialism everywhere else. While the emphasis is on history as economic innovation and expansion, at the expense of more traditional views of history as battles and regimes, Marx and Engels are nonetheless clear that commercially compounded greed, developing technologies of warfare, and timeless fantasies of vainglory all play a part in the modern urge to globalize.

Marx and Engels are quite sharp in showing how economic acquisitiveness moved on from looting to "trade" (i.e., the incorporation of noncapitalist economies of various kinds into capitalist patterns of production) in various ways. This moves class inequalities into an international arena where culture, nationality, nationhood, and all else fall victim to "development." Marx is also well-known for having a less than rosy view of life in low-technology, near-subsistence communities, though he was also disinclined to view the objects of colonialism (e.g., in India or Ireland) as anything other than victims of capitalists. Capitalists, of course, function through the "modern state," famously described as "a device for administering the common affairs of the whole bourgeois class."[2]

The *Communist Manifesto* clearly announces the existence and utility of ideologies—belief systems that define, justify, and reinforce the unequal holdings of power, both economic and political, for the benefit of some people at the expense of others. Often, though not always, this involves generational patterns of inheritance. Marx and Engels, of course, are quite sharp on the role that religious doctrines and institutions play in constructing and preserving these inequalities of production and exchange, and on the role of nationalisms in licensing colonial acquisitions and imperial protection of trade and industry. Perhaps if they had been more aware of racisms that do the same, they could have taken a view about the exploitation of women earlier on in their careers. Engels got on board in 1884 with his powerful but rather speculative announcement that the female sex was the first exploited class.[3] Nonetheless the outlines of the ideologies that commonly stimulate, accompany, and legitimate capitalist "development" are sketched in the *Communist Manifesto*.

What isn't sketched in anything other than passing terms is the specific ideology through which political economy instantiated capitalism as such. Capitalism is itself a conceptual system ("the economic categories," in Marx's terms), and without certain *categories* understood in certain ways, capitalism is by definition impossible and could never exist. Marx was fascinated with (and is fascinating on) the exact concepts that have to be socially current and performatively practiced in order for it to exist, and to exist in the dynamic and ruthless way that it does.[4] Interestingly the *Communist Manifesto* does not attempt to reproduce the basic arguments on this question that Marx undertook in *The Poverty of Philosophy* and the lecture version of *Wage-labor and Capital*, written just prior to the commission from the Communist League to draft them a manifesto for their Central Committee to consider. In the spirit of reaching out to the broader masses, which was in fact the strategy recommended by Marx and Engels, the ideas of their manifesto, as we have it, had another life of their own in the form of a shortened text published at large during the revolutionary events of 1848, notably in their native Rhineland.[5] Marx had the ability at this time to introduce his critical theory of capitalism because the central concepts of value in exchange, value in use, labor (even labor power), and capital as self-expanding value were all in place by 1847. What made the difference in *Capital* itself, as it originally emerged in 1867 (and then in its now familiar form only in the French edition and second German edition of the early 1870s), was the focus on the "commodity" and the "transformation of money into capital" that mark the Marxian critique of capitalism as we know it.

The theories of class, exploitation, and struggle exist independently of either frame through which Marx analyzed capitalism, whether the later sophistication of *Capital* or the earlier discussions in *The Poverty of Philosophy*. Arguably the outline theory that some people produce for the benefit of others and that this is exploitative—whether the system is capitalist, precapitalist monetary exchange, or nonmonetary "hoarding" or tribute—reaches back through Engels's early "Outlines of a Critique of Political Economy," to Rousseau's *Discourse on the Origin of Inequality* (surely Marx and Engels must have read this, but there is no record or reference), and ultimately at least as far in the past as Thomas More's *Utopia* of 1516. Most commentators, caught up in the intricacies of Marx's "discovery" that in capitalist society labor power produces more value than is required for its own reproduction, miss the *generality* of his overall theory of exploitation, and its necessary link to the longer lineage of class struggle, of which the current politico-economic tensions within capitalism (and outbreaks into a "more or less veiled civil war") were an instance, albeit a crucially defining and effectuating one for humanity as a whole, as we are told in the *Communist Manifesto*.

Marx, Engels, and Antiglobalism

Later on in 1865 Marx wrote up the "basics" of his "critique of the economic categories" as an address for the General Council of the International Workingmen's Association (in English), posthumously published (by Eleanor Marx) as *Value [or Wages], Price and Profit* (1898), thus incorporating his detailed "economic" views into his general strategy of political intervention, through writing, contact with radical elites, cross-class coalitions with liberals and democrats, always pushing them toward more democracy. In Marx's presentational terms critique as a discourse had to announce what belief systems he was against, explain why no one should believe them, reveal whose interests they served, and lead the reader through this criticism to an acceptance of other principles. The tricky thing was to gain the reader's confidence, on the one hand, with a reliable authorial narration of a received and probably somewhat familiar view, but on the other hand, to mount a clear and fierce criticism of that view, leading the reader to a set of quite different ideas, judgments, and values. A critique can be poor if it is too obviously partisan, so the reader rejects the analysis, or it can be poor if it is too obviously objective and generous, so the reader emerges more convinced than ever that the ideas under attack are good ones, or that the objections are really rather minor. Mostly, any critique runs risks of presuming too much knowledge and too much patience in its readership, and of preaching to the converted only, and never finding the right "hooks" or "darts" such that readers change their minds. Arguably Marx's later focus on his critique of political economy suffered from all these faults, and was probably destined to do so.

Marx had the job of presenting the "basics" of contemporary political economy both as the work of ideologues, who could be readily identified as toadies and apologists and so pilloried, further compounded with the self-serving character of their views. However, they had a further significance in his critique, since they were the key to the way that the ordinary concepts that define capitalism as a practice actually worked (so he claimed): commodity, money, capital. Political economists could thus be self-serving and class-biased precisely because their theories were in fact definitional or "scientific" refinements of commonplace understandings of the normal terms of trade: goods, wages, "stock." Trade, of course, includes wage laborers, exchanging time and effort for money, and it is on that point that Marx attempted an intricate reversal of definition and judgment. Political economy (of the Ricardian and Smithian varieties) presented the wage contract as a fair exchange, and the system of private property (e.g., in the means of production) as the way through which justice is defined and practiced. In the popular terms of the time, this was also a widespread perception, indeed among many socialists who opted instinctively for an egalitarian thesis and politically for reformist or transformationist strategies of equalization or at least redistribution.

Marx argued that this view, whether commonplace or specialist, was a self-serving hypocrisy because the political economists did not push their analysis beyond this point and so left the origin of profit a mystery. For Marx the "fair exchange" view was also a crime against wage laborers as a class, not least because so many of them believed that there could be no injustice in this inequality, and so no grounds for struggle and transformation. It is not too difficult to see Marx's critique of political economy (as an ideology) as itself an attack on globalism, conceived as an ideology of neoliberalism, an update of Ricardian and Smithian presumptions, and just as self-serving and class-biased.[6] These presumptions are that the contractual terms of trade, arrived at under "normal" circumstances of nonduress, are a paradigm of equal treatment, and moreover that justice is paradigmatically the enforcement of such contracts between those who are thus equal before the law. The trade between these legal equals is, of course, in resources, some of which are productive and require an input of labor, and some of which are merely labor itself, without the means to make an output. While Smith and Ricardo were not always sure that this system was inevitably to the benefit, or to the maximum benefit, of all those "freely" participating in it (as opposed to finding a life elsewhere . . .), later neoliberals have fewer doubts and promise more prosperity. The flip side of this "very Eden of the innate rights of man,"[7] as Marx described it, is a dystopia of exploitation and struggle, where there is fighting to get through layers of ideological mystification, normalization, and displacement (e.g., of troubles to "another world") in order to arrive at actions of the sort that challenge and eventually displace the very concepts through which capitalism operates and is thus "performed" by individuals.

By way of a counterattack on the theory and ideology of capitalism, Marx and Engels were utterly against invoking any countervailing religious or even moral "system," unlike many others in the nascent socialist and communist movements. Arguably the religious and moral wing of social "reform" has been more successful than Marxist atheism and "science" in challenging capitalist power structures and concentrations of wealth, but then no one so far has come at all close to the genuine abolition of capitalism. This would mark an end to the cash nexus and therefore a change to ability-based production and needs-based distribution. This was something to which Marx and Engels attempted to rally their communists, to be joined by déclassé middle classes and a "part of the bourgeois ideologists."[8]

At this stage it is an interesting question how the politics of resistance and transformation announced in the *Communist Manifesto* was to be performed, that is, enacted and promoted. Marx and Engels announced a curiously stealth-like strategy, given the grand sweep of their theory of globalization. Communists, they said, would not organize separately as a party but would seek to influence other parties, whether merely liberal and democratic or more radical and revolutionary. It is evident that this would take place through discussion and representation of views in political organizations. At the time most of these were by definition revolutionary, since they opposed the authoritarian and nonconstitutional monarchs then in power. Marx and Engels's paradigmatic political organization for the exploited is in fact the (banned) union movement, combining a commitment to democracy (so they thought) with an entrée to enlightenment through theoretical and practical modes of critique, and the potential for international solidarity (again, so they thought). What they did not mention, except to rule them out, were militarized authority structures, as opposed to popular force of arms. Indeed they had little to say about authority structures in revolutionary movements at all, fearing association with self-styled and self-serving conspirators.[9]

Summarizing, I would say that Marx and Engels produced a remarkably accurate picture of globalization as the relentless spread of production for profit, backed up by policies of imperialism and ideologies of fair trade. Imperialism includes both political and commercial bombardments and batterings; fair trade includes the introduction of "private" property systems and apparatuses to enforce contractual justice. Insofar as the two anticipated more recent theorizations of cross-cultural homogenization and instant flows of information, the *Communist Manifesto* puts itself presciently into this category, by calling for its own translation into numerous languages. This was achieved, in fact, though much more slowly than anticipated, by addressing the "workers of the world" on behalf of an international committee based in the then "world city," London.[10] Certainly their argument presumes a commonality of experience, or at least a commonality of reason, such that the forecasts of global transformation would be intelligible, not least in countries where primary production in agriculture and minerals was (usually unfreely) traded for a limited range of goods to benefit local elites (with higher profits retained, of course, in the "home countries" of "the West"). It took generations before this document reached even a fraction of the "non-Western" world and thus influenced key opinion leaders, one way or another. Communism stalks any land as a specter of fevered, right-wing imaginations more often than it does as the vision of globalization discussed here. But the ideas were already in place by the mid-1840s.

Globalism is rather more difficult to tease out of the *Communist Manifesto*, yet it is there in among the other ideologies that are purveyed by the capitalist class for their own protection and advancement. The text plays this out as a drama of proletarian rebellion and victory, against a class enemy, without detailing exactly how this exploiting class constitutes itself, how it operates, and what "science" (rather than political or religious "belief system") supports it. From Marx's later work it is evident that the commodity, money, and capital concepts were crucial, both in "ordinary life" at the bank and in the factory and in the works of the political economists, whom he sought so strenuously to expose as shallow thinkers and apologists for exploitation. Within political economy Marx went on to expose the naturalism and normalization that made contractual exchange and production for profit seem eternal and just, indeed progressive and good for all, or at least for "the industrious" (damn the lazy). His attack on globalism deployed a historical anthropology of production that is still valuable and a textual analysis of an apparently crucial issue: how does a presumed equality in the wage exchange give rise to realized profit in production? The political economists were prone to locate this production of surplus in the virtue, thrift, or abstinence of the capitalist-entrepreneur; Marx located it instead in the sweated brow of the uniquely endowed human laborer (compared with animals or machines, who also work). Political economists had the advantage of being rather fuzzy on the issue of profit and getting away with it. Their successors, the economists of subjective value and utility, have been even more successful because they jettisoned the problem altogether.

Neoliberal views are thus variations on the globalism of the political economists that Marx undertook to expound and explode. Current expositions of globalism vary from the Friedmanesque (capitalism produces a wealth of goods and services, via incentives to be unequal, that allow some people to excel) to the limply reformist (wealthy countries must pressure the IMF and World Bank to fund only policies and projects that empower the "third world" poor as against the elites of international corporations). Both kinds of work on globalism must present the view they see as correct and progressive versus an "other" against which this correct and progressive view is defined. In the case of Friedmanesque criticisms, the "other" is anyone wanting to curtail "market freedoms." In the case of reformists, the "other" is extreme neoliberalism requiring free trade, open doors for multinational companies, and low levels of "social services," ditto government borrowing. Friedmanites are for globalism, or their version of it; reformists and (misnamed) "antiglobalization" protesters are against it. As many of the so-called antiglobalization protesters embrace the communications strategy and international involvement that capitalist globalization makes possible (as presaged in the *Communist Manifesto*), they are perhaps better characterized as "antiglobalism" protesters instead, thus escaping the smears of Luddism and utopianism.

Hardt, Negri, and Globalization/Globalism

Hardt and Negri's vast study represents a kind of text and incorporates a textual dramaturgy very much at odds with the reading of Marx and Engels outlined above.[11] The discourse is that of academic referencing with great thinkers and intellectual debates (rather than a "manifesto" targeted at a group), and the textual dramaturgy presents a near dichotomy between order and anarchy (rather than a stimulus to struggle). The authors present a vision of a new world *order* drawn from rationalism and idealism that has (allegedly) found developed expression in the United Nations and even in great power campaigns for international stability.[12] The new systemic totality has its roots in ideas (so they say), namely, those of "right" and justice in the international sphere, and this realm of conceptual production is taken largely at face value. Hardt and Negri's account seems innocent of any unmasking or "ideology critique" that casts doubt on the universality and indeed definition of "empire as order" by evaluating the purported aspirations over time against the actualities of action (and inaction) linked to great power or "Western" economic interests.

In the second half of *Empire* Hardt and Negri self-consciously invoke Marx and Engels when they address themselves to production as such, indeed to globalizing capitalism. At that point they suggest that they are writing the book on "world market" that Marx never got to in order to finish off the books of

Capital.[13] Again, their focus is on presenting an order of concepts, indeed *orderly* concepts, that express and also (somehow) constitute a totalizing order in the world (and in the human subject). Struggle enters the picture as individualized resistance only in a paean to anarchic working-class (and middle-class) strategies of "resistance," which are only briefly and abstractly noted.[14] Hardt and Negri detect a decline in the vigor of empire and an openness in history to further transformations, but they posit no link between themselves, their writing, their (intellectual) audience, and transformational politics in any determinate sense.[15] Their evident strategy of writing for intellectuals, creating a conceptual realm of order with "a life of its own" and looking only to anarchic and inchoate resistance, surely resembles the "critical critics"—Bruno and Edgar Bauer, together with Max Stirner and others—whom Marx and Engels pilloried in the 1840s, notably in *The German Ideology*.

It is difficult to see Hardt and Negri's idealism and anarchism as even in outline a critique of globalism—the neoliberal ideology that capitalism is natural, inescapable, fair, and just. While they *say* that they oppose the effects of capitalist exploitation and inequality, there are no arguments at the level of the "economic categories" that would persuade us; indeed, the two merely gesture at deconstructing the underlying ideologies on which globalism itself relies for credibility: "The bizarre naturalness of capitalism is a pure and simple mystification, and we have to disabuse ourselves of it right away."[16] The sense of open-ended and risky struggle that infuses the *Communist Manifesto*, and to which its audience (of workers and intellectuals) was supposed to address itself in practice, is quite missing from Hardt and Negri's Olympian perspective. The idealism of order is simply announced and then supposedly supported with selective and specious histories (and philosophical citations, e.g., from Kant and Spinoza). The *Communist Manifesto*, by contrast, discusses the situation of communist groups in different countries and essentially views the process from the other end. An anarchic capitalism infuses itself with ideologies of order and rationality which—with a bit of help—everyday workers can deconstruct on the way to the practical solidarities of democratic action. This process was hardly unproblematic as it worked out, and the political efforts of Marx and Engels did not in themselves have an obviously effective outcome, but the linkages were there in the text. Hardt and Negri actually celebrate the anarchic character of resistance to globalized capitalism as it takes place *atheoretically* and thus innocently of any developed (and developing) antiglobalism as a circulation of signs that would challenge the present relations of exploitation.

Writing a book that contrasts with the project that I associate with Marx and Engels hardly makes Hardt and Negri wrong or ineffectual. However, contrasting them with the dramaturgy and strategy of the *Communist Manifesto* has the useful effect of aligning them very clearly with an idealism of questionable political efficacy and distancing them from the discourse and impetus of the texts that Marx and Engels actually produced. In this light *Empire* seems at times to be homage, parody, and transcendence. However we draw the lessons today, it is important to be clear that there are two quite different structural models here relating to the politics of antiglobalism. You have a choice.

Conclusion

Globalization is not much of a fact without globalism. Globalism is not much of an ideology without the normalizing concepts of nature, civilization, science, progress, and consumption that make it seem inevitable, incontrovertible, and good. Marx and Engels's sweeping view of globalization in the *Communist Manifesto* was remarkably prescient and stands up well as an analytical summary today. What distinguishes their work from other accounts is their antiglobalism, theorized elsewhere in Marx's writings. The kernel of that antiglobalism is a conception of exploitation that is simple and general, and can stand apart from the questionable orthodoxies of Marxist economics and "historical materialism." The whole theorization promotes struggle over easily understood issues and has a target audience among the exploited. The same cannot be said for Hardt and Negri's *Empire*, which announces a grandiose idealism of order and issues no credible call to political action. This chapter has argued for a reading of Marx and Engels that is adaptable to the present, in order to fill out the contrast between globalization and globalism and thus present a credible antiglobalism. Hardt and Negri rely on a Marxist Marx and Engels who are trapped in a conceptual systematization of the capitalist order, opposition to which is scarcely conceivable in effective terms. Hardt and Negri's antiglobalism is instead a gesture of unargued intellectual defiance of an almost apolitical character. They are themselves but an "other" to the Marxist Marx and Engels. I hope that my "political" reading of Marx and Engels speaks directly to our concerns today with globalism and the kind of globalization that it licenses and legitimates.

Notes

1. Karl Marx and Frederick Engels, "Manifesto of the Communist Party," in *Karl Marx, Later Political Writings*, trans. and ed. Terrell Carver (Cambridge: Cambridge University Press, 1996), 2.
2. Marx and Engels, "Manifesto of the Communist Party," 3.
3. Frederick Engels, *The Origin of the Family Private Property and the State* (New York: Penguin, 1985), 96.
4. See the discussion in Terrell Carver, *The Postmodern Marx* (Manchester: Manchester University Press, 1998), 24–86.

5. Terrell Carver, *Friedrich Engels: His Life and Thought* (Basingstoke, U.K.: Macmillan, 1989), 195.

6. I am following the distinction between "globalization" and "globalism" argued through in Manfred B. Steger, *Globalism: The New Market Ideology* (Lanham, Md.: Rowman & Littlefield, 2002), 1–80.

7. Karl Marx, *Capital*, trans. Ben Fowkes (Harmondsworth, U.K.: Penguin, 1976), 1:280.

8. Marx and Engels, "Manifesto of the Communist Party," 10.

9. Marx and Engels, "Manifesto of the Communist Party," 29–30.

10. Marx and Engels, "Manifesto of the Communist Party," 1.

11. Michael Hardt and Antonio Negri, *Empire* (Cambridge: Harvard University Press, 2000).

12. Hardt and Negri, *Empire*, 3–21.

13. Hardt and Negri, *Empire*, xvii, 205, 415 n. 4.

14. Hardt and Negri, *Empire*, 260–69.

15. Hardt and Negri, *Empire*, 393–413.

16. Hardt and Negri, *Empire*, 386–87.

GLOBALIZATION: IDEOLOGY AND MATERIALITY

Richard Terdiman

Pessimism of the intellect; optimism of the will.

—Antonio Gramsci[1]

Dominant ideology sells dominant interests: this maxim has been a commonplace of social theory at least since Marx.[2] It does not imply that a dominant ideology is the *only* ideology, but rather that, as Gramsci argued, the dominant ideology is "hegemonic." It is the beheld of all beholders, it defines the debate, *it calls the shots*. With regard to globalization—so intensely marketed and so strenuously contested over the past half decade or so—the ideology of transnational capitalism seems to be selling pretty well. The globalization product is being snapped up all over the world. But for many in the west and north, globalization is an abomination. Against it, numerous groups and movements have been seeking to formulate and propagate a counterideology. In the face of this condemnation—of the globalizing process, of its prospects, of its consequences—I want to look again at where *we* (in the West) stand, where we *ought* to stand, and where our *stand* comes from to begin with.

Objective 1

My first objective is to ask what can be said about the ideology of opposition to the hegemonic view in the West that markets—and profits from—globalization.

Beginning in Geneva in February 1998 and Seattle in November 1999, and continuing in Genoa, Davos, Québec, and most recently (at this writing) in Florence, tens of thousands of people have demonstrated against globalization and the institutions that promote it. Their commitment is admirable, and I want to subject their arguments and assumptions to a sympathetic but skeptical analysis.

The values and the reasoning that underlie these First World critiques of globalization need to be identified and articulated—something that has not been carefully done by their proponents.[3] In particular, the political and intellectual position that sees globalization as the exploitation of people and nations in the developing world needs a historicizing reconception. The following speculation seems to me the most salient point from which to begin a reconception of antiglobalization. First World opposition to globalization in the south and east is best understood as a powerfully overdetermined avatar of the long history of repudiation of capitalism in the *developed* world.[4]

This contestatory anticapitalist position, and the passion associated with it, first arose in nineteenth-century Europe. Such positions linked traditionalist conservatives like Burke and Balzac, Guizot and Carlyle on the one hand, and socialist thinkers from Saint-Simon, Proudhon, and Fourier to Marx and Engels on the other.[5] In its dream of a more humane world, on a more human scale, the ideology of contemporary antiglobalization combines elements of both of these strands.

But transnational capitalism, antiglobalization's antagonist, still dominates. We can feel the weight of its hegemony in the degree to which the arguments deployed against dominant neoliberal ideology today appear as a counter discourse automatically—almost involuntarily—denigrating the worldwide spread of capital.[6] Antiglobalizers thus find themselves playing on the field that globalization owns.

A reflex negation of a hegemonic view is an inadequate basis for policy or politics. We need to ask, What is the *practicable* socioeconomic paradigm that antiglobalizers could champion? What they repudiate is clear, and we may share their views and their hopes. But what is their positive program? Through what reorganization of the economy or society can such hopes be realized? What is the alternative?

Thinking through the question of alternatives is impeded—even imperiled—by two factors. The first is a misrecognition of the basis on which much popular opposition to globalization in the West rests. The claim I want to make about this basis is speculative, and substantiating it will require considerable empirical research. But the hypothesis nonetheless seems to me worth advancing: what people in the developed West most strenuously oppose, what most upsets them and pushes them most vigorously to action, are not the effects of globalization in the developing world, however unfortunate or destructive these may be, but the victory of capitalism in the developed world. This victory—particularly since

the revolutions of 1989–1990 in Central Europe and the former Soviet Union—
has so flattened opposition to the free market system in the West that fighting it
there (where most of those reading this essay are located) has become inconceiv-
able. Antiglobalism in the West must be construed as the only imaginable current form of opposition to the market system. Moreover, by projecting its castigation of capitalism beyond the West, such opposition emigrates from the area
of its analytical strength and concrete experience, and abandons that terrain for
a part of the world that, for most Western antiglobalizers, is not only geographically remote but empirically obscure.

The second factor undermining the effectiveness of antiglobalization protest
in the West (and elsewhere as well) is a disabling vagueness concerning the protagonists in this socioeconomic contention. In particular, the category *capitalism* referred to in virtually all antiglobalist rhetoric, in every program and strategy, tends to be framed as if everyone already knows what it is and has analytical
tools adequate to the power of the phenomenon itself. But impressionistic or
polemical framings of one's antagonist are not sufficient. We need to know better what capitalism is—not least because such knowledge bears critically on the
vexing problem of possible alternatives to it. The most coherent and capable paradigm for illuminating the matter is the Marxian category of the "mode of production" (*Produktionsweise* or sometimes *Produktionsprozess*).

By "mode of production" Marx means the overall way or manner by which
societies produce economic goods. The concept is intended to be understood
at a high level of structural generality.[7] Thus a given mode of production (e.g.,
capitalism) can persist across significant alterations in the production relations
that organize a social group.[8] A "mode" thus designates the fundamental technological, exchange, and distribution process by which production occurs: the
way human beings work with their productive forces and divide their labor categories among those doing the work. More technically, factors determining the
mode of production specify the distribution of social and economic power in
a group, the purpose of production (for immediate use or for exchange), the
form of labor (slave, serf, wage worker, etc.), and the means by which the value
of labor is extracted or expropriated in the production process (physical compulsion under slavery; legal compulsion in serfdom; "free" sale of labor power
in the capitalist labor contract).

The point of this terminological exegesis is simple. Antiglobalizers need to
specify clearly what aspects of the globalizing—of the more and more ubiqui-
tously capitalizing—process they contest. And most insistently and particularly, they need to say what alternative to these, what other socioeconomy, they
propose that the world adopt. But can they name another practicable mode of
production better adapted to the world's most urgent needs?

Capitalism has already had many forms and has many forms today. Some
are inherently brutal, some more benign. New forms are possible. The utility

of the "mode of production" concept is that it brings into fundamental relationship this diversity of historical, current, or possible capitalist forms ("free
market capitalism," "welfare capitalism," "market socialism," "socialism with
Chinese characteristics"), which, despite their diversity, make capitalism's fundamental characteristic—the production of commodities for exchange—central to social relations and economic activity.

The scandal is that capitalism *works*. It has increased the wealth of the
world dramatically. This is why so many people around the world today want
a market system to replace their current feudal or agrarian or sclerotic command socioeconomy. The people who don't want capitalism are those who
already have it. This is an uncomfortable (for some an unendurable) truth
because of the powerful investment since the nineteenth century in contesting
the system's very real cruelties and distortions. But the question remains: all
things considered, what would be a *better* system, what would be an authenti-
cally *different* mode of production? And on the basis of what values would we
order the practicable alternatives?

Because these questions have not even been seriously framed, what has
largely ensued is denegation of the answer that history and experience have so
far provided. Antiglobalizers appropriately continue the castigation of capitalist cruelty that has been a fundamental current in social thought since Carlyle
and Marx. But change within a mode of production is a very different thing
from change in mode of production. Projections of the latter transformation
today remain an empty set.

The effect is a static, even rigidifying, idealization of capitalism's contrary—
but what is that? Sadly, the antiglobalizers' projection is largely a politics of fantasy. We cannot even term such visualizations of an alternative to capitalism
"utopia" because they have almost no definition. They seek to chuck out what
is deplorable in capitalism—but without any notion of how a substitute socioeconomy could survive or prosper without capitalism's unique productivity.[9]
One interlocutor who heard a paper I once presented on globalization urged
conversion of the socioeconomy to traditional Native American cultural and
economic organization. I asked which half of us he would recommend be sac-
rificed, given the inability of such a mode of production—however mellow—
to support more than 50 percent of the world's population. Such hopeless projections are touching, but they are not politically or economically serious. In
this moment of the technological and social capacities of the world that we
know or can practicably imagine, I think we will look in vain for a contrastive
mode of socioeconomic production. There is a lot of charming romanticism in
antiglobalist contestation.

My claim is that, for the great majority of antiglobalization protesters, the
logic of opposition roots not in the reality of depredations exercised on the
Third World, but in the intellectual, ideological, and affective disaster of the

110

disappearance of any alternative to capitalism. There is no practicable contrastive political or social ideal that protesters fight for, or through which they seek to counter globalization's dynamic. Perhaps the only such ideal is a familiar (and entirely commendable) Enlightenment humanism, holding that people ought to be valued for themselves, that they must be respected and protected by the community of which they form a part. The flaw in this logic about globalization is that it has almost nothing to do with globalization's concrete process and material consequences. These I will consider in the next section of this chapter.

For now, I offer a brief suggestion of how we might interpret, react to, and deepen the logic of the antiglobalization struggle. My suggestion to recognize that what is happening in the developing world today under the influence of globalization is a capitalizing process parallel to the one that transformed the West from the mid-nineteenth century onward. All of the issues that characterized that massive process of transformation are recurring today. What Marx and Engels described in Europe around 1848 in the *Manifesto* is happening today in South and East Asia (in Singapore, South Korea, and Taiwan, among a number of other places, it has already happened).[10]

What is to be done? I'll put my suggestion briefly. In nineteenth-century Europe it was reasonable to believe that an alternative to capitalist development (or a more benign successor to it) was possible and could be fought for. Today that credo is virtually impossible to hold seriously. So our work must be to accept the domination of the mode of production in which our lives are lived—to recognize *what is the case*—and struggle to make it as humane as it can be. There is enough play in the system to make this possible.

The stage of the struggle at which the developing world finds itself today parallels the one in England at the beginning of Victoria's reign in 1837. Then as now, it is the *conditions of work and of the lives of those who work* that must be reformed. Reduction of hours, protection for children, assurance of worker safety, increases in the equity of wages, freedom of expression and association, and so on—these were the foci of intense social conflict in the 1830s and after. They must become the indispensable objectives of reform today. But the notion that we might revolutionize capitalism in this contemporary phase of its extension into the developing world, the idea that we can sweep away the market— these, unhappily, are daydreams.

Objective 2

My second objective in this chapter is to examine the most significant real-world consequences of the globalizing process. Attempts to see the development of the process in terms of the thin material choices and the stringent material constraints that face the south and east require hard-headedness and objectivity. For twenty-first-century Westerners, the world sometimes seems to have been solved. The bothersome limitations of materiality appear to have receded or to have been overcome; *language* appears to have replaced matter as the mode of interaction and the focus of absorption. But the world of human consequences is less forgiving than that. How do we represent the obstinate quality of a reality that language can't simply transform in a speech act?

Consider the following: "With a per capita income of only $210 per annum, Nepal is one of the poorest countries in the world. Nearly half of its population is living below the poverty line; and its social indicators are unsatisfactory."[11] Pace postmodernism, the material referent inexorably forces us beyond any possible containment within language. The reality of suffering reasserts its claims on representation. In the face of an average Nepali income of fifty-eight cents per day, the exquisite mobility and malleability of language, concept, and theory seems beside the point.

The Nepalis perish of starvation, of dysentery from contaminated water, of infections for which, given their penury, antibiotics are too expensive and wouldn't arrive in time anyway, since the average Nepali lives three and a half hours' trek from the nearest road, and many more hours from the nearest medical care.[12] However dispassionately reported, with whatever social-scientific objectivity (Nepal's social indicators are "unsatisfactory"), the horror of the story behind the words repels the distanciations of postmodern paradigms of understanding and calls for something to be *done*. The ethics of concern for our common humanity, the immediacy and immanence of the suffering referred to, make reading *this* description as if it were detachable from the suffering of bodies seem a tone-deaf metalepsis.[13]

My central claim is this: with globalization, materiality is forced back into brutal focus—*materiality becomes the case*. Globalization has turned the West's attention to parts of the globe beyond the comforts of per capita incomes above $15,000–$20,000 a year—recalling that Nepal's equivalent statistic is $210. How in our thinking did we lose touch with the suffering materiality of these distant places, with their bleak constraints and cruel challenges?

The standard account of how social and cultural theory veered toward the hypostasis of language goes something like this: as people in the north and west became richer and their lives became more comfortable, the refractoriness of materiality finally began to seem a problem close to resolution. It appeared that the grip of unmasterable circumstance and brute necessity had diminished to a point never been lower before. The world of labor-saving appliances, increasingly automated production, long-distance telephones, ubiquitous electronic communications media, and the seeming transparency of liberal democracy appeared increasingly convergent with the distinctive temporality and phenomenology of *language*, with its facility of exchange and control, its fluidity and its agility.

For Westerners things were getting easier. Not so for others elsewhere. Yet at the same time as the "language turn" was happening in the 1960s, the globalizing process was already gaining momentum and pursuing its transformation of the world. Yet given the empirical dispersion and obscurity inherent in the phenomenon, if you were living in Euro-America at that time you would have had to be looking well beyond your horizon to see it. Increasingly veiled in this conceptual and ideological inflection was the world of refractory *bodies*: of caloric deficiency and untreatable disease, of colonialist and totalitarian brutalities, of the millions of bodies dead on the stage of twentieth-century violence.

But today globalization has brought the reality of penury and deficient life chances back into contact with consciousness in the developed world. It has revealed the contingency of our theoretical projections and paradigms. In the United States and, with only a slight lag in Western Europe, the liberations of post–World War II "materialism" ironically freed thinking to turn its back on materiality. Exigencies that to most of the world and for most of the world's history have seemed unrelenting and immediate came to appear so transcendable that they ceased being theoretically active or effective at all. But the very facility of the processes of exchange that such paradigms were celebrating and modeling themselves on, and whose density was providing the ease that determined such inflections in thought, was simultaneously creating the conditions of possibility for the grittier challenges of globalization, and the consequent pressure that such developments exercise on theory itself.

Globalization may yet create for large numbers of people elsewhere on the planet a world of ease paralleling that of postwar years in the developed West. But getting there won't be painless. The process of such creation will be less like taking a call on your cell phone by the pool, and more like the brutal primitive accumulation of early capitalism that Engels chronicled in *The Condition of the Working Class in 1844* or that Marx theorized in *Capital*, volume 1, part 8. The process is ugly.

In the end, as in the historical cycle of colonization, violence, and eventual decolonization, globalizing capitalist process may *not* produce the leap in standard of living that First World advocates and ideologues anticipate or at least argue for. As it has in the past, what comes out of these developments might follow the familiar law of unintended consequences. Globalizers in the developed West may achieve their objective of penetrating and transforming the socioeconomies of less favored parts of the world. But what might flow from such domination in the medium and the long term is considerably less certain. It's not clear that even today's advanced cybernetic capitalism can control the forces that globalization will assemble and enable.

This uncertainty was already perceptible at the moment of incipience in the eighteenth century. In 1776 in *The Wealth of Nations*, Adam Smith saw it clearly.

He wrote: "At the . . . time when [European colonization of America and the East occurred], the superiority of force happened to be so great on the side of the Europeans, that they were enabled to commit with impunity every sort of injustice in those remote countries. Hereafter, perhaps, the natives of those [formerly colonized] countries may grow stronger, or those of Europe may grow weaker."[14] The implications of such a revolution in relative power would be as incalculable for the West as for the "Rest."

Still, based on what happened over the past two hundred years, we can imagine what may happen in the rest of the world as an outcome of the coming of capitalism. It seems reasonable to suppose that, as it did in Europe, capitalist development in the rest of the world will produce real improvements in a series of consequential "social indicators"—caloric intake, median life expectancy, per capita income, average educational level, and other statistics that bear directly on the well-being and life chances of real people.

Some data points: In 1960, India and China had equivalent per capita GNP. Today the numbers are *twice as high* in China. In 1960, per capita incomes in India and South Korea were identical. Today South Korea's per capita income is *twenty times higher* than India's. In the late 1960s, Singapore's political and economic survival was doubtful. Today Singapore's per capita income is *higher* than Britain's.[15]

To be sure, the new wealth in these societies is not distributed evenly or equitably. But it would be fatuous to imagine that many if not most of those who live in the countries benefiting from such explosive growth in productivity do not see their life chances improve. And consider the least advantaged. Even assuming the most retrograde attitude of exploitation on the part of those who will invest their capital in these mutations and derive their profits from them (as was the case with Euro-American capitalist development), they will find it in their longer-term interest to improve the lives of the workers who will also be their consumers.

The process will result in accentuated inequities and maldistributions of power, wealth, health, leisure, and reward—and in the perception of them. This is the place where the humanism—the respect for persons and rights—that the Enlightenment refined as a polemical and philosophical tool for combating the irrationalities of absolutist medievalism still resonates in our globalizing world today. Who could risk repudiating these Enlightenment values? In the face of considerations like Nepal's disastrous demographic, caloric, and economic statistics, it becomes harder to rail against the coming of global capital if such a transformation will ameliorate the penury of large numbers of human beings.

The job of reformists is to help make the process of these transformations as humane as two centuries of experience with the contrary have helped us comprehend. And if such reformist initiatives find wide support, the globalizing system will have little trouble accommodating them. Just as they did in the face of workers' struggle against the deplorable conditions of labor in nineteenth-century Euro-America, the transnationals will add the cost of minimalist humanism to the calculation of their prices. Such a calculus is completely coherent with the assumptions and practices of free market business, and with elasticity and adaptability of the capitalist mode of production.

It is *not* progressive to fail to analyze and foresee the consequences of one's own practices, theories, or ideology—particularly when these, projected onto a world of 6–7 billion people, could have the effect of relegating to ongoing destitution those billions not already privileged by modern market production. However seductive its bucolic imagery may be, the Native American economy model won't work—nor have any of the noncapitalist others that the south and east have tried. If we seek to deny the path of development that is capitalizing Third World economies today, allegedly for the illegitimate benefit of the First World—and there's no doubt that the First World makes out like a bandit in this process—we must have a *better* idea about how to save the poor Nepalis from starvation. Currently existing socialisms—with Indian or Chinese characteristics—have not found solutions to the problem outside of capitalism.[16] Capitalist globalization is coming because nothing else that anyone has tried has provided the amelioration of conditions that people all over the globe are demanding.

Objective 3

Now to my final objective. What can be said *critically* (if very briefly) about the critique of globalization? What should our attitude toward it be? Let me begin on the ground in the developing world. When people leave their villages to work in the new globalized factories of Asia and the Southern Cone, we need to credit their choices. It is too easy to suppose that in their naïveté they have been hoodwinked or forcibly driven from their villages and their land (if they had any) by some version of the dispossessing "enclosures" that Marx chronicled in Britain (*Capital*, 1:885–89). These people are not dumb or deluded. Today, however deplorable the working conditions (and many are deplorable), the globalized factories of Bombay and Bangkok offer many people a better life than the one they left to join the capitalist workforce. Just try visiting Bihar.[17] This is a detestable perspective to the extent that it identifies a degree of privation that seems unconscionable in a world where many enjoy affluence. But as always, we need to know *what is the case*.

When the results of globalizing processes are compared with the reality of the countryside in Asia, the picture can look quite different from the way we tend to conceive it. I considered Nepal earlier. There the specialists' conclusions are dispiriting: "there has been *little tangible progress in reducing widespread poverty.* . . . At best, Nepal appears to have stood still."[18] The deeper down you drill into the data—for Afghanistan, India, Pakistan, Bangladesh, Thailand, Cambodia, and a dozen other countries—the worse things get. Just as in the First World in the nineteenth century, in these places starvation is still a quotidian fact. People *die* of underdevelopment—as in the Enlightenment's century in Europe they died of malnutrition, not to speak of arbitrary authoritarian violence, imprisonment, and physical and psychological torture. Such horrifying experiences have faded from the conscience of many in the West, in large part because the normalization of Enlightenment values themselves over the past two centuries has increasingly made intolerable the treatment of human beings that such values stigmatize—and in part because capitalism has made such depredations, at worst unproductive, at best obsolete.

The neoliberal ideology of globalization must be subjected to the critique of humanist intellectuals East and West whose commitments to the humane treatment of human beings everywhere must become the primary focus of progressive struggle in our age.[19] But we won't foster that task if we fail to subject antiglobalizing ideology to an equally hard-headed critique. Brecht famously put the moral principle that must guide progressive programs in relation to globalization as it does for many other struggles: *"first grub, then ethics."* It's terrible when these two objectives pull in opposite directions. But how could we possibly say that we'll choose "ethics" if it means that *other* people will starve?

Notes

1. The maxim was originally coined by Romain Rolland. Gramsci made it into a programmatic slogan. See Antonio Gramsci, *Selections from the Prison Notebooks*, trans. Quintin Hoare and Geoffrey Nowell Smith (New York: International, 1971), 175.

2. "The ideas of the ruling class are in every epoch the ruling ideas, i.e. the class which is the ruling *material* force of society, is at the same time its ruling *intellectual* force." Marx and Engels, *The German Ideology* (1845–1846; Moscow: Progress, 1968), 67. I use the term "ideology" here in a neutral and descriptive sense to mean the system of conceptions through which individuals and groups comprehend the world.

3. Part of the difficulty of accomplishing such analysis arises from the disparate nature of the organizations that have grown up to oppose globalization, and the fluid character of the positions they espouse. A Google search on the term "antiglobalization" will turn up about 52,000 sites. Many of them are moribund or entirely dead, as currents in the movement have changed under the pressure of events (particularly after 9/11), and because of the generally low

level of centralizing organization in this extremely variegated movement. Hence any characterization of the antiglobalization movement must seek to identify underlying assumptions active in significant portions of it. Such positions cannot be totalized because the movement is too diverse. But an attempt at analysis is nonetheless vital because of the stakes of this contention, and its consequences for billions of people throughout the world.

4. The following is the first (there are five in total) of the "hallmarks" that define the objectives of Peoples Global Action: "1. *A very clear rejection of capitalism*, imperialism and feudalism; all trade agreements, institutions and governments that promote destructive globalisation . . ." (emphasis added; see NADIR, "Hallmarks," Peoples Global Action, www.nadir.org/nadir/initiativ/agp/en/#hallmarks [April 22, 2003]). The self-description of the group's policy continues by describing its "clearly anti-capitalist (not just anti-neoliberal) stand." "Peoples Global Action against 'Free' Trade and the World Trade Organisation" was founded in February 1998 in Geneva. PGA has coordinated Global Action Days around the world "to express the global resistance of popular movements to capitalist globalisation"; see www.agp.org. The group has been a major organizing network for the demonstrations in Geneva (February 1998), Seattle (November 1999), Prague (September 2000), and Doha (November 2001).

5. The figures in the former, "conservative" group must be distinguished from classical free market liberals like Adam Smith, Condorcet, Benjamin Constant, Jean-Baptiste Say, or Frédéric Bastiat. These latter thinkers argued (with diverse nuances) for unfettered economic exchange. On the other hand, traditionalist conservatives were scathing about the dislocations in the social fabric and the deterioration of older forms of human relations that early capitalism produced.

6. The notion of "counter discourse" here refers to Richard Terdiman, *Discourse/Counter-Discourse* (Ithaca, N.Y.: Cornell University Press, 1985). Michel de Certeau illuminated the early nay-saying, "negative" stage in dissident or oppositional movements. See Michel de Certeau, "May 1968," in *The Capture of Speech and Other Political Writings*, ed. Luce Giard, trans. Tom Conley (Minneapolis: University of Minnesota Press, 1997), pt. 1, 1–87.

7. See, for example Karl Marx, *Capital*, vol. 1, trans. Ben Fowkes (Harmondsworth, U.K.: Penguin-New Left Books, 1976), 505, 602, 617. See also G. A. Cohen, *Marx's Theory of History: A Defence* (Princeton: Princeton University Press, 1978), 79–84. Cohen's account is particularly helpful because of its analytical clarity.

8. Thus in early capitalism the social relations of guild production were maintained for a long period.

9. If wishes were horses, then beggars would ride. The fantasy that the problems of a socioeconomy might be resolved through supernatural transformation is not new. Antiglobalizers want a system that will be productive but

not burdensome; human-scaled but sufficiently forceful to remedy the millennial destitution of more than half of the world's population. Such imperatives, however attractive in themselves, are socioeconomic oxymorons. We know no way to make them real. The flight into magic that they enact bears an uncanny resemblance to Marx's satire of the early capitalist bourgeoisie's fantasy that the problems of their own mode of production might resolve themselves by a miraculous disappearance of its primary inconvenience: "They wish for a bourgeoisie without a proletariat." Karl Marx and Frederick Engels, *The Communist Manifesto* (London: Verso, 1998), 70.

10. Marx, *Manifesto*, 37–39.

11. World Bank, *Nepal: 2000 Economic Update*, "World Bank Poverty Reduction and Economic Management Unit, South Asia Region," www-wds.world bank.org/servlet/WDSServlet?pcont=details&eid=000094946_0004050243 1820 (April 22, 2003).

12. Of course with many Nepalis living in cities, this means that these average distances are much higher for those living in the villages. World Bank, *Nepal 2000 Economic Update*, 11; World Bank, *Nepal: Poverty in Nepal*, 4.

13. In Nepal for the 1992–1997 period the child malnutrition rate (ages 1–5) was 47 percent. In South Asia as a whole the mortality rate for children under five is 100 per 1,000 births; for adults 15–59 it is approximately 215 per 1,000 population. In Nepal the corresponding rates are approximately 117 and 290. World Bank, *Nepal 2000 Economic Update*, 11. See also World Bank, *Nepal: Poverty in Nepal at the Turn of the Twenty-First Century*, "Poverty Reduction and Economic Management Unit, South Asia Region," www-wds.world bank.org/servlet/WDSServlet?pcont=details&eid=000094946_990 31910543371 (April 22, 2003).

14. Adam Smith, *An Inquiry into the Nature and Causes of the Wealth of Nations*, ed. Kathryn Sutherland (New York: Oxford University Press, 1998), 364.

15. See Daniel Yergin, with Joseph Stanislaw, *The Commanding Heights: The Battle for the World Economy* (New York: Simon & Schuster, 2002); and, most recently, Daniel Yergin, "Giving Aid to World Trade," *New York Times*, June 27, 2002, A27.

16. For example, the political economist and theorist Amartya Sen, a man of the left, estimated that socialist engineering of the Chinese economy starved some *30 million people* to death in the early 1960s. See Jonathan Steele, "Amartya Sen," *Guardian*, March 31, 2001. "Although by most indicators, from life expectancy to literacy, Mao's China was ahead of Nehru's India, China had had a catastrophic famine between 1958 and 1961 in which up to 30m people starved to death. There was no free press or alternative political parties to give early warning" (6). Nor can India be said to have successfully abolished destitution despite the remarkable degree of centralized government regulation of development there. These are particularly dispiriting facts, since when we talk about

India and China we are referring to about one-third of the people on our planet. From Sen more generally, see *Development as Freedom* (New York: Anchor, 1999).

17. Or most of the rural areas of Asia. Bihar is the poorest state in India, with more than half of its population below the official Indian poverty line. The dispiriting preferability of capitalist "exploitation" in urban factories is particularly true for women living under archaic conditions of patriarchal domination. Here is a poignant example to help counter any tendency toward unthinking romanticization of village socioeconomies in the poorest parts of the world.

18. World Bank, *Nepal 2000 Economic Update*, 11. Emphasis in original.

19. See, for example, Manfred B. Steger, *Globalism: The New Market Ideology* (Lanham, Md.: Rowman & Littlefield, 2002).

ANTICAPITALIST CONVERGENCE? ANARCHISM, SOCIALISM, AND THE GLOBAL JUSTICE MOVEMENT

Mark Rupert

In recent years neoliberal capitalist globalization and its hegemonic project—seeking to realize a privatized and putatively depoliticized, market-centered vision of global social life—have faced a series of transnational mass protests.[1] It has become increasingly apparent that many segments of the resistance movement (especially in North America and Europe, but also in "non-Western" locales) are animated by political imaginaries drawn as much or more from the anarchist than the Marxian socialist traditions of the left. In light of the historical love–hate relationship between these radical siblings[2] the resurgence of anarchism in an "anticapitalist convergence" poses theoretically interesting and politically consequential questions. In this chapter I will address the following question: Is an anarchist-led counterhegemonic bloc an oxymoron, or are we witnessing an emergent form of radical politics for the twenty-first century?

The Movement for Global Justice

Reverberating throughout the movement for global justice is the influence of the Zapatistas of Chiapas. Bringing Maoist-inflected Marxism and North American indigenous cosmologies into a syncretic political vision,[3] Subcommandante Marcos clearly linked the Zapatista struggle against neoliberalism—inaugurated on the very day NAFTA went into effect (January 1, 1994)—to the five-hundred-year history of European colonialism and North American imperialism: "Renamed as 'Neoliberalism' the historic crime in the concentration of privileges, wealth and impunities, democratizes misery and hopelessness."[4] The Zapatistas denounced neoliberalism as the vehicle for capitalism's commodification of social life and the imposition of a universal model of development that would result in "cultural assimilation and economic annihilation" of alternative ways of life—including their own.[5] Survival of the indigenous communities of Chiapas was understood to depend on struggles at multiple levels: "A world system makes it possible to transform crime into government in Mexico. A national system makes it possible for crime to rule in Chiapas. In the mountains of the Mexican Southeast, we struggle for our country, for humanity, and against neoliberalism."[6] Forging political connections between centuries-old anti-indigenous racism, the corrupt postrevolutionary Mexican state, and global neoliberalism, Marcos and the Zapatistas effectively articulated the identities of indigenous peoples, Mexican peasants, members of civil society, and global resistors.

With great effect, they reached out in solidarity to various persons and communities who felt their distinctive economic and cultural existences threatened by neoliberal capitalism: "we are all the same because we are different."[7] Marcos and the Zapatistas imagined a world of dialogic democracy, of mutual respect across social and cultural differences, a world whose inhabitants "know themselves equal and different" and who therefore recognize "the possibility and necessity of speaking and listening," realizing "a world made of many worlds."[8] In such a world, democratic communities would govern themselves and their leaders would "rule by obeying."[9] Eschewing the conquest of state power, the Zapatistas practiced a complex multilevel politics that involved organizing self-determining base communities, resisting the military and ideological power of the Mexican state, coordinating with social movements and civil society groups across Mexico, and transnational networking among autonomous but related nodes of resistance. In Marcos's words, "We are the network, all of us who speak and listen. . . . We are the network, all of us who resist. . . . This intercontinental network of resistance, recognizing differences and acknowledging similarities, will strive to find itself in other resistances around the world."[10] And so it has.

The emergent movement for global justice is complex and multifarious, aptly characterized as "a movement of movements," but there are significant commonalities on the basis of which we may describe these movements as forming a sort of confluence. Highlighting the most important factor bringing these various movements and agendas into (at least partial) alignment, Michael Hardt and Antonio Negri wrote:

The protests themselves have become global movements, and one of their clearest objectives is the democratization of globalizing processes. This should not be called an anti-globalization movement. It is pro-globalization, or rather, it is an alternative globalization movement—one that seeks to eliminate inequalities between rich and poor and between the powerful and the powerless, and to expand the possibilities of self-determination.[11]

Expressing precisely this democratizing impulse, one street protester told the *New York Times* (February 3, 2002), "There's no magic solution, but we have to struggle and build a more democratic world from the ground up."

Influential Canadian author-activist Naomi Klein suggests that the movement coalesces around "a radical reclaiming of the commons"—slowing, halting or reversing tendencies toward privatization and commodification that effectively colonize and consume public space, thereby displacing grassroots processes of democratic deliberation. "There is an emerging consensus," she writes, "that building community-based decision-making power—whether through unions, neighborhoods, farms, villages, anarchist collectives or aboriginal self-government—is essential to countering the might of multinational corporations."[12] This common thread, woven through what they call the "new democracy movement," is underscored by long-time author-activists Maude Barlow and Tony Clarke: "the most persistent theme underlying the mobilization of popular resistance to corporate globalization is opposition to the systematic assault on democracy and the commons," which they name as "a form of global class warfare." "Developing a new democracy along these lines at local, national and international levels is the only possible antidote to corporate globalization."[13] On the broad terrain of formulations such as these—all of which presuppose a view of the world economy as a sphere of social power relations that can and should be reconstructed in more democratic, pluralistic and enabling forms—community activists, indigenous people's groups, peasants and landless laborers, feminists, progressive unionists, anarchists, socialists and autonomist radicals, as well as a plethora of other social forces, have found sufficient common ground to converge for collective acts of resistance.

Anarchism and the Movement for Global Justice

Among those most actively engaged on these grounds of resistance are many persons and groups inspired by anarchist traditions of social thought and practice. These traditions are diverse and, in some respects, divergent. Although anarchism as a whole defies straightforward summary, some major streams of anarchist thinking can be identified. Rudolf Rocker summarizes the political horizon of social anarchism in the following terms:

For the anarchist, freedom is not an abstract philosophical concept, but the vital concrete possibility for every human being to bring to full development all the powers, capacities, and talents which nature has endowed him with, and turn them to social account. . . . the problem that is set for our time is that of freeing man from the curse of economic exploitation and political and social enslavement.[14]

Since Proudhon, social anarchists have argued that the social form most consistent with human freedom and self-development is the small-scale, directly self-governing voluntary association. These associations, in turn, may join into larger federations or networks of associations, but these latter must respect and facilitate local autonomy if they are to avoid degenerating into an implicitly tyrannical hierarchy. Between social anarchists and their communitarian political horizon stands the modern state with its formidable coercive apparatus. Anarchist-socialists in the tradition of Bakunin and Kropotkin have understood the state and capitalism as interdependent aspects of a system of domination. The coercive power of the state is deployed for the protection of private property and the defense of capitalist domination embedded in the economy. Accordingly, anarchists have represented parliamentary democracy as little more than a veneer masking these relations of domination. The state and capitalism have been objects of anarchist antipolitics aimed at the realization of freedom through struggle against institutionalized oppression. Anarchists distinguish themselves from Marxian socialists not only by their opposition to social hierarchy in all its forms (and a concomitant refusal to privilege class-based politics), but also by a practical emphasis on grassroots democracy instantiated in small-scale communities.[15]

Contemporary anarchist thinking and practice has found inspiration in the widespread outbreaks of popular rebellion against the brutalizing market discipline imposed on much of the developing world by the IMF and World Bank in the pluralistic, dialogic, and democratic political vision of the Zapatistas, and in the creative and flexible direct action of Reclaim the Streets (United Kingdom) and the German and Italian autonomist groups.[16] As Barbara Epstein explains, North American anarchists have incorporated a "distinctive style of politics" developed over the past few decades by the nonviolent Direct Action Movement (especially its antinuclear and environmental wings), "drawing the concept of the affinity group from the history of Spanish anarchism, the tactic of large-scale civil disobedience from the US civil rights movement [with roots in the Gandhian tradition of nonviolent resistance], and the process of decision-making by consensus from the Quakers."[17]

Anarchists were highly visible in the landmark 1999 Seattle protests largely due to the disproportionate media attention devoted to the tactic of corporate property destruction adopted by the (relatively few) participants in the militant

Black Bloc, a kind of ad hoc anarchist tactical grouping.[18] This, however, was but the most obvious—and arguably the least significant—manifestation of anarchist influence within the new movement. In fact, much of the training, preparation, and coordination for the nonviolent direct action that briefly shut down the WTO in Seattle was carried out by groups such as the Direct Action Network and the Ruckus Society, which were influenced by anarchism.[19] Invoking traditional anarchist values, the Direct Action Network invited us to "imagine replacing the current social order with a just, free, and ecological society based on mutual aid and voluntary cooperation. A NEW WORLD IS POSSIBLE and we are part of a global movement that is rising up to make it happen."[20] In the years since Seattle, the profound influence of anarchist ideas and practices, especially on the North American and European wings of the heterogeneous global justice movement, have been widely noted.[21]

The Montreal-based Anti-Capitalist Convergence (CLAC) played a crucial role in organizing the April 2001 mass demonstrations at the Quebec Summit of the Americas. They envisioned "a society that is radically equal" and explicitly linked this political horizon with the organizational practices of the movement: "such a project can only come about in the absence of hierarchical dynamics. . . . we believe in putting into practice this basic principle within resistance groups themselves." Asserting their autonomy from authoritarian political forms (parties, unions, etc.) they also rejected "reformist" strategies "such as lobbying within the framework of negotiations of free trade accords." Instead, they adopted a self-consciously "confrontational" posture embracing "a variety of creative initiatives, ranging from popular education to direct action."[22]

People's Global Action (PGA) has been engaged in militant struggle against neoliberal globalization since the 1998 Geneva mass demonstrations targeting the WTO. Emerging out of intercontinental Zapatista support networks, the PGA founding conference in Geneva (February 1998) was attended by over three hundred representatives of grassroots resistance groups from seventy-one countries around the world. "Despite great material differences," they wrote, "the fights are increasingly similar in every part of the global empire, setting the stage for a new and stronger sort of solidarity." Self-consciously avoiding institutionalized forms of organization based on centralized structures, official leadership, membership rosters, or permanent finances, PGA represents itself as a *process* rather than a social fact—"an evolving coordination" of grassroots groups working together to "realize our dreams of self-governance, freedom, justice, peace, equity, dignity and diversity."[23] Among the "defining documents" of the PGA are its five hallmarks, clearly indicating its anarchist heritage:

1. A very clear rejection of the WTO and other trade liberalization agreements (like APEC, the EU, NAFTA, etc.) as active promoters of a socially and environmentally destructive globalization;

2. A very clear rejection of all forms and systems of domination and discrimination including, but not limited to, patriarchy, racism and religious fundamentalism of all creeds. We embrace the full dignity of all human beings.
3. A confrontational attitude, since we do not think that lobbying can have a major impact in such biased and undemocratic organizations, in which transnational capital is the only real policy-maker;
4. A call to non-violent civil disobedience and the construction of local alternatives by local people, as answers to the action of governments and corporations;
5. An organizational philosophy based on decentralization and autonomy.[24]

PGA has achieved transnational influence. Its network includes many of the best-known direct action groups around the world: the Direct Action Network and the CLAC in North America, the KRRS peasant farmers movement in India, in Europe Ya Basta (Italy) and Reclaim the Streets (UK), the MST landless peasants movement of Brazil, and a broad and variegated network of associated groups on every populated continent.[25] As a coordinating element linking networks of grassroots resistance, PGA has called for Global Days of Action in support of protests in particular locales aiming at institutions of global capitalist governance. During the September 2000 protests against the IMF/World Bank in Prague, PGA's call for global action was rewarded with demonstrations in 110 cities around the world.[26]

In many of its anarchist inflections, the global justice movement's ends and means are related in a vision of *prefigurative politics* in which more democratic forms of social organization are seen as immanent. David Graeber—an activist-intellectual closely associated with the anarchist wing of the new global movement—is at pains to disassociate anarchism from its frightful popular reputation, partly earned by the violence of historical anarchist tactics of "propaganda of the deed" and partly the cumulative result of over one hundred years of antianarchist caricature and calumny.[27] Graeber describes anarchism as "a social movement . . . founded above all on opposition to all structures of systematic coercion and a vision of society based on principles of voluntary association, mutual aid and autonomous, self-governing communities":

> In North America especially, this is a movement about reinventing democracy. It is not opposed to organization. It is about creating new forms of organization. It is not lacking in ideology. Those new forms of organization *are* its ideology. It is about creating and enacting horizontal networks instead of top-down structures like states, parties, or corporations; networks based on principles of decentralized, non-hierarchical consensus democracy. Ultimately, it . . . aspires to reinvent daily life as a whole.[28]

126

The character of the global justice movement as a decentered yet transnational democratizing project is emphasized by George Katsiaficas: "Our alternative to the top-down globalization of huge multinational corporations and their militarized nation-states is an internationalism founded upon autonomous nuclei of popular participation."[29] Kevin Doyle likewise emphasizes democratic processes, the "politics of means and ends," at the core of the anarchist alternative to capitalist globalization.[30]

In many of its avatars, this revivified anarchism embraces a dual commitment to *both* grassroots democracy and socialism, identifying anarchy with "self-managed stateless socialism."[31] Many anarchists take the cooperative associations of the Spanish Civil War period as exemplars of anarchist socialism and signposts toward future possible worlds. According to Doyle, the two key exemplary features of the Spanish workers collectives were production for human need rather than for profit and workplace self-determination. Anarchist-socialists such as the workers solidarity movement (publishers of *Red & Black Revolution*) see freedom and socialism as necessary complements—neither is realizable in the absence of the other: their masthead features Bakunin's maxim that "socialism without freedom is tyranny and brutality."[32]

Anarchism, Socialism, Global Justice: Tensions and Possibilities

Anarchists have been among those most consistently and strongly critical of authoritarian potentialities within Marxism, especially Leninist vanguardism and Bolshevik dictatorship.[33] Anarchists have long rejected both authoritarian socialism and the reformist politics of social democratic and other electoral parties; indeed, their self-understanding derives in large part from situating themselves in the nexus of this dual refusal. These long-standing tensions between anarchism and other forms of left politics now echo through the global justice movement.

At the broadest level of strategy, the movement has been divided by disagreements that center on the question of reforming, reconstructing, or abolishing global economic institutions in the course of constructing future possible worlds. In particular, the role of nongovernmental organizations (NGOs) in the movement has been highly controversial.[34] Many anarchist-inspired activists are bitterly critical of the perceived reformism and hierarchical politics of NGOs seeking to renegotiate in more egalitarian and democratic forms the institutions of the global economy.[35]

Underlying these disputes are theoretical questions of enduring significance. From a historical materialist perspective, anarchism is profoundly limited by the absence of a consistently relational or dialectical understanding of human beings and their social relations. Ironically, the persons whose *natural* "powers, capacities, and talents" anarchists wish to liberate and "turn to social account" (Rocker) are closer to the transhistorical abstract individuals posited by capitalism than the historically conditioned and contradictory *social* beings whom Marxians have sought to further develop and empower through the actualization of capitalism's one-sided and self-limiting—but nonetheless real—historical potentialities.[36] Bookchin is archetypal:

> A basic sense of decency, sympathy, and mutual aid lies at the core of human behavior. . . . there is nothing in this society that would seem to warrant a molecule of human solidarity. What solidarity we do find exists despite the society, against all its realities, as an unending struggle between the innate decency of man and the innate indecency of society.[37]

Constructing in this way an abstract opposition between human nature and social relations of domination, and neglecting the historically concrete ways in which (contradictory) capitalist social relations both generate and constrain new forms of sociality and new social powers, anarchists have tended to take the state and the capitalist workplace at face value even as they rebel against them.

Since Proudhon, anarchists have treated the state and politics as if these could be straightforwardly and universally equated with domination. In Bookchin's historical metanarrative, "Domination fulfills its destiny in the ubiquitous, all-pervasive State."[38] Opposing domination, therefore, would seem to entail steadfast opposition to the state and refusal to engage in "political" activity on the terrain of the state or political parties.[39] Abstracted from the historically particular social relations which generated it—and the *processes of contestation to intrinsic to these relations*—the state is understood as a (reified) thing to be smashed, and politics as subjection to the thing and therefore to be avoided.

There are good theoretical reasons to suppose that structures of social power—social relations generating collective capacities to act, namely, "power to"—need not be reducible to domination, "power over."[40] If this transhistorical reduction is resisted, then it becomes possible to interpret the material forms of the present in terms of a concrete dialectic of "power to" and "power over" in which historically generated human social powers continually struggle against their actualization/containment/distortion within particular forms of domination.[41] As Scott Solomon (2002) has emphasized, for Marx capitalism is not a black hole of oppression that negates light as it assimilates into itself all matter within its reach, but rather represents a contradictory life of "dual freedom." Capitalism entails liberation from the relations of direct politico-economic dependence characteristic of feudalism and other precapitalist forms, and hence presents possibilities for social individuation and "political emancipation" within the parameters of republican forms of state; but capitalism simultaneously limits the historically real emancipatory possibilities it brings into

128

being by (re-)subjecting persons to social domination through the compulsions of market dependence and the effects of fetishism and reification, as well as the privatization of class-based social powers and the concomitant evisceration of political democracy.[42]

All of this suggests not evasion but *transformation* of politics and the state along with the social relations in which those historical forms are embedded. This would entail the democratization and expansion of politics into putatively depoliticized and implicitly market-governed spheres of social life—explicitly political self-activity that would construct new relations of solidarity from within the historical forms of capitalism, transgress reified social boundaries in order to (re-)unify and democratize politics *and* economics, state *and* civil society, and in the process realize new kinds of persons with new social powers and freedoms.

Marx advocated not the abolition or diminution of control but the extension of a certain kind of control, not the abolition of all norms and sanctions but their reintegration into areas of human life that under capitalism evade conscious social control. What is aimed for is not the disappearance of anything that might be termed authority but, on the contrary, the reassertion of conscious social control by men [sic], associated with one another, over their own lives, creations, and relationships.[43]

With its valorization of militant direct action and phobia of "reformism," anarchism has not generally understood social transformation as a dialectical process in which self-activity aimed (in the near term) at achieving meaningful reforms in existing social relations can create a dynamic of social self-empowerment and expanded political horizons, leading toward rather than away from social transformation.[44] For example, the boycott tactic used by the "fair trade" and "no sweat" segments of the movement have been subjected to anarchist critique as just another form of consumerism. "This type of activism accepts the category of consumerism, suggests that we control capitalism with capitalism, and puts the burden of change on the individual."[45] Anarchist critique such as this fails to see the ways in which the explicit linkage of social production and consumption can challenge the fetishism of commodities and its attendant identity of apolitical individual consumer. In combination with other tactics that aim at the core separations effected by capitalism in order to (re-)politicize economic life and to (re-)unify social production and consumption, this is a potentially powerful democratizing strategy.

Conclusion

I return to the question with which I began: Is an anarchist-led counterhegemonic bloc an oxymoron, or are we witnessing an emergent form of radical politics for the twenty-first century? In good dialectical fashion, I want to suggest that the answer to both questions could be yes.

Anarchism has made historically significant contributions to left politics and to the nascent global justice movement. "At their best," writes socialist scholar David McNally, "anarchists have injected a real energy and enthusiasm into the global justice movement while promoting participatory forms of organization."[46] They have contributed to the realization of the Zapatista vision of decentralized and pluralistic networks of resistance to neoliberal globalization. Without the active influence of anarchist-inspired organizations on every populated continent, it is doubtful that the movement would have achieved the visibility and significance that it has. Their tactical innovation and commitment have propelled a movement that has, in effect, called into question the political reproduction of global neoliberal capitalism.[47] Yet I would maintain that while the movement as a whole has contributed to an opening of political horizons, anarchist (anti-)politics is in itself insufficient to realize emancipatory possibilities in the concrete circumstances of contemporary capitalism.

As the global justice road show has unfolded, anarchists have become increasingly aware that direct action of this kind is not enough and, as a consequence, many have turned away from peripatetic protest and back toward community organizing at the grass roots.[48] Linkages of global and local—constructed along participatory democratic lines—are indeed crucial to the future of this movement of movements, and anarchism has important contributions to make here. But if they are to contribute to a transformative project, these nodes need to be strategically coordinated in such a way that they are part of a larger movement seeking to overcome capitalism's disabling social separations and reifications, and this will require a marriage of the democratic forms beloved of anarchists with Marxian socialist theorizations of transformative process. This, in turn, will require of anarchists a recognition that Marxism is not a monolithic doctrine of vanguardist authoritarianism but a rich and evolving body of theory with potentially emancipatory and democratizing political horizons; and it will require of Marxists an appreciation of the force of anarchist critiques of authoritarian Marxisms, and a willingness to engage anarchists in a diverse political movement that both speaks and listens. Such a dialogical process offers transformative possibilities that are necessary (if not sufficient) for getting beyond the historical divisions between anarchist and Marxian socialist politics, for negotiating thorny issues surrounding the scale(s) of democratic community, as well as for articulating these new political forms with political projects aimed at overcoming gendered, racialized, and other forms of oppression internalized within globalizing capitalism.

Notes

I am grateful to Adam Morton, Bill Robinson, Scott Solomon, Manfred Steger, Franke Wilmer, and the participants of the conference on *Ideological Dimen-*

sions of Globalization for offering thoughtful comments on earlier drafts of this chapter.

1. For a Gramscian interpretation of neoliberal capitalist globalization as a contested hegemonic project entailing "reciprocal siege" and ideological struggle, see Mark Rupert, *Ideologies of Globalization* (London: Routledge, 2000); and from a different but consonant perspective, Manfred Steger, *Globalism: The New Market Ideology* (Lanham, Md.: Rowman & Littlefield, 2002).

2. James Joll, *The Anarchists* (Boston: Little, Brown, 1964), 84–114; Daniel Guerin, *Anarchism: From Theory to Practice* (New York: Monthly Review Press, 1970); Paul Thomas, *Karl Marx and the Anarchists* (London: Routledge, 1980).

3. I am grateful to Adam Morton for suggesting this syncretic understanding of Zapatista ideology. See also Harry Cleaver, "The Chiapas Uprising and the Future of Class Struggle in the New World Order," *Riff-Raff*, January-February 1994, 133–46; Manuel Castells, *The Power of Identity* (Oxford: Blackwell, 1997); John Holloway and Elofna Pelaez, "Introduction: Reinventing Revolution," in *Zapatista: Reinventing Revolution in Mexico*, ed. John Holloway and Elofna Pelaez (London: Pluto, 1998), 1–18; John Holloway, "Dignity's Revolt," in *Zapatista*, 159–98; John Ross, *The War against Oblivion* (Monroe, Me.: Common Courage, 2000); Marcos, *Our Word Is Our Weapon* (New York: Seven Stories, 2001); Marcos, "The Seven Loose Pieces of the Global Jigsaw Puzzle," *Chiapas Revealed, Irish Mexico Groups* (1997), www.struggle.ws/mexico.html; A. Morton, "'La Resurreccion del Maiz': Globalization, Resistance and the Zapatistas," *Millennium* 31, no. 1 (2002): 25–27.

4. Zapatistas, *Documents from the 1996 Encounter for Humanity and against Neoliberalism* (New York: Seven Stories, 1998), 11; also Marcos, "Seven Loose Pieces."

5. Cleaver, "Chiapas Uprising."

6. Marcos, *Our Word*, 90.

7. Zapatistas, *Documents*, 30.

8. Zapatistas, *Documents*, 43, 47, 45.

9. Marcos, *Our Word*, 18, 33, 44, 49, 72.

10. Zapatistas, *Documents*, 52–54.

11. Michael Hardt and Antonio Negri, "What the Protesters in Genoa Want," *Global Policy Forum*, www.globalpolicy.org/ngos/role/globdem/globprot/2001/0720rens.htm (April 22, 2003). Originally published in *New York Times*, July 20, 2001, A21.

12. Naomi Klein, "Reclaiming the Commons," *New Left Review* 9 (2001): 82; and "The Vision Thing," in *The Battle of Seattle*, ed. E. Yuen, G. Katsiaficas, and D. Rose (New York: Soft Skull, 2001), 312.

13. Maude Barlow and Tony Clarke, *Global Showdown* (Toronto: Stoddart, 2002), 125–26, 208.

14. Rocker, quoted in Noam Chomsky, introduction to Guerin, *Anarchism*, vii, viii.

15. Helpful overviews of historical and contemporary expressions of the antiauthoritarian impulse include Joll, *Anarchists*; Guerin, *Anarchism*; April Carter, *The Political Theory of Anarchism* (New York: Harper Torchbooks, 1971); Paul Avrich, *Anarchist Portraits* (Princeton: Princeton University Press, 1988); Darrow Schecter, *Radical Theories: Paths beyond Marxism and Social Democracy* (Manchester: Manchester University Press, 1994); Peter Kropotkin, "Anarchism," in *Kropotkin: The Conquest of Bread and Other Writings*, ed. Marshall Shatz (Cambridge: Cambridge University Press, 1995), 233–47; Emma Goldman, *Red Emma Speaks*, ed. A. Shulman (Amherst, N.Y.: Humanity, 1998). Among the leading contemporary interpreters of this tradition is Murray Bookchin, "Anarchism: Past and Present," in *Reinventing Anarchy Again*, ed. Howard Ehrlich (San Francisco: AK Press, 1996), 19–30; and Murray Bookchin and Janet Biehl, eds., *The Murray Bookchin Reader* (London: Cassell, 1997). Note that my discussion focuses on "social anarchism" rather than more individualist variants.

16. Andrew Flood, "What Is Different about the Zapatistas?" in *Chiapas Revealed*, Irish Mexico Group (Dublin: Irish Mexico Group, 2001), www.struggle.ws/mexico.html; and the essays collected in Eddie Yuen, George Katsiaficas, and Daniel Rose, eds., *The Battle of Seattle: The New Challenge to Capitalist Globalization* (New York: Soft Skull, 2001).

17. Barbara Epstein, "Anarchism and the Anti-Globalization Movement," *Monthly Review*, September 2001, www.monthlyreview.org/0901epstein.htm.

18. Seth Ackerman, "Prattle in Seattle: WTO Coverage Misrepresented Issues, Protests," *Fairness and Accuracy in Reporting (FAIR) 2000*, www.fair.org/extra/0001/wto-prattle.html (April 22, 2003); David Graeber, "The Riot That Wasn't," *In These Times*, www.inthesetimes.com (May 29, 2000); Infoshop, "Frequently Asked Questions about Anarchists at the Battle of Seattle," www.infoshop.org/octo/a_faq.html (April 22, 2003); Yuen, Katsiaficas, and Rose, *Battle of Seattle*, sec. 2; R. Cunningham, "Bashing the Black Bloc?" *Red and Black Revolution* 6 (2002), www.struggle.ws/wsm.html.

19. Starhawk, "How We Really Shut Down the WTO," in *Globalize This*, ed. Kevin Danaher and Roger Burbach (Monroe, Me.: Common Courage, 2000), 35–40; S. Guilloud, "Spark, Fire, and Burning Coals: An Organizer's History of Seattle," in *The Battle of Seattle: The New Challenge to Capitalist Globalization* (New York: Soft Skull, 2001), 225–31; John Sellers, "Raising a Ruckus," *New Left Review* 10 (2001): 71–85.

20. DAN quoted in LaBotz, "Moving," 4.

21. On anarchism as a guiding philosophy and general ethos of some of the most dynamic segments of the global justice movement, see William Finnegan, "After Seattle: Anarchists Get Organized," *New Yorker*, April 17, 2000, 40–51;

David Graeber, "Anarchy in the USA," *In These Times*, January 10, 2000, www.inthesetimes.com; David Graeber, "The New Anarchists," *New Left Review* 13 (2002): 61–73; David Graeber, "Reinventing Democracy," *In These Times*, February 19, 2002, www.inthesetimes.com; M. Albert, "Anarchists," in Emma Bircham and John Charlton, eds., *Anti-Capitalism* (London : Bookmarks, 2001), 321–27; Epstein, "Anarchism and the Anti-Globalization Movement"; James Harding, "Counter Capitalism: Inside the Black Bloc," *Financial Times*, October 15, 2001, http://specials.ft.com/countercap/FT3BG4GLUSC.html; Naomi Klein, "Vision Thing," in *Battle of Seattle*; Esther Kaplan, "Keepers of the Flame," *Village Voice*, January 29, 2002, www.villagevoice.com/issues/0205/kaplan.php.

22. CLAC/CASA, *The Summit of the Americas from the Bottom Up* (Montreal: CLAC, 2001); also Organization for Autonomous Telecommunications, "What Is the CLAC?" www.tao.ca/~clac/who_en.php (April 22, 2003).

23. R. Ellis, "Globalizing the Resistance and Bringing It Back Home," *Social Anarchism*, December 31, 2001; Peoples Global Action, "Third International Conference of Peoples' Global Action," Cochabamba, Bolivia, 2001, www.nadir.org/nadir/initiativ/agp/cocha/cocha.htm.

24. Peoples Global Action, "Third International Conference," 2.

25. For affinities with PGA, compare Direct Action Network, "DAN Continental—Who We Are and How We Work," www.agitprop.org/artandrevolution/missionprinciples.htm (April 22, 2003); Anti-Capitalist Convergence—Montreal, "What is the CLAC?" www.tao.ca/~clac/who_en.php (April 22, 2003); J. Singh, "Resisting Global Capitalism in India," in *Battle of Seattle*, 47–50. PGA received applications to attend its September 2001 Conference at Cochabamba, Bolivia, from seventy-seven groups originating in Latin America, six from Africa, thirty-four from Asia and the Pacific, fourteen from Eastern Europe, twenty-two from Western Europe, and eight from North America: PGA, "List of Applicants for PGA Conference," www.nadir.org/nadir/initiativ/agp/cocha/applications.htm (April 22, 2003).

26. In good anarchist fashion, PGA disclaims any leadership or initiative in organizing these worldwide demonstrations. Rather, they claim to have facilitated the coordination of activities initiated and organized by autonomous localized nodes of resistance: see PGA, "Third International Conference," 8.

27. Joll, *Anarchists*, 11–48; Guerin, *Anarchism*, 73–75; B. Weisberger, "Terrorism Revisited," *American Heritage* 44, no. 7 (1993).

28. Graeber, "Anarchy," 70; compare Bookchin, "Anarchism," 28–29; *Reader*, 131.

29. G. Katsiaficas, "Seattle Was Not the Beginning," in *Battle of Seattle*, 32.

30. K. Doyle, "The Anarchist Economic Alternative to Globalization," in *Fighting Global Capitalism* (Dublin: Workers Solidarity Movement, 2001), www.struggle.ws/wsm.html.

31. L. van der Walt, "Revolutionary Anarchism and the Anti-Globalization

Movement," in *Fighting Global Capitalism* (Dublin: Workers Solidarity Movement, 2001), www.struggle.ws/wsm.html; also Anti-Capitalist Convergence, New York, "Why We Are Not Making Demands of the World Economic Forum," 2002, www.accnyc.org/issues_wefdemands.html.

32. Doyle, "Anarchist Alternative," 8; Bookchin, *Reader*, 158–63; Workers Solidarity Movement, "About the WSM," *Red and Black Revolution* 6 (2002): 2.

33. Joll, *Anarchists*, 84–114, 174–93; Guerin, *Anarchism*, 20–27; Bookchin, "Anarchism," 21–22; *Reader*, 124–42.

34. Compare J. Davis, "This Is What Bureaucracy Looks like," in *Battle of Seattle*; M. Williams, "Towards more Democracy or More Bureaucracy?" *Social Anarchism*, July 31, 2001; Barlow and Clarke, *Showdown*, 27–28; Graeber, "New Anarchists," and "Reinventing Democracy."

35. Documents such as *The People's Hemispheric Agreement* (1998) reflect iterative dialogues among transnational coalitions of NGOs and social movement groups in order to produce initial strategies for reconstruction of transnational economic relations and institutions: see Rupert, *Ideologies*, 83–85. See also the International Forum on Globalization, *Alternatives to Economic Globalization* (San Francisco: Berrett-Koehler, 2002).

36. On the abstract individual as the contradictory form of social subjectivity characteristic of capitalist modernity, see D. Sayer, *Capitalism and Modernity* (London: Routledge, 1991), chap. 2.

37. Bookchin, *Reader*, 115, also 23–24, 104; for Bookchin's *social* anarchism, see 166–69.

38. Bookchin, *Reader*, 97.

39. Joll, *Anarchists*, 78–81; Guerin, *Anarchism*, 14–20; Carter, *Political Theory*, 25–26, 105; Bookchin, "Anarchism," 25; *Reader*, 97–98, 105–6, 148–49, 170.

40. J. Isaac, *Power and Marxist Theory* (Ithaca, N.Y.: Cornell University Press, 1987).

41. J. Holloway, *Change the World without Taking Power* (London: Pluto, 2002).

42. S. Solomon, "Marx's 'Dual Freedom' Thesis and Globalization" (paper presented at The Politics of Protest in the Age of Globalization workshop at the University of Sussex, United Kingdom, September 26–27, 2002). The *locus classicus* is Karl Marx, *Capital*, vol. 1 (New York: Vintage, 1977), 272–74, 874–85; on fetishism, chap. 1. On capitalism's hollowing out of democracy: Karl Marx, "On the Jewish Question," in *Early Writings* (New York: Vintage, 1975), 211–41; Thomas, *Karl Marx*, 56–122; Sayer, *Capitalism*, chap. 2; and E. Wood, *Democracy versus Capitalism* (Cambridge: Cambridge University Press, 1995).

43. Thomas, *Karl Marx*, 349.

44. D. McNally, "Mass Protests in Quebec City: From Anti-Globalization to Anti-Capitalism," *New Politics* 8, no. 3 (2001); although see Albert, "Anarchists," on "nonreformist reforms."

45. R. DeWitt, "An Anarchist Response to Seattle: What Shall We Do with Anarchism?" *Social Anarchism*, January 31, 2001.

46. McNally, "Mass Protests."

47. On the neoliberal capitalist bloc's recognition that their global project faces a significant political challenge, see Rupert, *Ideologies*.

48. R. Ellis, "Globalizing the Resistance and Bringing It Back Home," *Social Anarchism*, December 31, 2001; C. Dixon, "Finding Hope after Seattle: Rethinking Radical Activism and Building a Movement," *Z net*, www.zmag.org/dixonseattle (April 22, 2003); B. Dominick, "Toward an Anti-Capitalist Globe: We Know Why, the Question Is How?" *New Politics* 32 (2002), www.punj.edu/newpol/issue32/domini32.htm.

GLOBALIZATION AND THE NEW
REALISM OF HUMAN RIGHTS

MICHELINE ISHAY

If the advance of a more integrated world has enabled many to envision the idea of a global citizenship sharing newly ascendant values of human rights and dignity, these very advances have exacerbated the fear that national, cultural, and economic differences will overwhelm such universalist aspirations. As the pendulum of globalization continues to swing between fostering cosmopolitan values on the one hand and more particularist cultural or national security agendas on the other hand, human rights advocates must carefully identify the advantages provided by those divergent trends. This chapter will argue for an approach to human rights policies that, going beyond railing at the darkest implications of globalization, imperialism, and the pursuit of national security, seizes opportunities within that context, generating an approach that may be described as a new human rights realism.

As human rights activists criticized globalization from an internationalist perspective—trying to reconcile competing conceptions of rights from different regions of the world to resist nationalism and to overcome strategic obstacles—bin Laden and al Qaeda launched a far more telling blow against the United States, the main architect of globalization, though hardly in the name of democracy or individual liberties. As progressive supporters of the antiglobalization movement were drawn toward solidarity with the United States, tension within the human rights community (HRC) intensified, reaching a potentially crippling impasse. Globalization has brought together strange bedfellows, fighting against the same enemy but using different means for different ends. The mobilization of Western society against antiglobalization terrorism by religious fundamentalists has posed daunting quandaries for progressive critics of globalization. How can the hitherto successful strategy of mass protests at globalization summits avoid perceptions that progressives and terrorists have overlapping agendas? How will the movement cope with the suppression of civil and human rights in the name of wartime requirements? How can the case be made that when countries are threatened, security and human rights concerns are not always antithetical?

If the first critical test for the human rights community in our globalized era is to renew its universalist aspirations, bridging developed and developing world concerns and reasserting the inalienability and indivisibility of civil-political and socioeconomic rights, the HRC is confronted with another test. As the major powers continue to shape, mediate, and resolve conflicts consistent with their geopolitical, imperial, and other interests, the second challenge for the HRC, and the subject of this chapter, lies in its ability to confront a narrow national security agenda associated with the decline of civil liberties in wartime, and to offer instead a realistic human rights alternative, drawing on a legacy that extends to the Enlightenment.

Civil Liberties and Other Human Rights in Wartime

The war against terrorism has indisputably affected civil liberties and other human rights in the West, and offered new license for governments around the world to crush dissidents in the name of a global war against terrorism. The Patriot Act, passed in the aftermath of the September 11 attacks, provides U.S. authorities with greater invasive power in the private realm. It expands the federal government's ability to conduct electronic surveillance and issue nationwide search warrants, permits detaining immigrants for a week without charging them for a crime or immigration violation, and broadens FBI access to private records (including library, bank, motel, and grocery store records). While the act includes a sunset provision and expires in 2004, civil rights watchdog groups fear that such laws will have a chilling effect on free speech, as the government is tempted to apply the Patriot Act to political dissidents. John Sellers, a leading organizer of the Seattle 1999 antiglobalization protest, warns that the act "will be wielded as a very blunt weapon against a lot of very important movements for justice in this country that happen to disagree with the status quo."[1]

While the Europeans have long enshrined privacy rights, both in their comprehensive 1950 European Convention of Human Rights and in the 2000 Charter of Fundamental Rights, the calamity of 9/11 has ignited European debate over whether such privacy guarantees are compatible with security objectives. "The principle of protecting the people's personal data must not stand in the way of fighting against crimes and terrorism," recently stated Otto Schiller, the German interior minister.[2] His concern has been echoed in fifteen European countries, where new rules would subject everyone who uses the Internet or a telephone to greater surveillance. These laws, human rights custodians worry, would have the effect of creating a massive electronic data bank containing information about everyone's private activities.

Other countries have jumped on the antiterrorism bandwagon as an opportunity to justify greater internal repression. A month after 9/11, Chinese Foreign Ministry spokesman Sun Yuxi conveyed his government's new antiterrorist stand, blurring the distinction between al Qaeda terrorism and Muslim separatist claims. "We hope that efforts to fight against East Turkistan terrorist forces will become a part of the international efforts and should also win support and understanding," he stated, in hopes of heading off an international outcry as China detained, tortured, and executed Muslim (Uighurs) separatists.[3] Russia also made use of America's war on terror, invoking the danger of Islamic extremism to legitimize its own brutal military occupation of Chechnya. Finally, the Israeli government similarly used the opportunity to characterize its conflict with the Palestinians as part of the international war on terror, as it applied increasingly harsh measures against the population of the occupied territories.[4] In retrospect, it hardly seems surprising that countries such as Russia and China, with weak civil liberties traditions, would use September 11 as a pretext for human rights abuses. More unsettling, the aftermath of 9/11 brought renewed awareness that liberal democracies, where protection of civil rights is a foundation of governance, are also prone to impinge on well-established rights at times of economic crisis and war.

Are all human rights, by implication, jeopardized in times of scarcity and conflict? Historically, freedom of expression and other civil rights were undermined in the West during the World Wars, the Great Depression, and the Cold War, although conversely, during these same periods, liberal governments increased their attention to welfare rights programs. War and serious economic crises tend to create xenophobia, increase repression against all forms of domestic dissent, and encourage a political climate in which free speech and privacy rights are muted by patriotic fervor. These circumstances also favor stronger governmental intervention in the economy. Efforts to increase military expenditures, limit inflation and unemployment, and stimulate consumer confidence and purchasing power are a daunting task for any state. Since governments must give priority to retaining popular legitimacy during times of crisis, there is a strong incentive to focus on the social and economic welfare of their citizens.

Unsurprisingly, during the Great Depression, full employment became the cornerstone of European and U.S. economic policies, as John Maynard Keynes became the new prophet of democratic capitalism. If assistance to the poor and the unemployed had hitherto depended on the discretion of whichever leadership happened to be in power at the time, welfare programs were more systematically instituted as legal, social, and economic rights under the Roosevelt administration, and were strengthened with the development of the welfare state during World War II and the Cold War, while spreading throughout the Western world. Yet if wars and depressions stimulate welfare rights institutions as prophylactic measures to temper the whims of the market, they also erode the edifice of fundamental liberties that liberal states enjoy in peacetime.[5]

Following the 1941 Japanese attack on Pearl Harbor, the Roosevelt administration presided over the wartime internment of 110,000 innocent Americans of Japanese descent. The Cold War revival of anticommunist fervor produced the notorious demagoguery of Senator Joe McCarthy and the House Un-American Activities Committee, as the blacklisting of accused communist sympathizers left dissidents fearful of expressing their views. Finally, mounting opposition to the Vietnam War inspired the Nixon administration to infiltrate and disrupt antiwar organizations, authorize the auditing of tax returns of prominent opponents of the war, and hire a secret group (the Plumbers) to conduct illegal actions against troublesome politicians, journalists, and antiwar activists.[6]

If each of these episodic civil rights setbacks coincided with a new drive toward the fortification of welfare rights, should we then concur, as hundreds of innocent sons of Allah were unjustly detained after 9/11 without appropriate legal representation in the United States and elsewhere, that the state is about to resume a more redistributive role? Will war once again lead Western states to intensify efforts to address economic inequity? In his recent history of upper-class American politics, the historian Kevin Phillips predicted a domestic reawakening of mass militancy, as the social gap between rich and poor has widened and as corporate corruption has reached a level last encountered during the early decades of the twentieth century.[7] If Phillips is right, then today's junction between growing popular resentment and the government's need for wartime social cohesion should result in a revival of New Deal–style programs, designed to curtail the power of the rich and provide greater economic security for ordinary Americans.

As of 2003, conservative voices led by the Republican administration of President George W. Bush are still claiming that these domestic social issues are of marginal concern, as the United States faces a formidable enemy from without that now threatens the lives of millions of Americans with weapons of mass destruction. Security concerns, they insist, as did George Kennan at the outset of the Cold War, must always prevail over the spectrum of human rights considerations.[8] Some realists were eager to point out in the aftermath of 9/11 that the seemingly enhanced post–Cold War role for human rights in foreign policy had now been reversed, revealing the true face of a history condemned, like Sisyphus confronting his eternal curse, to the struggle of power against power.[9] In our globalized era, as before, according to this view, human rights must be seen as subordinate to security objectives and at worst as antithetical to security.

With security concerns now central to the foreign policy agenda, should we agree with John Mearsheimer, Paul Kennedy, and other like-minded scholars that realism is the only sound worldview, and that the history of world politics is characterized by a never-ending Vichean cycle of national growth and decline? Accepting this position, which implies that the entire struggle for universal human rights is quixotic, overlooks the historical record of progress in human rights.

Of course, the advance of human rights is slow and suggestive of unfinished labor. Yet it can be argued that global justice and human rights belong now more than ever at the center of any strategy that hopes to achieve long-term security. Those drawn to that argument may find it useful to consider how security and human rights have been connected since the origins of the modern system of states, and how a current human rights agenda might continue to build on that tradition.

Linking Human Rights and Security: The Historical Legacy

The history of the interdependence of human rights and security as associated with the nation-state began with the spread of the Reformation wars and mercantilism. In this historical context the realist political thinker Thomas Hobbes argued in 1652 that the state, the Leviathan, would become the framework in which individuals could seek protection from war. Hobbes linked the right to security and allegiance to the state rather than papal authority, which was revolutionary in its implications. By basing sovereignty on natural rights (today called human rights), Hobbes also opened the door to liberalism—to what was later called the first generation of civil and political rights—and to three centuries of debate over the human rights basis for state legitimacy.

John Locke further developed the liberal conception of human rights, inquiring more deeply than Hobbes into what constituted natural rights and hence what was required to justify the state. Coeval with the emergence of the English bourgeoisie, he proposed in 1690 to add to Hobbes's concern for security (or life), the rights to political liberty and private property—views that greatly influenced the founders of the American republic in 1776. Seven decades later, Rousseau's social contract identified and legitimized for the first time the nation-state as the embodiment of the "general will" of the people, a collectivist view that influenced the *Declaration of the Rights of Man and Citizen*

(1789). Since that time, Robespierre, Paine, and Kant justified the raison d'être of the state, only insofar as it secured these "vital" universal rights domestically and internationally.[10] Many other great visionaries maintained with them that with the development of republican institutions and commerce, human rights would prevail around the world.

But was the state able to secure the rights of all people or even the rights of its own citizens? The industrial revolution created new conditions, in which it became increasingly clear that rights to life, liberty, and property were insufficient to legitimize the state. As capital increasingly was able to escape the boundaries of states, some began to insist that the liberal state and the free market economy were preventing the realization of the universal rights advocated during the French Revolution. The unlimited pursuit of property rights, socialists now argued, would mainly benefit a minority who were initially advantaged. Put another way, the instruments of state power were being used to preserve the security of the capitalist class, while depriving ordinary working people of security and other human rights. The familiar prescription offered by Karl Marx and Engels maintained, particularly after the February revolution of 1848, that the betrayed working proletariat should seize the reins of state power in order to promote socialist rights worldwide.[11]

Over time, that call for global revolution faced increasing competition from those who sought to reform the state, a possibility enhanced by the spread of labor movements and the passing of social welfare laws. In Germany, the socialist Ferdinand Lassalle argued in 1862 that the state was the sole possible promoter of freedom and human rights. In England and elsewhere, Fabian and other evolutionary socialists espoused a similar perspective. The eloquent French socialist Jean Jaurès echoed their views, suggesting that the state would advance the moral and socialist development of humankind slowly but ineluctably.[12]

Fear of communist rebellion now spurred reform. In 1883, at the zenith of German expansionist policies, German Chancellor Bismarck secured the passage of social legislation, including compulsory health insurance for workers, an accident insurance plan, and a comprehensive pension for the aged and disabled. In a sense, Bismarck set the stage for what would become the standard response of realist statecraft to the problem of reconciling human rights and security in the world's industrialized states. Domestic workers would be appeased with redistributed wealth and ultimately universal suffrage, making it safe to ignore the economic and political aspirations of the remainder of the world's poor.

An enormous problem confronted this realist conception of universal rights being achieved domestically while power politics prevailed in international affairs. That problem was the twentieth-century emergence of the phenomenon of world war. The scale of wartime destruction was so immense that security seemed to demand some sort of effective international organization. The first to reach this conclusion were the socialists, who not only proclaimed that universal human eights were the only way to prevent world war but established the First International (1864–1876) to gather representatives from around the world for the purpose of creating a global regime based on human rights and peace.

After World War I, liberals also arrived at the idea that human rights and security require an international organization. One of the two organizations set up after World War I, the International Labor Organization (ILO), grafted socialist convictions onto liberal thought by insisting that world peace could only be preserved if workers' rights were respected in all countries. The other concurrent attempt to construct a liberal peace, the League of Nations, like its successor, the United Nations, placed the goal of nonaggression at the center of its search for international peace. Building on the failure of the League, the United Nations sought to combine practical recognition of the world's division into large and small powers, with a more developed vision of universal human rights, as witnessed by the 1948 U.N. Declaration of Human Rights.

Each historical cycle of world violence created the need to develop stronger mechanisms to protect individual rights within and between nations. If the Enlightenment introduced into world politics the notion that the state exists to secure the universal rights of its all inhabitants, and by extension to exemplify those rights for all humankind, the Industrial Revolution planted the seeds for a more interventionist state and a stronger international organization to promote human rights and counter conflicts between states. Last, the twentieth century was an era in which the establishment of the welfare state presented an improvement over the purely greed-driven capitalist state, and the United Nations an advance over the impotent League of Nations. Just as the wars and social revolutions of the eighteenth and nineteenth centuries strengthened the capacity of the state, and the two world wars and the Cold War institutionalized the domestic welfare state, the mounting potential for violence incubated by globalization may well bring the task of securing global welfare into the realm of practical politics in this historical era.[13]

Today's realists, seeking only security, find themselves drawn toward policies designed to advance human rights: a lesson that even the sole superpower can no longer afford to overlook. National Security Adviser Condoleezza Rice argued before 9/11 that realism required U.S. foreign policy to avoid humanitarian and human rights efforts. Reversing that view after 9/11, she stressed the complementarity of realism and idealism, so that "to continue to build . . . a balance of power that favors freedom, we must extend as broadly as possible the benefits of liberty and prosperity that we in the developed world enjoy. We have a responsibility to build a world that is not only safer but better."[14] Even if the first realist impulse after 9/11 was to seal U.S. borders and attack the ter-

rorists in their caves, the second reaction was the realization that such measures are hopeless if they ignore universal aspirations for justice and rights. As
a result, the Bush administration, rejecting much of the foreign policy platform
of candidate Bush, found itself committed to nation building in Afghanistan,
to celebrating the rights of Afghan girls to go to school, and to increasing
sharply the foreign aid budget, all because, as the president expressed it, "hope
is the answer to terror." Thus the United States vowed to become the new
Jacobin soldiers of universal rights and democracy.

One may disparage these discourses as merely another step toward a more
enlightened imperialism. Noam Chomsky, Antonio Negri, Michael Hardt, and
Michael Ignatieff have all argued recently (though from different perspectives)
that we have entered a new stage of globalization orchestrated by American
imperialism.[15] For Ignatieff, it is not the imperialism of the past, "built on
colonies, conquest and the white man's burden," but one reveling in a "global
hegemony whose grace notes are free markets, human rights and democracy,
enforced by the most awesome military power the work has ever known."[16]
While imperial greed should always be denounced, the moral evaluations of
empires, Ignatieff reminds us, get complicated when the policies of empire
benefit the Kosovars, Afghanis, Iraqis, and others.

As foreign policymakers, preoccupied after 9/11 with security, begin to
acknowledge the relevance of human rights, the HRC should be prepared to
offer a substantive agenda linking human rights and international security.
The following considerations should be seen as a point of departure for shaping what one may call a new realist human rights agenda for the twenty-first
century.

Toward a New Realism of Human Rights

Considering Human Rights Opportunities amid Great Power Politics

When security concerns bring major powers into conflict with brutal
regimes, human rights activists should work to ensure that intervention serves
to advance human rights. In this respect, the war against the Taliban, if not
undertaken to liberate women from feudal slavery, had considerable beneficial
consequences for women's rights, just as NATO's intervention in Kosovo might
well have averted a repetition of Serbia's genocidal war, dramatized by Sre-
brenica, against Muslims in Bosnia. While human rights rhetoric often masks
other motives and the United States routinely maintains a double standard
favoring regimes committing gross human rights violations wherever its serves
U.S. interests (e.g., Saudi Arabia and China), a new realism of human rights
should nevertheless seize opportunities to advance the cause whenever Western powers confront repressive governments. Certainly human rights activists

144

should condemn repressive regimes with equal fervor regardless of whether they are seen as friend or foe by the United States or the European Union. While it remains critically important to draw attention to grave human rights abuses that are ignored by the media and appear on no one's political agenda, human rights advocates should not shrink from actively opposing Saddam Hussein's cruel regime simply because he was the *bête noire* of the United States or other major powers. One can deplore the long record of human rights abuses in the foreign or domestic policies of the five permanent members of the Security Council and still support those instances when their common cause advances human rights.

Considering the Appropriate Means toward Human Rights Ends

Human rights activists have traditionally condemned shortsighted great power foreign policies that breed human rights abuses. For instance, many rightly criticized U.S. support of the mujahideen during the Afghan war against the Soviet Union, and U.S. indifference to the Afghans' plight after Soviet withdrawal. Yet such critical stands are hardly sufficient. The human rights community should feel obligated to offer viable policies, whether for liberating women from the Taliban regime or for freeing individuals in current repressive and authoritarian regimes. When power politics or the "CNN effect" draws the world's attention toward the brutality of particular regimes, a new human rights realism will assess in critical instances whether war is a legitimate last resort, and whether the cost in likely casualties outweighs the prospective ends.

Just as the question of means and ends divided early-twentieth-century socialists, pitting on the one hand Karl Kautsky and Rosa Luxemburg, and on the other hand Trotsky and Lenin, over what means were justified for achieving a socialist vision of rights, the question of the appropriate means to forward human rights principles is today equally divisive.[17] For instance, while there may be broad agreement that toppling Saddam Hussein's dictatorial regime and restoring democracy and human rights for Iraqis was an honorable goal, the difficult question remained whether an intervention in Iraq might override the envisioned ends, namely that a U.S.-U.N. military intervention might instead escalate into an intractable Middle Eastern conflict, while inflaming anti-American sentiments in the Arab world. Obviously critics of military intervention would have been fewer if the short-lived resistance and the low cost in human lives could have been foreseen. While no one knows with certainty the outcome of any impending war, reflexive judgments are no substitute for sober assessments of whether ongoing political and military operations are consistent with human rights objectives, and whether the considered means justify the envisioned ends.

Considering the Limit of Imposing Human Rights from Outside

Even if human rights abuses can be greatly reduced at the cost of very low casualties, the question remains whether external forces are sufficient for sustaining
improvements in human rights. If, for instance, one can applaud U.S. policies
in Afghanistan that freed women from their burkas, the U.S. intervention
against the Taliban regime would not have been possible without the Northern
Alliance. Although the groups composing the Alliance were hardly democratic,
they nevertheless represented a vital source of support for a new post-Taliban
government. Generally, finding viable local or exiled sources of resistance
remains imperative whenever outside military intervention to redress human
rights is under consideration. Not only is domestic support for intervention
important in the short term, in its absence the long-term task of creating the
infrastructure to maintain democracy in societies devastated by civil war is
prone to be seen as another form of imperialism, resulting in growing resistance.

Thus Michael Walzer's warning that outsiders' attempts to improve from
outside are unlikely to take hold absent strong local support is eminently reasonable.[18] Unfortunately, Walzer's position implies that short of an unfolding
genocide, the world should refrain from interfering in cases of severe human
rights violations.

That position provides an unacceptable reward for effective totalitarian-
ism—ensuring that once the iron fist of tyranny has silenced all internal resistance, all hopes for outside help disappear as well. In practice, Walzer's view
marks an unacceptable retreat from the conviction that the inalienable, indivisible perspective of human rights, including their political, social, and economic dimensions as endorsed by the Universal Declaration of Human Rights,
are not a Western privilege but should be enjoyed by everyone everywhere.
Hence the task confronting a human rights realist is to carve a space between
the charge of indifference linked to a noninterventionist position and the possible accusation of imperialism associated with humanitarian intervention.

Considering a New Human Rights Realism in
Our Globalized Economy

If security strategies need to be understood in the framework of our globalizing economy, a new human rights realism should not shy away from supporting initiatives, wherever voiced, that integrate security, economic development,
and human rights, such as one the discussed in July 2000 in Okinawa, Japan.
Under the Miyazaki initiatives, the G8 foreign ministers called for "a culture of
prevention" in addressing security threats. That culture would be based on "the
U.N. charter, democracy, respect for human rights, the rule of law, good governance, sustainable development and other fundamental values, which consti-

tute the foundation of international peace and security."[19] Although these statements may be characterized as cosmetic rhetoric, a new human rights realism would hold accountable the merchants of human rights ideals and press for the implementation of their decisions.

A campaign to apply that public pressure implies a clear rejection of the conviction shared by many human rights scholars and activists that globalization is simply antithetical to the advancement of human rights. There are aspects of capitalism that represent dramatic improvement when compared to the feudal arrangements that prevail in much of the global south: its progressive capacity, its formidable power to develop the forces of production, to regenerate new needs, and to kindle humans' unlimited possibilities.[20] That hardly entails an endorsement of neoliberal ideology, which can be held accountable for rules imposed on developing countries by the institutions controlling globalization (e.g., the IMF) that have perpetuated—or even worsened—poverty.

How then could a new human rights realism free globalization from its destructive trends? A new human rights realism must always condemn the harsh conditions of workers in sweatshops; however, the often romanticized alternative of self-sufficient feudalism may be even worse. In reality, millions of young women beyond the reach of globalization are left with no choice but to be subjugated under patriarchal domination or the arbitrary tyranny of local mullahs in countries such as Pakistan or Nigeria. For women and other destitute people in the most impoverished regions of the world, opportunities for change offered by market-driven economic growth should be welcomed when synchronized with redistributive policies that ensure real opportunities to escape poverty and achieve democratic aspirations.

While economic growth is vital to rescuing the poor, so are the institutions of the state. Realizing the advantage of a market economy, a human rights realist perspective calls for more state intervention and not less to develop economic infrastructure, public health and education, and civil institutions[21] and, in the same vein, for the implementation of supportive regulatory mechanisms in international financial institutions. Extending the campaign to forgive the debts of Third World countries, for instance, could help many developing countries combine economic development with a measure of social justice. Needless to say, keeping people alive, combating the spread of epidemics, and providing clean water cannot be left solely to the work of the "invisible hand." In this respect, from the perspective of a new human rights realism, globalization is not an end, as its proselytes would like to have it, but a means to advance political, civil, social, and economic rights—not just merely for the privileged but also for the wretched of the earth.

One cannot relegate the task of building such a global welfare mechanism, bridging security, economic development, and human rights concerns to policymakers or the providential caprices of history. That task belongs to the active

147

intervention of the HRC, which in the current climate of fear must vigilantly resist narrow, shortsighted security, cultural, and economic pressures. These forces always result in the fragmentation of what should remain the inalienable and indivisible mission of the HRC, namely, its relentless fight for civil, political, social, and economic rights for the visible, less visible, and conveniently unnoticeable among us, within and beyond every national border.

Notes

This chapter is indebted to comments made by various people, notably David Goldfischer. I also want to thank Manfred Steger for his editorial suggestions; David Ost, John Vail, and those who attended the Ideological Dimensions of Globalization convention at the Globalization Research Center, University of Hawai'i–Manoa, Honolulu, Hawai'i, December 9–12, 2002.

1. Kevin Galvin, "Rights and Wrongs, Why New Law-Enforcement Powers Worry Civil Libertarians," *Seattle Times,* December 7, 2001, A3; see also Ann McFeatters, "Bush Signs New Anti-Terror Bill," *Pittsburgh Post-Gazette*, October 27, 2001, A6; Edward Helmore, "The US Refuses to Either Charge or Free those Suspected of Terrorism," *Guardian*, May 7, 2002; Bob Egelko, "FBI Checking Out American's Reading Habits," *San Francisco Chronicle*, June 23, 2002, A5; and Frank Gardner, "Muslims Condemn US Terror 'Profiling,'" *BBC News*, June 26, 2002.

2. Lee Dembart, "Privacy Undone; The EU's Internet Plan Takes Liberties with Personal Rights," *International Herald Tribune*, June 10, 2002, 11.

3. Amnesty Fears, "Terrorist Crackdown Could Mean Repression in China," *Agence France Press*, October 12, 2001.

4. "EU/Chechnya: MEPS Say Russia Uses Terrorism as Excuse for Human Rights Abuses," *European Report*, April 12, 2002.

5. See Bruce Porter, *War and the Rise of the State: The Military Foundations of Modern Politics* (New York: Free Press, 1994).

6. See also Paul L. Murphy, *World War I and the Origin of Civil Liberties in the United States* (New York: Norton, 1979).

7. Kevin Phillips, *Wealth and Democracy: the Politics of the American Rich* (New York: Broadway, 2002).

8. "Government is an agent, not a principal. Its primary obligation is to the interests of the national sovereignty it represents, not to the moral impulses that individual elements of that society may experience." George F. Kennan, "Morality and Foreign Policy," *Foreign Affairs*, Winter 1985, 206.

9. See, for example, Fareed Zakaria, "The End of the End of History," *Newsweek*, September 24, 2002, www.msnbc.com/news/629514.asp.

10. Immanuel Kant, "The Metaphysics of Morals," in *Kant's Political Writ-*

ings, ed. Hans Reiss (Cambridge: Cambridge University Press, 1970); see also Micheline Ishay, *Internationalism and Its Betrayal* (Minneapolis: University of Minnesota Press, 1995), 59.

11. Karl Marx, "The Class Struggles in France, 1848–1850," in *Collected Works*, trans. Richard Dixon et al. (New York: International, 1975), 10:203.

12. Ferdinand Lasalle, *Der Staat ist es welcher die Funktion hat, diese Entwicklung der Freiheit, diese Entwicklung des Meschengeschlechtes zur Freiheit zu vollbringen* (Stuttgart: Reclam Dietzing, 1973), 43; Sidney Webb, "English Progress toward Social Democracy," in *Fabian Tracts* (London: Fabian Society, 1892), 3, 9; Jean Jaurès, "Idealism in History 1895," in *Socialist Thought*, trans. and ed. Albert Fried and Ronald Sanders (New York: Columbia University Press), 410.

13. Excerpt from this previous section are drawn from Micheline Ishay, *The History of Human Rights from Ancient Times to the Era of Globalization* (Berkeley: University of California Press, forthcoming).

14. Condolezza Rice, "America Has the Muscle, but It Has Benevolent Values," *Daily Telegraph*, London, October 17, 2002, 26.

15. Noam Chomsky, *The New Militarism, Lessons from Kosovo* (Monroe, Me.: Common Courage, 1999); Michael Hardt and Antonio Negri, *Empire* (Cambridge: Harvard University Press, 2000).

16. Michael Ignatieff, "The Burden," *New York Times Magazine*, January 5, 2003.

17. See Rosa Luxemburg, "The Russian Revolution," in *Rosa Luxemburg Speaks*, ed. Mary-Alice Waters (London: Pathfinder, 1970), 387; Karl Kautsky, *Selected Political Writings*, ed. and trans. Patrick Goode (New York: St Martin's, 1983), 147; Leo Trotsky, "Their Morals and Ours," in *The History of Human Rights Reader*, ed. Micheline Ishay (New York: Routledge, 1997), 338; see also Ishay, *History of Human Rights*, chap. 4.

18. Michael Walzer, *Just and Unjust War* (New York: Basic, 1977).

19. Japan Ministry of Foreign Affairs, "G8 Miyazaki Initiatives on Conflict Prevention," www.mofa.go.jp/policy/economy/summit/2000/documents/initiative.html (February 10, 2003).

20. Karl Marx, *Capital* (London: Penguin Classics, 1993), 1: pt. I, 8.

21. See on this subject, Leo Panitch, "Globalization and the State," *Socialist Registrar,* 1994.

PART III
GLOBALISM IN A GLOBAL CONTEXT

GLOBALIZATION AND NATIONAL DEVELOPMENT: FUTURISM AND NOSTALGIA IN CONTEMPORARY POLITICAL ECONOMIC THINKING

Arif Dirlik

In this chapter I will take up a problem that is elided in most discussions of globalization—national development under the regime of globalization. The juxtaposition of the terms "globalization" and "national development" points to a deep contradiction in contemporary thinking or a nostalgic longing for an aspiration that may no longer be relevant. But it is powerful enough to disturb the forces relegating it to the past.

I am referring here to the contradiction between the global and the national. Arguments for globalization suggest that national development may be achieved through globalization, which in turn would be expected to contribute to further globalization, and so on and so forth into the future, which goes against the tendency of these same arguments to set the global against the national, as a negation of the latter. While it may not be a zero-sum relationship, the relationship between globalization and national development is nevertheless a highly disturbed one. Understood as the persistence of commitments to autonomy and sovereignty, most importantly in the realm of the economy, the national obstructs globalization, just as globalization erodes the national, at the same time rendering irrelevant any idea of development that takes such autonomy and sovereignty as its premise. If globalization is taken seriously, in other words, the very idea of national development becomes meaningless.

On the other hand, if national development is taken seriously, as it was for most of the past century, then globalization appears as little more than an ideological assault on the nation, to rid the present of the legacies of the past. I suggest that we take this contradiction seriously, inquire into some of its implications, and consider resolutions that avoid entrapment between the past and the present or an ideological erasure of the past by the present, and instead seek ways to guide the forces of globalization in directions that do not erase but rather presume the central importance of the local in globalization.

I am concerned mostly with Third World circumstances in globalization. The term "Third World" is a reminder of the distance between the present and the past, but is still a convenient way of mapping shifts in global power and inequality. The Third World may not constitute an entity identifiable on a geographical or cultural map, but arguably three or four decades ago there was a shared Third World response to questions of national development, identifiable with some kind of national liberation socialism.

In this chapter, I will sketch out the outlines of these strategies of national development. I will then outline what some influential analysts see as the defining characteristics of a mapping of the global political economy under the regime of globalization. The differences between the two mappings of political economy and economic development, I suggest by way of conclusion, should be the point of departure for any consideration of a political economy that aims to get past political slogans to address concrete economic, social, and political problems. This requires close attention to questions of class interest and power in the organization of the global economy, not just to technical economic questions.

National Development and Social Revolution in
Early Chinese Marxist Thought

The subheading for this section is the title of the first article I ever published nearly three decades ago.[1] It expresses cogently an ideal of national development that was expressed by Chinese Marxists of various stripes in the 1920s and became quite prevalent in Third World ideas of development, as well as efforts to explain Third World difficulties with development in such alternatives to modernization discourse as dependency theory and world system analysis.

Despite internal differences in their diagnoses of the problems of national development, Chinese Marxist analyses were uniformly inspired by V. I. Lenin's analysis of the contradictory role imperialism (understood as "the highest stage of capitalism") played in colonial and semicolonial societies: although imperialism was responsible for introducing the progressive forces of capitalism into these societies, it also created structural impediments to the realization of capitalist development as in Europe and North America.

There were two major aspects to these impediments. One was economic. Development in these societies did not result from the logic of the national economy responding to internal demand and needs but followed the logic of a globalizing capitalist economy, the search of imperialist powers for markets for commodities and capital, as well as the conflict generated by the competition among them in this search. As imperialists had little or no interest in the national development of these societies, what development there was contributed not to national economic integration and an economic structure that answered the various needs of the national economy, including subsistence needs of the population, but to a bifurcated economy with a modern capitalist sector increasingly integrated into a global capitalist economy. A much larger sector remained mired in premodern economic practices and was subject to the exploitative forces of the modern sector, just as the national economy as a whole was subject to the exploitative forces of global capitalism. Spatially speaking in the case of the Chinese economy, this meant the lopsided development of coastal areas and a few coastal cities such as Shanghai, and the increasing "underdevelopment" of vast areas of the interior and their populations. Economic bifurcation, needless to say, also undermined efforts to achieve integration at the political level.

The other aspect was social: the creation of a new class structure. As capitalism was introduced into China from the outside, the emergent Chinese bourgeoisie was itself a foreign product, aligned in its interests with the outside forces that produced it and having little commitment to the interests of the nation as a whole. True, there was some distinction between an overtly "comprador" bourgeoisie and a "national" bourgeoisie that strove for autonomy within the structural context of imperialism. But even the latter was more closely integrated structurally with the forces of global capitalism than with the national economy. These people were condemned in their very activities, so to speak, to contribute to the deepening of the almost inevitable structural bifurcation of the economy. This was the major reason that any hope for national development had to be preceded by a social revolution that would transfer power to social forces that had an investment in the creation of a national economy, represented most importantly by the working class and the peasantry. Ultimately, this meant the creation of an autonomous state that could use political means to establish boundaries around the national economy and the basis for national economic integration; an autonomous economy that answered to internal needs.

At its most insistent, such an analysis led to demands not only for autonomy but for economic autarky too, as during the Cultural Revolution in the 1960s. We know in hindsight that such autarky could be achieved only through the institutionalization of state control and coercion in everyday life, if not the substitution of state interests in development for popular needs and aspirations. There is an additional complication, perhaps less evident in a well-established society such as China than in many other Third World societies: the assumption that there already was in place a nation whose economic integrity had to be safeguarded, when the creation of an integrated national entity was itself one of the goals of economic development.

The underlying spatial assumption of this argument—that the nation is composed of a space, defined by a bounded surface, with little tolerance in that space for uneven development—is very important, for such unevenness calls into question not just economic integrity but the political existence of the nation. If the search for autarky carried the logic of national integration to its extreme, its very extremeness is a reminder that the anxiety over unevenness in the national economy was a characteristic of not just extremist revolutionary regimes but all political economic thinking that took the nation as the unit of analysis. Marxist revolutionary regimes did not invent so much as inherit the use of state power to regulate economic relationships and, until the 1960s and the 1970s, import substitution seemed to be the preferred route to development against export-oriented development.

This is not so much a difference between liberal nationalism and a revolutionary fundamentalism, but a difference in power that is embedded in the very structure of the capitalist world economy as it has taken shape over the last few centuries—the powerless have very few options in their struggle for national economic and political integrity other than shutting out the world economy and, with it, the promise of development that comes at a very high social and political price. It may not be very surprising that radical social scientists through the 1970s (and to the present) have concurred that national economic development may not be possible except through some measure of delinking from the global capitalist economy dominated by nations of the First World.[2] But shutting out the world has proven to be an impossible task. The controlling powers in the world economy are prepared to use all the coercive means at their disposal to force open economies that sought to shut out a globalizing capitalism, or whenever it seemed that they might be vulnerable to dependency on others—most notoriously in the case of energy dependency, which continues to serve as an important factor in the First World's seemingly endless war against the Third World.

I am interested in globalization not as some kind of historical process, which is not particularly new, but as an ideology that came to the fore in response to the contradictions generated by the very processes of development.[3] Globalization discourse provides its own mapping of the process of development which, in its contrast with earlier mappings of national development, points not so much to the failure of the latter as to the contradictions they presented. The resolution of these contradictions that finds expression in the discourse of globalization, it needs to be underlined, does not represent the only resolution possible, but rather the most preferred resolution that sustains the structure of power under the capitalist world system while containing the oppositional forces generated by the system itself.

The Network Society

In the first volume of an ambitious three-volume study of contemporary global transformations, *The Rise of the Network Society*, Manuel Castells offers a revealing analysis of the respatialization of the political economy of development, both as concept and as practice.[4] His theorization of the new situation of globality is important not because what he has to say is particularly unusual, but because he is able through the metaphor of the "network society" to synthesize much that has been written on the question of globalization. His work is particularly relevant to my argument here because a spatialization of the global capitalist economy around nodes in a network provides a cogent contrast to the spatialization around bounded surfaces that I discussed above. It may or may not describe accurately the processes at work in the contemporary world economy, but it has much to say about a shift in ways of thinking about the world economy that has taken place over the last two decades, and does so without an apparent ideological commitment to globalization.

One of the most impressive aspects of Castell's analysis is its ability to account for an intensified mobility of capital while retaining a strong sense of the persistence of structural relationships in power. Castell's metaphor of networks in the description of contemporary capitalism is derived from the central importance he assigns to information technologies, which then serve as the paradigm for the reconfiguration of global relations. The metaphor of "network" offers ways of envisaging the new global capitalism in both its unities and disunities, in its pervasiveness as well as in the huge gaps that are systemic products of the global economy. The network metaphor shifts attention from surfaces to "highways" that link nodes in the global economy. A network has no boundaries of any permanence but may expand or contract at a moment's notice and shift in its internal configurations as its nodes move from one location to another. Marginality to the global economy may mean being outside of the network, as well as in the many spaces that are in its many gaps. Marginality does not imply being untouched by the networks, as the inductive effects of network flows affect even those who are not direct participants in its many flows. Finally, the network metaphor offers new ways of accounting for power. It is possible to state that the most powerful nodes in the global economy (e.g., Saskia Sassen's "global cities")[5]—may be locations where nodes of economic, political, and cultural power coincide. The network militates against neat spatialities, but it also allows for their inclusion in considerations of power. While any location may be included in the network, the most powerful, and controlling, nodes are still located in the national spaces of commanding global presence.

Castells identifies North America, Europe, and East Asia as the locations of such commanding power, which determine "the basic architecture" of global relations. "Within this visible architecture," however, "there are dynamic processes of competition and change that infuse a variable geometry into the global system of economic processes." As he explains it,

> What I call the newest international division of labor is constructed around four different positions in the informational/global economy: the producers of high value, based on informational labor; the producers of high volume, based on lower cost labor; the producers of raw materials, based on natural endowments; and the redundant producers, reduced to devalued labor. . . . *The critical matter is that these different positions do not coincide with countries. They are organized in networks and flows, using the technological infrastructure of the informational economy.* They feature geographic concentrations in some areas of the planet, so that the global economy is not geographically undifferentiated. . . . Yet the newest international division of labor does not take place between countries but between economic agents placed in the four positions that I have indicated along a global structure of networks and flows. . . . all countries are penetrated by the four positions. . . . Even marginalized economies have a small segment of their directional functions connected to a high-value producers network. . . . And certainly, the most powerful economies have marginal segments of their population[s] placed in a position of devalued labor. . . . The newest international division of labor is organized on the basis of labor and technology, but is enacted and modified by governments and entrepreneurs.[6]

Castells observes that while nation-states are by no means irrelevant to the functioning of the new global economy, national spaces no longer serve as meaningful economic units, crisscrossed as they are by economic activities of various sorts between nodes that are as much parts of a variety of global structurations (subject to chaos though they may be) as they are of the national space in which they are located. As he focuses almost exclusively on labor and technologies, Castells has less to say about the organizational aspects of such structurations; on the alternative spatializations produced, for instance, by transnational corporations as well as a host of transnational organizations from NGOs to universities. His analysis is nevertheless at one with most other analyses of globalization that are premised on the insufficiency of the nation as a unit of analysis in the analysis of the contemporary global economy.

While to an analyst such as Castells this may present a problem in regard to the social, political, and cultural implications of globalization, ideologues of global capitalism perceive in it the end of the nation-state and a need to respatialize politics to conform to the essential "borderlessness" of a globalized economy. Analyst Kenichi Ohmae suggests that "the nation-state has become an unnatural—even a dysfunctional—organizational unit for thinking about economic activity."[7] The alternative is to rethink political units in terms of "region-states" that correspond to the "regional economies" that are emerging with globalization (that also correspond, we might note, to the more stable nodes in the global networks). What Ohmae proposes for China (and which plays a large part in his analysis) provides a sharp contrast to the economic thinking of Chinese Marxists that I described above:

> the people of Guangzhou [in Southern China] know that they cannot deny a significant, ongoing relationship with the rest of mainland China. That connection is real—and is part of their strength and appeal. What they cannot afford is to be victims of tight, centralized control. But they can productively be—in fact, they would do well to be—part of a loose grouping of Chinese regional states, a kind of Chinese federation or commonwealth.[8]

Unfortunately, Ohmae has little to say on what the mutual responsibility would be of the "region-states" in such a federation, or what role a central government would play in enforcing those responsibilities. We may glean what he has in mind, however, from his discussion of "the civil minimum," the provision of equal services, including those that entail subsistence needs, to all the citizens of the nation-state, which in his view is inconsistent with the efficient allocation of resources. As he puts it,

> the alignment of government power with domestic special interests and have-not regions makes it virtually impossible for those at the center to adopt responsible policies for a nation as a whole, let alone for its participation in the wider borderless economy. . . . No matter how understandable the political or even social pressures behind these alignments, they make no sense economically. Investing money inefficiently never does. In a borderless world, where economic interdependence creates ever-higher degrees of sensitivity to other economies, it is inherently unsustainable.[9]

Ohmae does not tell the reader what "an explicit commitment to heightened regional autonomy within a 'commonwealth' of China" might leave of a "commonwealth of China" when the regional economy acts or aspires to act "as a local outpost of the global economy."[10] The message, however, is clear. Globalization means the supremacy of the market in shaping all relations, social and political; the nation-state in its social and political concerns is an impediment to the efficient functioning of the market. The nation-state must allow the regional autonomy that permits successful regions to participate in the global economy, unhampered by obligations to other parts or constituencies of the nation guaranteed earlier by the state. What he does not say is why the nation-state might be needed at all under the circumstances, except to guarantee the success of its global "nodes" in the global economy—and perhaps to suppress the dissent that might result from its own participation in the "bifurcation" of the economy. The state here becomes something more than a mere promoter of economic development; it appears as an enforcer of the interests of the "local outposts of the global economy" and, we might add, of those in charge of the "local outposts." This is the state of global capitalism.

For all their vaunted internationalism, socialist states, in their real or imagined responsibility to their popular constituencies, produced a totalistic empowerment of the nation-state. It is equally interesting that capitalism, which experienced its embryonic growth within the womb of the nation-state, would return the nation-state to an earlier alliance between capital and the state, where the state is no longer responsible to constituencies other than those who manage the global economy, rendering the nation more or less into an empty shell or a mere geographic or cartographic expression. The contrast provides a clue to the predicament facing us all at the present.

Public Responsibility in an Age of Globalization

At a time when the nation no longer serves as an exclusive or even a viable unit of economic activity, when the ties between the state and the nation are once again being blurred, what is in question is not merely the viability of the nation-state, yearning for which may simply be the product of nostalgia for the past, but the more substantial question of the relationship between forms of political governance and public welfare. This question inevitably invites thinking about the relationship between corporate activity and public welfare, as the behavior of corporations in a context of global economic competition has much to do with the erosion of the power of the state to be responsive to its constituencies at large. The transnationalization of corporate activity implies, moreover, that such responsibility is not restricted to constituencies in the country of affiliation, but wherever the particular activity is conducted. Should a U.S.-based corporation, for example, be responsible for the welfare of populations in India, where the corporation may be active? If claims to globalization are to be taken seriously, globalization should not mean just the globalization of activity but a globalization of responsibility as well. The question is how such responsibility may be enforced, which raises further questions about the unevenness of power that is often elided in discussions of globalization. It has become painfully evident over the past decade, following the fall of socialism, that such unevenness of power has assumed even greater sharpness than before with the expansion of the coercive power of the United States, to the point where globalization appears to be little more than the universalization of U.S. sovereignty (and suzerainty) globally.

The problem with an analysis such as Ohmae's is its obliviousness to the different consequences of marketization in different social and political contexts, most importantly in the differences between societies that occupy the architectural centers of global power, as Castells puts it, and those who are powerless or marginal. Such unevenness, as is cogently manifested in Ohmae's analysis, applies not just to political relations between countries but to social relations within countries. Paralleling inequality between countries, in other words, are inequalities in class and gender relationships that cut across countries and are in the process of being globalized as well.

Equally problematic is the rather cavalier dismissal in such an analysis of the surfaces implied by "national development," which comes into sharp relief when contemporary analyses of globalization are placed against earlier ideas of national development. There is much to support such a position empirically. Back in 1987, the People's Republic of China premier Zhao Ziyang suggested (contrary to what the socialist revolution had hoped to achieve) converting all of coastal China into a special economic zone to encourage foreign investment. While coastal China has not become a special economic zone, it has developed rapidly over the past decade and a half, producing the economic bifurcation feared by earlier revolutionary nationalists. Indeed, analysts such as Dean Forbes have perceived in the development of Southeast and East Asian economies of an urban corridor, increasingly remote from its hinterland.[11]

The problem is deciding what meaning to assign to this restructuring of national economies into networks that cut across national boundaries. There is a difference between a city-state such as Singapore and a continental nation such as the People's Republic of China in judging the consequences of an urban corridor that unites them. The latter has to face the politically divisive consequences of a structural bifurcation in the national economy, which presents questions of not only national sovereignty but also the very viability of the nation. These questions are not likely to go away so long as nations exist, which is also an empirical fact. The PRC government, with a century of nationalist/socialist revolution behind it, has so far refused to accept the bifurcation of the economy and has made some effort to promote the development of western China. Whether the effort will be successful remains to be seen.

The rapidly developing parts of the national economy in the "urban corridor" are not without deep problems either. There is little need here to dwell on the ecological destructiveness of rapid growth facilitated by foreign investment, by investors who have little interest in the ecological welfare of places in which they invest. Likewise, the exploitation of labor has reached levels where slave-like or even slave labor has made a comeback. A recent study by Anita Chan documents the horrendous condition of Chinese labor in the most rapidly developing areas, which not only does not receive much help from the state but suffers from the oppressive collaboration between Chinese officials and foreign investors.[12] The situation is obviously worse in the so-called developing economies, but similar phenomena are by no means absent from the most developed economies, such as the United States.

These problems, elided in celebrations of globalization and regional states, call for difficult policy decisions by states, transnational corporations, and local businesses, as well as public interest groups. However, fundamental to any consideration of solutions is an ideological and cultural transformation of attitudes toward the notion of development. Celebration of globalization, or preoccupation with contemporary configurations as a given empirical fact, too often leads to a dismissal of insights derived from the past, especially when that past is associated with seemingly failed or discredited attempts to open up alternative paths to the future. Such a dismissal may be described properly as ideological. Although past paradigms may no longer be relevant, the problems that produced them are still with us, even more critically than before. Those paradigms need to be reexamined in order to produce out of them new paradigms appropriate to the present.

Certain considerations are crucial to any contemporary cultural transformation, or even a cultural revolution, and should be a point of departure in confronting the seemingly intractable problems we currently face. First is the ideology of development itself, what we may call developmentalism, which has become something of a "global faith," driven not only by corporate and government greed but also by a globalized cultural desire to participate in endless cycles of consumption.[13] Second is an attention to places, concrete locations of everyday life. Rather than meaningless statistics of growth at the national or state level, they ought to be the measure of economic health, social welfare, and political democracy—a measure of the claims of states and corporations to fulfill the promises of popular welfare off which they thrive. This requires reconsideration of governance at all levels, beginning with places, and guaranteed public participation not only in the political process but in corporate decision making as well.[14] Finally, as I noted above in passing, if globalization is to serve as more than an excuse for intensified and uncontrolled exploitation of labor globally, it must be accompanied by the cultivation of global responsibility on the part of global actors, that a corporation, say, should be responsible not only to its stockholders, or the nation or location from which it hails, but to every location where it conducts its activities.

This is a wish list no doubt. There are seemingly insurmountable ideological and material obstacles to each of these propositions, especially at a time when we seem to be entering a period of endless war, unprecedented imperial arrogance on the part of the United States with its commanding role in global affairs, and corporate contempt for not only human welfare but even the welfare of stockholders. But it is precisely the continuous crisis that we seem to be living in that calls forth an insistence on such a wish list. The alternative is hopelessness and, possibly, catastrophe for all.

Notes

1. Arif Dirlik, "National Development and Social Revolution in Chinese Marxist Thought," *China Quarterly*, April–June 1974, 286–309. The Chinese Marxist arguments I discuss below are described in greater detail in this article.

2. The term "delinking" is derived from the title of a volume by Samir Amin, *Delinking: Towards a Polycentric World*, trans. Michael Wolfers (London: Zed, 1990). The analytical basis for the idea is to be found in a whole range of theorists of development from H. R. Cardoso (more recently a prime minister in Brazil and a convert to global capitalism) to Andre Gunder Frank (another convert) to Immanuel Wallerstein and Immanuel Arrighi.

3. For a comprehensive discussion of the ideological dimension of globalization, see, for example, Manfred B. Steger, *Globalism: The New Market Ideology* (Lanham, Md.: Rowman & Littlefield, 2002).

4. Manuel Castells, *The Rise of the Network Society*, vol. 1 of *The Information Age: Economy, Society, and Culture* (Malden, Mass.: Blackwell, 1997).

5. Saskia Sassen, *The Global City: New York, London, Tokyo* (Princeton: Princeton University Press, 1991). Needless to say, the nodes of the network economy are not restricted to these major centers. For an elaboration, see Saskia Sassen, ed., *Global Networks, Linked Cities* (New York: Routledge, 2002).

6. Castells, *Rise of the Network Society*, 146–47.

7. Kenichi Ohmae, *The End of the Nation State: The Rise of Regional Economies: How Capital, Corporations, Consumers, and Communication Are Reshaping the Global Markets* (New York: Free Press, 1995), 16.

8. Kenichi Ohmae, *End of the Nation State*, 97.

9. Kenichi Ohmae, *End of the Nation State*, 57.

10. Kenichi Ohmae, *End of the Nation State*, 74, 94.

11. Dean Forbes, "Globalisation, Postcolonialism, and New Representations of the Pacific Asian Metropolis," in *Globalisation and the Asia-Pacific: Contested Territories*, ed. Kris Olds, Peter Dicken, Philip B. Kelly, Lily Kong, and Henry Wai-cheung Yeung (London: Routledge, 1999), 238–54.

12. Anita Chan, *China's Workers under Assault: The Exploitation of Labor in a Globalizing Economy* (Armonk, N.Y.: Sharpe, 2001).

13. I owe the term "global faith" to Gilbert Rist, *The History of Development: From Western Origins to Global Faith*, trans. Patrick Camiller (London: Zed, 1997).

14. For discussions of the significance of "place," see Roxann Prazniak and Arif Dirlik, eds., *Places and Politics in an Age of Globalization* (Lanham, Md.: Rowman & Littlefield, 2001).

GLOBALIZATION AND AFRICA'S
INTELLECTUAL ENGAGEMENTS

ZINE MAGUBANE AND
PAUL TIYAMBE ZELEZA

Globalization seems to be everywhere, as rhetoric and reality, as process and project. It is propagated simultaneously as an intellectual concept and an ide-ological commodity, describing concrete conditions and prescribing particular futures. Often absent from the celebrations and conceptualizations, critiques and condemnations of globalization, however, is Africa as a spatial and epis-temic presence. Africa is claimed, with various degrees of glee and gloom, to be marginal and in crisis both in epistemological and economic terms, African polities, economies, societies, and studies are irrelevant to globalization. Over the past decade, there have been vigorous debates about the dimensions and dynamics of Africa's alleged marginality and crisis. However, what strikes us— a historian and a historical sociologist—is how old these debates are. The lan-guage of crisis and marginality, so deeply embedded in the Western imaginary since the first tragic encounter between Africa and Europe in modern times, is attractive for its equal-opportunity ideological possibilities. To those on the right, it evokes a death wish for a continent seen as beyond the pale of human-ity. For the left, it kindles hope for the redemption of the downtrodden.

Tade Aina, a Nigerian scholar, has argued that African intellectuals should beware of northern globalization discourse: "Globalization theories imagine and

165

envision the world within a limited scope which is place-determined in terms of privileging a particular Eurocentric (Northern) positioning or understanding which undervalues, ignores or rejects non-European, non-Northern visions and knowledge."[1] Thandika Mkandawire, a Malawian scholar, shares Aina's views. Analyses of globalization and Africa are dismal, he believes, because most of the nuances that characterize the debate elsewhere "disappear; as a result, the dominant view emphasizes the hyper-globalists on one hand and the incomprehensible marginalization of the continent on the other."[2]

We need to differentiate between historical and ideological globalization and Africa's links with it. Understood as a historical process, the world has been globalizing for a long time, although the process accelerated rapidly during the course of the twentieth century. Africa has been an integral part of these processes, central to the construction of the modern world in all its ramifications—economic, political, cultural, and discursive—over the last half millennium. This is not to argue that Africa's engagements with and contributions to globalization have necessarily been beneficial to its peoples. On the contrary, Africans have paid a high price over the last half millennium in the construction of a more integrated world.

In this chapter we seek to understand what globalization means for Africa and African intellectuals, concretely and conceptually. First, we seek to provide a historical account of Africa's intellectual engagement with globalization, describing four key episodes—slavery, colonialism, independence, and the postcolonial era. Each of these episodes marks an important moment whereby Africa and Africans became integrated into global economic, political, and cultural networks. Our purpose in comparing and contrasting these key moments is to highlight both the continuities and discontinuities that characterize Africa's global engagements.

Second, because our mandate is to look at the ideological dimensions of globalization, we seek to mark the complicity between economic globalization and the spread of ideologies about African character, capabilities, and potential. Specifically, we seek to document the ways in which globalization and the spread of racial ideologies have been intertwined.

Third, in documenting African responses to globalization, we seek to demonstrate that, at least where Africa is concerned, any response to globalization necessarily entailed a response to racism. These responses took varied forms that incorporated ideologies from Europe and America in unique and interesting ways. Thus we also highlight the manner in which responses to globalization were reliant on ideologies that circulated through global networks.

Fourth, we wish to draw attention to the ways in which African responses to globalization necessarily entailed a discussion of the state. Globalization has played a key role in the formation and disintegration of the African state. African intellectuals' varied responses to globalization have always entailed discussion of the state, its role in the economy, and its relationship to global forces and networks.

Slavery, Mercantilism, and Abolitionism:
Africa's First Confrontation with Globalization

Writing in 1663, Renatus Enys declared that the Negro slaves were "the strength and sinews of this western world."[3] As such, African people were also the strength and sinews of the first wave of capitalist globalization. If we understand globalization to mean the interpenetration and interdependence of national economies, a global division of labor, and "a coalescence of varied transnational processes and domestic structures, allowing the economy, politics, culture, and ideology of one country to penetrate another," then slavery and the mercantilist economic system of which it was a part certainly qualify as one of its manifestations.[4] Mercantilism, as an economic system, was one of the first instances of global economic interpenetration and dependence. Its guiding premise was that the economy of the colony should be completely subordinated to that of the metropole, its exports being sold solely to the "mother country" and its imports emanating from that single source as well.

The triangle trade, the linchpin of the mercantilist system, marked the emergence of both a global economy and a globalized division of labor. According to Eric Williams, slavery "stimulated capitalism, provided employment for British labor, and brought great profits to England."[5] Brought from Africa to labor in the Americas, slaves created wealth by producing raw materials like sugar and cotton that were worked into finished materials in the metropole. Slave labor thus constituted a critical component of British manufacturing as it provided a basis for the employment of hundreds of thousands of Englishmen—particularly those engaged in shipping, shipbuilding, cotton manufacture, sugar refining, and metallurgy.

Ideologically speaking, slavery was responsible for the emergence of both racism and the ideology of race. Simply put, "slavery was not born of racism: rather, racism was the consequence of slavery."[6] It was also the impetus for antislavery sentiments that celebrated the ideas of equality, sovereignty, and democracy. Indeed, these two impulses proceeded together. As Pieterse explained, "Race emerged as the buffer between abolition and equality."[7] The manner in which slavery and abolitionism shaped the culture and ideology of African people was quite profound. Indeed, the antislavery impulse can rightly be considered the first formal African intellectual response to globalization. It is possible to identify in African-generated antislavery discourses the roots of the two principal intellectual traditions that continue to inform African intellectual responses to globalization.

The first response, typified by Creole populations in Senegal and mission-educated West Africans in the Gold Coast, emphasized the value of African assimilation to European culture and the importance of economic cooperation between European and African economies. Robert July explains that "with the settled communities of Gorée, Saint-Louis, and the entrepôts along the Senegal, the French efforts at cultural assimilation were received with cordiality by both the *métis*, or mulattoes, and the small number of Africans who, like the mulattoes, were engaged in the [international] river traffic."[8] Likewise, Samuel Ajayi Crowther, a former slave and graduate of Fourah Bay College, which was established in Liberia by the Church Missionary Society in 1827, argued that abolition would be hastened if the interior of Africa was opened up to legitimate trade from Europe. He argued for establishing permanent missions in the interior of Africa, which would establish trade treaties with local chiefs while providing training in crafts and modern agricultural methods for local people.

The second key intellectual response to slavery challenged the assimilationist view. The opinions of Edward Blyden, a West Indian who migrated to Liberia, contrasted sharply with those of Crowther. Blyden strongly repudiated the idea that Africans were inferior to Europeans or needed European assistance to develop. Instead of preaching assimilation, Blyden promoted the idea of an "African personality." In a speech delivered in Freetown in 1893 he argued that "it is sad to think that there are some Africans, especially among those who have enjoyed the advantage of foreign training, who are blind to the radical facts of humanity as to say, 'Let us do away with the sentiment of Race, let us do away with our African personality and be lost, if possible, in another race.' "[9]

The ideas of James Africanus Beale Horton, the son of a repatriated Ibo slave, echo those of Blyden. Horton argued that there were no significant intellectual differences between Africans and Europeans. Thus it could reasonably be expected that education and economic development would bring political and commercial equality. Horton dreamed of the day when the people of West Africa would achieve economic independence and take charge of a series of independent, self-governing, modernizing states. Horton's dreams were not realized, however, as the colonial powers gradually became aware of the immense economic and social gains they could realize through permanent colonial occupation of Africa.

Neomercantilism and the Scramble for Africa: African Intellectual Responses to Colonialism

Following the spread of industrial capitalism from England to the United States and other European countries during the latter half of the nineteenth century, international trade became increasingly important and competitive. The economic response to this development was neomercantilism, a system of protection for the infant industries of Europe and America that made the markets of the colonies the exclusive monopoly of the metropole and ensured that the colonies remained their exclusive suppliers of raw materials like cotton, rubber, palm oil, and minerals. The scramble for Africa was the inevitable result of the ensuing competition among the principal industrial states for control over these markets.

Boahen describes this process as an "almost hysterical reaction to the crisis in industrial capitalism, feeding on fear that the economic and hence political future of an industrial country rested on the exclusive control of markets and raw materials."[10] Colonialism, Boahen explains, resulted in the integration of the African economy "into the world economy in general and into the capitalist economy of the former colonial powers in particular."[11] Colonialism also meant that most African economies wound up being monocrop economies oriented toward producing cash crops for export, as the colonial powers made no attempts to either diversify African economies or make them efficient producers of goods for internal consumption. Finally, all the colonial currencies were tied to those of the metropolitan countries and all of their foreign exchange earnings were expatriated and not used for internal development.

The ideological dimensions of colonialism and the scramble for Africa were both profound and enduring. The idea of race as a permanent, immutable, biological characteristic by which the humanity of populations could be ranked found its highest expression in the ideologies used to justify conquest and subjugation. Thus anticolonial resistance must be understood as having emerged in part as a response to the racial ideologies that provided support and justification for colonialism. As was the case with slavery and mercantilism, African responses to colonialism and its accompanying ideologies took two main divergent forms. On the one hand, a cadre of African elites equated progress in Africa with mastery of the European (particularly French) way of life and closer economic relationships between metropole and colony. Although they opposed racialist ideas that cultural differences between Europeans and Africans were both permanent and unbridgeable, they nevertheless agreed that European culture was superior to African and that African economic salvation lay with the continent's increased global interpenetration and integration. Hence they urged that French West African colonies continue to base their economies on the export of raw materials to France.

The social philosophies of Blaise Diagne are typical in this regard. Diagne was born on the Senegalese island of Gorée and educated in France. As the Senegalese representative in the French Chamber of Deputies, Diagne fully supported Bordeaux merchants' economic prerogatives in Senegal. According to Boahen, Diagne "became more and more conservative in his demands; he died in 1934 an ardent defender of the colonial system."[12] Indeed, Diagne defended France's colonial labor program at the conference on forced labor held by the International Labor Organization in 1930. In a 1921 speech, Diagne declared that independent African advance was impossible: "to isolate the black race and let it work out its own evolution is ridiculous. . . . The evolution of our race . . . requires the cooperation of everybody."[13] Diagne was not alone in his views. A number of Senegalese politicians, including Galandou Diouf and Lamine Guèye, shared his opinion that "we Frenchmen of Africa wish to remain French."[14] Thus assimilationists, although conservative, subscribed to a vision of the relationship between the state and the citizen that was somewhat revolutionary. They saw citizenship much more broadly, refusing to limit it to being a function of one's location in a geographically fixed state. Hence one could be "French" by virtue of culture, language, and upbringing and a "citizen" of France, despite living in a far-flung geographical locale.

Not everyone who experienced French colonialism shared the assimilationist philosophy, however. An equally strong legacy of the French colonial experience found expression in the doctrine of negritude, which borrowed and combined ideas from French existentialism and the Harlem renaissance. Negritude argued for the importance of a simultaneous movement toward political and cultural independence. It also stressed the importance of appreciating and valuing the uniqueness of the "African personality." Although it might not be able to claim superiority on the same registers as did the European, it nevertheless could claim superiority in its own right.

According to Léopold Sédar Senghor, one of the Senegalese founders of the negritude movement, "we, the creators of the new generation, want to give expression to our *black personality* without shame or fear."[15] One of the key tenets of negritude was that colonialism, instead of demonstrating the superiority of European civilization, actually proved its moral and spiritual bankruptcy. As Aimé Césaire explained in his *Discourse on Colonialism*, "colonization dehumanizes even the most civilized man. Colonial activity, colonial enterprise, colonial conquest, which is based on contempt for the native and justified by that contempt, inevitably tends to change him who undertakes it. The colonizer, who in order to ease his conscience gets into the habit of seeing the other man *as an animal,* accustoms himself to treating him like an animal, and tends objectively to transform *himself* into an animal. It is this result, this boomerang effect of colonization, that I wanted to point out."[16]

Although defenders of negritude fully supported the idea of African political and economic independence, negritude, as a social philosophy, had little to say about the specific forms of state and economy that would be necessary to achieve this end. Hence Frantz Fanon sharply criticized the fact that supporters of negritude articulated their opposition to colonialism primarily in culturalist terms. Fanon wryly observed that "all the proofs of a wonderful Songhai civilization will not change the fact that today the Songhais are under-fed and illiterate, thrown between sky and water with empty heads and empty eyes."[17]

A clearer connection between cultural and economic emancipation is found in the writings of pan-Africanists who argued that international cooperation among Africans was the most effective way of achieving African cultural self-determination. Pan-Africanists, some of whom attended W. E. B. DuBois's pan-African congresses in 1919 and 1921, were strongly influenced by the conference organizing theme that the basis for self-government in Africa was racial equality and declared Africa the natural leader of worldwide pan-Africanism. At the suggestion of W. E. B. Dubois, some African devotees of pan-Africanism pursued the idea of an internationalized Africa formed of the former German colonies, to which the colonies of Portugal and Belgium would one day be added. Others became devotees of Marcus Garvey and sought to build an independent African financial empire.

Pan-Africanism was unique in globalizing the idea of the citizen. According to its tenets, Africa could and must count the entire African diaspora among its citizens. Although the devotees of pan-Africanism had no desire to challenge the autonomy or integrity of African states, their philosophies clearly put more value on fostering a continental and global consciousness that transcended, indeed superseded, attachments to a single state.

Independence and the Fight against Neocolonialism

The independence period witnessed the reemergence of the dual impulses of assimilation and economic integration on the one hand and pan-Africanism and economic independence on the other. Because colonialism resulted in the uneven integration of African economies into the global system, the leaders of some independent African states responded by pointing out that economic independence was the necessary basis for true political freedom. Indeed, many African intellectuals and politicians argued that formal political independence was essentially meaningless in Africa precisely because of the failure of most African leaders to gain control over national economic assets. Sékou Touré of Guinea, Kwame Nkrumah, first independent leader of Ghana, Modibo Keita, the president of Mali, as well as the radical leadership in Algeria, are all well-known for their critiques of what they called neocolonialism. Neocolonialism was a broad umbrella term describing a wide variety of economic activities and devices used by the former colonial powers to maintain their control over African economies. These devices included, but were not limited to, economic infiltration through loans, structural adjustment programs, control over currency, and the support of puppet independent regimes sympathetic to their former rulers.

One popular response to neocolonialism was the dual call for pan-Africanism and "African socialism." Sékou Touré, for example, argued that African countries must band together to gain control of their economies in order to reserve the continent's wealth for its citizens. Nkrumah agreed that African governments should work together to mobilize surplus production for investment, accepting foreign aid only when it furthered the goal of national development. Julius Nyerere of Tanzania was famous for his support of state planning and regulation in the form of "East African socialism." His famed Arusha Declaration of 1967 rejected the idea that inter- and intraclass warfare was a motivating force in African politics and abjured traditional European socialism while embracing the idea that equal access to economic resources was a fundamental human right and that societies should strive to eliminate class inequality. Nyerere first put forth the idea of the *ujamaa* village community, which encouraged African farmers to produce cooperatively with minimal foreign assistance, in the declaration.

The opposite view can be found in the writings of the Kenyan leader Jomo Kenyatta, as well as in those of Félix Houphouet-Boigny of the Ivory Coast. Abjuring the idea that close economic integration or even subordination constituted neocolonialism, both sought to establish close and productive relations with their former rulers postindependence. In *Facing Mount Kenya* Kenyatta argued that Kenyan national development would best proceed if Africans concentrated on agricultural production while leaving industry in the hands of Europeans, to be sustained by infusions of private capital from abroad. Houphouet-Boigny agreed that the Ivory Coast should remain in the French Union and should concentrate on becoming a major exporter of primary products to France. Thus, the economy of the Ivory Coast remained firmly in the hands of the French, who established close working relationships with the local African bourgeoisie. Industry remained under European control and the French expatriate community dominated commercial activity. In short, both Kenya and the Ivory Coast evolved into countries whose primary economic roles were to supply raw materials and financial profits to their former rulers.

Capitalist Globalization in the Postcolonial Era

Most contemporary African intellectuals share the view that contemporary globalization is neither a new nor a unilinear phenomenon. According to Dani Nabudere, contemporary globalization is a process driven by the West, which has supplanted the globalizations of other civilizations. He traces globalization's origins to the Christian universalism of the Crusades and the trading voyages of the European Middle Ages, through the scientific stage of the early modern period, to the subsequent eras of the industrial and capitalist revolution, capitalist imperialism, and internationalization. The latter stage, characterized by so-called globalization, is marked by denationalization, deregulation, and the expansion of a post-Fordist economic system.

Claude Ake, the renowned Nigerian political economist, agrees with Nabudere that "uneven globalization is not only a process but also an ongoing structuration of power . . . [it] is the hierarchization of the world—economically, politically, and culturally—and the crystallizing of a domination. It is a domination constituted essentially by economic power."[18] For Ake, globalization is both a destructive phenomenon and a coercive ideology from the north that, despite some of its novelties, is only slightly different from previous forms and phases of capitalist imperialism. Samir Amin, an Egyptian scholar, also regards globalization as the manifestation of contemporary capitalism's chaos, which "is visible in all regions of the world and in all facets of the political, social and ideological crisis."[19] In Amin's view, globalization is "responsible for the erosion of the three subsystems that formed the basis of postwar growth, the national welfare state in the West, the national bourgeois project of Bandung in the Third World, and Sovietism in the Eastern bloc."[20]

For Africa, globalization has meant structural adjustment programs that have derailed postindependence development efforts, leading to what Nabudere calls the "third colonial occupation," distinguished by the downsizing of the postcolonial state.[21] Aina has likewise argued that the economic restructuring process embodied in structural adjustment programs begs the question of "what globalization means for economic development and whether this is still a possibility for African economies."[22] Given the ways in which integration into the global economy has handicapped African economies, a number of African scholars have called for a radical restructuring of the economic world order. As Aina observed, while the bulk of Western-centered analyses "emphasize 'time-space compression,' 'shrinking world,' new technologies, integrated markets, global inter-dependence and global flows albeit within a framework implicitly underwritten by Western dominance, 'non Western knowledges' struggle with two related sets of elements," namely, "the question of inequality, unevenness, and injustice embodied in the New World Order."[23]

Likewise, Claude Ake has argued that globalization will not survive "without solving the problem of uneven development and the poverty of much of the world's population. The North would do well to resist the temptation that it can appropriate at will and pay no heed to even development and the rule of law in global governance. The ghetto is too large and the haven it inhabits is small and shrinking."[24] Amin agrees that globalization via the market must be countered by "developing an alternative humanistic project of globalization consistent with a socialist perspective."[25] He thus argues for a new global political system that would ensure equitable access to the planet's resources, ensure open and flexible economic relationships between the world's major regions, and reengineer north–south relations by restructuring international financial and trade institutions while regulating global financial markets.

To be sure, some African intellectuals accept globalization as "an omnipresent and inescapable fact" and even welcome it for its potential to liberate African economies, politics, and social sciences from the suffocating grip of statist nationalism. One of the proponents of this argument has been Achille Mbembe, a Cameroonian scholar who rejects the idea that globalization is tantamount to imperialism. He dismisses this idea as "intellectual laziness" and argues that globalization is "full of possibilities that Africans should seize and exploit."[26] He also has serious disagreements with pan-Africanist and Afro-centrist views, which he dismisses as "nativism" or "a racist and authoritarian approach which, on the pretext of protecting cultural specificity, consists in reasoning as if black Africa were all of Africa and all Africans were negroes."[27]

A third way perspective has been articulated by Nelson Mandela and Thabo Mbeki, the president and former president of South Africa, who have argued for the necessity of global economic integration but have also remained firmly committed to pan-Africanism and inter-African cooperation. The latter ideas are actualized in the notion of an African renaissance, which Mbeki introduced in a speech to the United States Corporate Council on Africa in April 1997.[28] Nelson Mandela elaborated on Mbeki's ideas the following July in a speech at Oxford University, in which he described the African renaissance as encompassing both regional and global economic integration. According to Mandela, "the pooling of sovereignty in the consolidation of regional economic associations, as building blocks of an African Economic Union, will help make Africa's voice heard in the capitals of a world increasingly defined by regional blocs within the global economy."[29]

The ideology of an African renaissance seeks to bring together what in the past were generally seen as oppositional ideologies. "The very term 'African Renaissance' has proved a useful marketing tool in both organizing an increased share of global trade while stimulating Africans to seek greater control over the Continent's human and material wealth."[30] Thus, on the one hand, a constitutive part of the renaissance ideology is the idea of African economic and political autonomy, achieved via pan-African cooperation. Mbeki stated this in an October 1995 speech before the Eleventh Conference of Heads of State of Governments of Nonaligned Countries, proclaiming that "South–South cooperation is, among us, an article of faith."[31] At the same time, Mbeki argues for continued—indeed extended—cooperation between European and African economies, pointing to the fact that "history has tied the two continents of Africa and Europe by an umbilical cord which cannot be severed."[32] Hence pan-Africanism is married to a reconstructed African capitalism, not to African socialism. As Mbeki noted in a 1995 speech before the Business and Finance Forum:

Steps have been taken in the direction of reducing protective tariffs in line with our commitment to the Uruguay round of the General Agreement on Tariffs and Trade. . . . In the same context, we have signed on to the World Trade Organization and are fully committed to extensive though gradual tariff reforms, we are taking steady steps towards the removal of exchange controls, and are also introducing changes in our monetary and fiscal policies with the objective of creating a climate conducive to local and foreign investment.[33]

At first glance, it might appear that the concept of an African renaissance is seeking to bring together the mutually exclusive objectives of claiming more of Africa for Africans and claiming more of Africa for the West. However, as Durham points out,

this convergence of strategies does not mean that the objectives of African leaders of their rendition of an African Renaissance are the same as their Northern counterparts. For instance, regionalization serves African interests by building economies of scale to resist Northern hegemony while it is establishing a global power base of South-South alliances. Only from such a broader base of global power, can Africans hope to restructure the space economy of Africa in ways that serve Africans. This includes finding a way to influence the rules of global trade, i.e., taxes on buying and selling foreign exchange, regulation of finance, and debt cancellation.[34]

Conclusion: In Defense of Intellectual Engagements

Africa and globalization have a long, unhappy history. Africa's purported marginalization by globalization means that the continent has been integrated into the world in a subordinate position. For Africa, globalization represents an old problem in new contexts: the hegemony of northern processes, practices, and perspectives. Part of the intellectual challenge is to contest this provincialization of world history, to transcend the writing of histories of the south as transitional narratives to globalization, much as once their histories were written as transitional narratives to modernity, as histories of absence, of lack, of becoming. As African intellectuals, we have a responsibility to bring to globalization discourses the experiences and expectations of our societies. We must refrain from becoming mindless parrots for northern perspectives, preoccupations, and paradigms, not in pursuit of narrow nationalisms or the dangerous myths and essentialisms of what Paul Gilroy calls raciology, but as part of the struggle to create a global civilization in which we as Africans, for so long victims of oppressive forces emanating from elsewhere, can feel at home.

Notes

1. Tade Aina, *Globalization and Social Policy in Africa: Issues and Research Direction* (Dakar: CODESRIA Working Papers Series, 1997), 19.

2. Thandika Mkandawire, "Globalization and Africa's Unfinished Agenda," *Macalaster International* 7 (1997): 74.

3. Quoted in Eric Williams, *Capitalism and Slavery* (Chapel Hill: University of North Carolina Press, 1994), 30.

4. James Mittelman, *Globalization: Critical Reflections* (Boulder: Lynne Rienner, 1996), 3.

5. Williams, *Capitalism and Slavery*, 65.

6. Williams, *Capitalism and Slavery*, 7.

7. Jan Nederveen Pieterse, *White on Black: Images of Africa and Blacks in Western Popular Culture* (New Haven: Yale University Press, 1995), 59.

8. Robert July, *A History of the African People* (Prospect Heights: Waveland, 1992), 230.

9. July, *History*, 22.

10. A. Adu Boahen, *African Perspectives on Colonialism* (Baltimore: Johns Hopkins University Press, 1987), 32.

11. Boahen, *African Perspectives*, 100.

12. Boahen, *African Perspectives*, 84.

13. July, *History*, 378.

14. July, *History*, 378.

15. Léopold Sédar Senghor, "Negritude: A Humanism of the Twentieth Century," in *Colonial Discourse and Postcolonial Theory*, ed. Patrick Williams and Laura Chrisman (New York: Columbia University Press, 1994), 27.

16. Aimé Césaire, *Discourse on Colonialism* (New York: Monthly Review Press, 1972), 20.

17. Frantz Fanon, "On National Culture," in *Colonial Discourse and Postcolonial Theory*, ed. Patrick Williams and Laura Chrisman (New York: Columbia University Press, 1994), 37.

18. Claude Ake, "The New World Order: A View from Africa," in *Whose World Order: Uneven Globalization and the End of the Cold War*, ed. H. Hans-Henrik and G. Sörensen (Boulder: Westview, 1995), 23.

19. Samir Amin, *Capitalism in the Age of Globalization* (London: Zed, 1997), 2.

20. Amin, *Capitalism*, 34.

21. Dani Nabudere, *Globalization and the Postcolonial African State* (Harare: SAPES, 2000), 53.

22. Aina, *Globalization*, 21.

23. Aina, *Globalization*, 20.

24. Ake, "New World Order," 42.

25. Amin, *Capitalism*, 5.

26. Achille Mbembe, "Getting Out of the Ghetto: The Challenge of Internationalization," *CODESRIA Bulletin* 3–4 (1999): 3.

27. Mbembe, "Getting Out," 3.

28. Thabo Mbeki, *Africa: The Time Has Come* (Cape Town: Tafelberg, 1998).

29. Nelson Mandela, "Renewal and Renaissance: Towards a New World Order," www.anc.org/ancdocs/history/mandela/1997/sp970711c.html (April 22, 2003).

30. A. Durham, "Designing Boundaries for a Continent: The North-South Geopolitics of an African Renaissance," www.webpro.co.za/clients/ipt/durham paper.htm (April 22, 2003).

31. Mbeki, *Africa*, 213.

32. Mbeki, *Africa*, 215.

33. Mbeki, *Africa*, 49.

34. Durham, "Designing Boundaries," 7.

EMERGENT GLOBALISM AND
IDEOLOGICAL CHANGE IN
POSTREVOLUTIONARY CHINA

KANG LIU

The Chinese Communist Party (CCP) concluded its sixteenth National Congress on November 14, 2002. Its political discourse and the media coverage and commentaries of the event offer a glimpse of the ideological change in China today in the context of globalization. Although some critical distance is preferable, the following observation of the ongoing process in China suggests the necessary provisionality and difficulty of conceptualizing an emergent ideological formation that bears all the contradictions of its time. Media coverage of the congress illustrates these contradictions. The English online edition of the *People's Daily*, the most important state media of China, tries to convey the message in a matter-of-fact, businesslike tone:

> The week-long 16th National Congress of the Communist Party of China (CPC) ended Thursday morning. . . . The 16th Central Committee of the Communist Party of China (CPC) was elected. . . . Some 180 out of the 356 members and alternate members of the new CPC Central Committee are new faces, sources said. Some of the members are CEOs and chairmen of China's huge enterprises, a signal that the Party embraces Jiang Zemin's "Three Represents" idea and begins to include professional business managers in its top decision-making body.[1]

On the same day, the *People's Daily*'s editorial, however, has an entirely different style:

> The 16th National Congress of the Communist Party of China has come to a successful close. . . . The theme of Comrade Jiang Zemin's report is holding high the great banner of Deng Xiaoping Theory, comprehensively implementing the important thought of "three represents," carrying on the past and opening a way for the future, keeping pace with the times, building a well-off society in an all-round way, accelerating the advance of the socialist modernization drive and striving to create a new phase in the cause of socialism with Chinese characteristics, the report conforms to the tides of the times, accords with the aspirations of the Party and the people, and was thus unanimously endorsed by delegates to the Congress and enjoys the whole-hearted support of comrades of the whole Party and people of the whole country.[2]

The English online news aims at the global audience, while the editorial is for the domestic consumption of the Chinese public, which has seen immense changes in China's economic and social life, but little if anything in the way the state political discourse represents these changes. The glaring contrast between China's political reality and state discourses filled with ideological platitudes of the Maoist past, as exemplified by the *People's Daily*'s editorial, is further accentuated by Western media coverage that carries a different ideological baggage. The *New York Times* covers the news on the same day with a dramatization of the inner circle power struggle and reshuffle:

> Hu Jintao, a 59-year-old insider known as brilliant and bland, will be named chief of the Communist Party today, the point man in a sweeping generational shift of the nation's leadership that was achieved through the most orderly transition in the 53-year history of the party. . . . Mr. Hu takes over a country of dazzling economic growth and social change, one that is taking a more confident place in world affairs. But he must also cope with official corruption, spreading unemployment, a widening gap between rich and poor and bubbling demands for political change that may severely test the party. . . . Mr. Hu has survived as heir apparent by revealing little of his inner leanings. In any case, analysts say, it may take years for him to consolidate power and strike out in new directions.[3]

I quote these news stories and editorials at length in order to show that the political and ideological landscape in China is not only filtered through but also significantly affected by a global media network under U.S. hegemony. The Chinese media is taking an almost schizophrenic turn in the global media network, trying to keep up with the "global" (i.e., U.S.) standard of businesslike objectivity, on one hand, but unable to give up a discursive formation deeply entrenched in the revolutionary communist ideology, on the other.

In ideological and cultural domains in China, intense conflicts occurred between the revolutionary legacy of the Mao era and various ideologies of neoliberalism and developmentalism. Mao's revolutionary ideology constituted the core of his utopian project of alternative modernity that aimed to transform both the political and economic orders and social consciousness. This ideological hegemony prevailed during Mao's era, and it has an enduring impact even today, as the hegemonic discourse of revolution still provides the ruling Chinese Communist Party (CCP) with ideological legitimacy. This is largely because the post-Mao leadership of the 1980s and 1990s was not able to create new discourses and ideologies to justify its practices and policies that espoused free market, privatization, economic development, and efficiency at the expenses of social justice, democracy, and economic equality. The continuing deployment of the revolutionary ideology and discourse by the state is intended to maintain political and ideological stability. Yet the very content of the revolutionary ideology itself—egalitarianism, collectivism, and idealism—clashes sharply with what has already become the dominant social values in China, namely, the pursuit of individual material wealth and the fulfillment of personal, instinctual desires.

In this chapter, I explore China's present endeavors to reinvent an ideology and a discourse—at the crucial moment of China's full-blown integration into the capitalist world system or globalization. In this chapter I, first, briefly review the historical process of China's *gaige kaifang* (reform and opening up) in the context of globalization. Second, I examine the theory of Three Represents, coined by CCP General Secretary Jiang Zemin in 2000–2001 and included in the CCP constitution, as amended at the sixteenth Congress. The theory is said to have laid the foundation for a fundamental political and ideological change by substituting Marxist principles of class struggle with political governance and management of an emergent "corporate empire." I argue that a globalism with "Chinese characteristics" has emerged, which draws essentially on neoliberal ideologies and reinscribes a nationalist discourse into a universal developmentalism as the guiding principle of China's modernity.

Globalization and *Gaige Kaifang* in China

The watershed in China's recent history is widely known as Deng Xiaoping's *gaige kaifang* (reform and opening up) project, which began in 1979. Unlike Gorbachev's now almost forgotten perestroika, which led to the collapse of the Soviet-style socialism, *gaige kaifang* has succeeded in bringing economic development and material prosperity while keeping the political status quo under the rule of the CCP. The last two decades witnessed not only phenomenal economic growth but also spectacular political crises and unrest (which culminated in the

Tiananmen events in 1989), as well as profound social, ideological, and cultural changes.

New political and social formations, new sets of values and beliefs, new social identities, and subjectivities have emerged. These emergent formations, transformations, and reformations cannot be comprehended merely as the result of China's unique experiments, or "socialism with Chinese characteristics" as labeled by communist ideologues. They must be seen within the broad context of globalization. Globalization is not simply a new international or global conceptual framework for understanding changes in China. It is both a historical condition in which China's *gaige kaifang* has unfolded and a set of values or ideologies by which China and the rest of the globe are judged. Only immanent knowledge or "cognitive mapping" seems to be capable of deciphering the intrinsic tensions and contradictions of globalization and offering alternative visions by way of a critique.

Globalization constitutes a fundamental paradox in the sphere of culture, or tension between the trend toward cultural homogenization through global cultural production and distribution (media, popular culture, and entertainment industry) and the opposite trend toward cultural diversification in terms of local, ethnic, and national cultural projects and agendas. The paradox signals the basic contradiction of globalization as a new phase of capitalism that tends to penetrate and dominate every corner of the globe and social life with unprecedented intensity and velocity. Global expansion of capital has eroded political sovereignty of the nation-state and national economies, and has brought about dynamic cultural interactions as well as new schisms between the global and local, the center and the periphery, the developed West and the developing world, and the intellectual elite and the public. Cultural changes in China, especially in the 1990s, are the results of these interactions. As China further integrates itself into the capitalist world system, a new cultural formation is emerging—a hybrid postrevolutionary culture that embodies the fundamental contradictions of globalization. It cannot be solved by a Hegelian dialectic leading to an overarching synthesis, nor by Mao's handling of the "principal contradictions" by means of a univocal, totalizing move. In an overdetermined and enormously complex situation like the present globalization, there seems no singular way of resolution but rather plural and multiple movements and countermovements.

Given its revolutionary legacy—with socialism still as its state-sanctioned ideology—China's struggle is more with capitalism than with other aspects of globalization. It is, after all, a struggle between capitalism and its ideologies and cultural practices and past and present alternatives. These alternatives and experiments have been completely rejected and abandoned in the former Soviet bloc, and radically altered in China. Given that China's economy, unlike those of its East Asian neighbors such as Japan and South Korea, has not become thoroughly

globalized, the impact of economic globalization on China cannot be overemphasized. Yet China is perhaps most enthusiastic about globalization, from its leadership to the general public. It seems to many Chinese political, intellectual, and
other power elite that globalization may lead China out of its political and ideological impasse and eliminate the last vestige of revolutionary culture, ultimately
allowing China to embrace capitalism without rekindling the old ideological warfare between socialism and capitalism.

Under the leadership of Deng Xiaoping, China abandoned Mao's revolutionary idealism and instead adopted an economic developmentalism in order to
build a modern, market-oriented, postsocialist nation. This postsocialist project of modernization has inevitably resulted in the intellectual and cultural
diversification and pluralization of the past two decades. The "Deng theory," or
developmentalism, is a highly pragmatic and expedient policy, focusing exclusively on economic sectors while willfully neglecting changes in political, social,
and cultural spheres.[4] Mao's revolutionary ideological hegemony has been thoroughly deradicalized and hollowed out of its meaning and content. Still, its discursive formations and rhetoric continue to provide the necessary legitimation
for the Deng regime and its successors.[5] However, the legitimating discourse is
simply incommensurable with actual economic policies because it is predicated
on Maoist ideologies of revolution, mass democracy, and egalitarianism, which
are diametrically opposed to the endless accumulation of capital as the utmost
aim of capitalism. Consequently, ever since the beginning of the reform, ideological tensions and various legitimation crises have haunted China.[6]

For roughly half a century, from the 1930s to the 1970s, Mao drew a revolutionary blueprint for China's modernity, or alternative modernity, under the
condition of Western pressure and its own historical tradition of the old empire.
Mao recognized the centrality of culture and ideology in the revolutionary struggle. Over decades of political struggles leading to the establishment of the People's Republic of China (and, in the ensuing years, the struggles to reconstruct
a modern state and society), a revolutionary ideological hegemony was constituted. This revolutionary hegemony served as a legitimating force for CCP rule,
forging social cohesion and consensus by, first, often brutally suppressing dissent among the intellectual elite and, second, gaining the broad consent of the
working classes—the peasantry and the urban proletariat.

Post-Mao China under Deng Xiaoping's *gaige kaifang* witnessed the debunk-
ing of Mao's cultural and ideological hegemony and the adaptation of developmentalism. In the West developmentalism assumes the forms of development
theory as well as underdevelopment and dependency theories. The Chinese
modernization plan under Mao took the form of self-reliance and autonomous
development, akin to the delinking and isolationist notions of dependency theories and underdevelopment theories. *Gaige kaifang* rejects the premises of isolationist self-reliance and relies on the hypothesis that China, like other develop-

ing countries, will follow the same pattern of modernization as modernized countries in terms of marketization and full integration into the world system.

Deng Xiaoping's *gaige kaifang* represents a strategy of modernization and globalization without offering a real alternative vision. It retains the discursive forms of Mao's revolutionary hegemony, but not a revolutionary globalism as its ideological core. Capitalist globalization, by contrast, has both a vision (albeit assuming a variety of ideological guises) and enormous material and institutional power. Yet the neoliberal vision of the free market—the dominant ideology of globalization—cannot rationalize and camouflage growing rifts between the wealthy and the dispossessed, the powerful and disempowered, which is, in the final analysis, the fundamental and irreconcilable contradiction of globalization. The global/local, universal/particular, or homogenizing/diversifying dichotomies or paradoxes are different manifestations of this fundamental contradiction.

The Dilemma of Representation: A Critique of the Theory of Three Represents

The "Theory of Three Represents"—a new ideological hallmark of CCP—was first formulated in February 25, 2000, in a speech delivered by Jiang Zemin in Guangzhou during his tour of Guangdong Province, to a gathering of village and township cadres. Jiang stated that

> summarizing the more than seventy-year history of our party, an important conclusion can be reached—our party as the vanguard of the working class—won the support of the people because throughout the historical stages of revolution, construction and reforms, our party has always represented the development demands of China's advanced productivity, the forward direction of China's advanced culture, and the fundamental interest of China's broadest populace.[7]

This speech inaugurated what has become the new reigning doctrine of the CCP, namely *sange daibia lilun* (theory of Three Represents). On July 1, 2001, Jiang Zemin delivered the speech marking the eightieth anniversary of the CCP, in which he explicated the theory of Three Represents at length. While the speech was touted in China as the definitive document of the new theoretical innovation by the state media, it made headlines in the Western media because it accepted private entrepreneurs into the ranks of the CCP. Ironically, Western media either sidestepped or simply ignored the Three Represents formula and called Jiang's speech a "New Deal for China's capitalists."[8] For a while *sange daibiao* in Western media was translated "three representatives," but the official English version by China's state media—Three Represents—gradually prevailed, no matter how awkward it may look in English.

At the sixteenth CCP Congress, the Theory of Three Represents was formally enshrined in the CCP constitution as the "guiding ideology the Party must follow for a long time to come."[9] The state has waged an intense propaganda campaign to promote the theory since its announcement, and most of the public discourse of the sixteenth CCP Congress concentrates on its implications for China's development. It is perhaps too soon for Western China watchers to articulate any critical assessment, and Chinese intellectuals have so far remained silent on its meaning. Neoliberals in China have expressed their "satisfaction" that the CCP is now admitting capitalists into its ranks and effacing Marxist class analysis and the principle of class struggle. Conversely, the Chinese New Left is said to suffer "aphasia" as to the political comments of the new ideology.[10] Nevertheless, a critical assessment of the new theory's historical significance and its central dilemmas, no matter how preliminary, is urgently needed.[11]

What some Western media describe as the pressing problems of China—official corruption, spreading unemployment, a widening gap between rich and poor, and bubbling demands for political change—embody the country's fundamental contradictions of capitalist globalization. The Theory of Three Represents says virtually nothing about these difficulties. A Marxist analysis insists that the struggle results in exploitation and resistance on a global scale, and adopts a resolution of opposition, confrontation, and revolution. The Chinese Communist Party and Mao's revolution was first based on a Marxist model emphasizing the revolutionary struggles in the first half of the twentieth century and during Mao's reign over the People's Republic. However, as Deng and post-Deng leadership under Jiang Zemin set a course irreversibly transforming the CCP from a party of insurgency and revolution to a party of political governance of a modern nation-state, Marxist class analysis, Leninist theory of the state, and Maoist political strategies were abandoned not only as epistemological models but as practical guidelines.

Whether or not today's CCP can be considered a Marxist party of revolution is practically irrelevant. Despite the revolutionary rhetoric deployed by the CCP in its political and ideological discourses, the CCP has transformed itself into a gigantic, powerful conglomerate. High on its agenda is the construction of a corporate culture,[12] as it were, or a new ideology that legitimates the CCP in its efforts to monopolize political decision making and manage the economic, social, and cultural life of the entire country as a mammoth corporation or a corporate empire. In the United States, some marginally positioned literary scholars and philosophers tried to identify the ideological formations of a global empire in the U.S. Constitution, hybrid identities, and expanding frontiers, and so on.[13] In China, by contrast, the CCP ruling elite has been making self-conscious attempts to find a new ideological trademark for a fledgling corporate empire.

As I invoke the notion of empire in the Chinese case, a caveat is needed: at present, the CCP ruling elite can only imagine an economic empire within Chinese territories and perhaps within the network of a Chinese diaspora. In this regard, it is no rival to the global, U.S.-centered empire, be it imagined or real. I prefer the notion of a "corporate empire" because all signs indicate that the CCP ruling elite now aims at corporatizing not only the economy but social life in China, retaining the supreme power of corporate rule without adopting Western-style multiparty electoral democracy. The transition from Maoist "democratic centralism" to corporate culture as the political principle of the CCP, however, does not constitute an abrupt cleavage. It is a strategic shift that bolsters CCP political power, whereas the democratic participation of the citizenry is deferred indefinitely.[14]

Let us examine in more detail the Three Represents. The first Represent refers to "advanced productive forces." The CCP is the "representative" of advanced productivity instead of revolutionary idealism that ultimately leads to a communism justified by a Hegelian, teleological view of history: "The development of human society is a historical process of advanced productive forces replacing the backward ones."[15] But this productivist version of Marxism is invoked merely as an obligatory gesture of deference to the "ancestors," so to speak. The bulk of Jiang's elaborations on the First Represent dwells on strategies of maximizing productivity and promoting economic efficiency and performance. In the documents of the Sixteenth Congress, Jiang and the CCP strategists spared no effort in delineating the blueprint for microeconomic development, marketization, privatization (or "the development of nonstate economy," a coded phrase used in the state discourses), and growth of the middle class.

The tenet of the Second Represent is that of the CCP "representing China's advanced culture." It singles out the "national and scientific" as the locus of cultural development, charging that the CCP should promote a "national spirit" and a "culture industry" that aims to construct a strong, state-sponsored nationalism and social cohesion in the face of the multiple, centrifugal ideological trends under globalization.[16] The rising tide of Chinese nationalism has provoked an enormous reaction in the West, whose popular media sensationalizes the nationalist sentiment of the Chinese to conjure up a new version of the "yellow peril" or the "Chinese threat." Yet Western mass media invariably fail to mention the crucial link between the espousal of global capitalism by the Chinese state and the state-sponsored nationalism.

The last of the Three Represents points to the CCP as "representing the fundamental interests of the Chinese people." This fully embodies the intrinsic contradiction of the CCP's ideological legacy and its current revisionist agenda. On one hand, it preserves the rhetorical Maoist injunction to "serve the people," which used to be the essence of what the CCP stood for. On the other hand, the real thrust of this last tenet lies in the changing nature of the CCP—

a change that is both fundamental and structural. Simply put, the CCP is trans-forming itself from "the vanguard of the working class" into the condensed essence of "the Chinese people and the Chinese nation"—a political party that can purportedly represent the interests of the Chinese public as a whole.[17] This assertion not only shores up the party's overriding goal of maintaining its polit-ical monopoly but also signals a complete rejection of the Leninist model of the Communist Party—a model that Deng Xiaoping was unable to challenge throughout his period of leadership.

Because the key word in the Theory of Three Represents is *daibiao* (repre-sentation) and the theory's intrinsic contradictions lie primarily in the notion of *daibiao*, a critique ought to begin with a scrutiny of the connotations and ram-ifications of this concept. The core of the matter is the contradiction between its ideological representation and its practical objectives and goals, as well as the strategies employed to reach these goals, not the party's willingness to jettison its Marxist principles. *Daibiao* in Chinese means "speaking for," but it also stands for "representative" or "political delegate." Its connotation approximates Karl Marx's German term *Vertretung*, commonly understood as the political rep-resentation as proxies and agents of power. Famously, Marx addressed political representation and class formation in *The Eighteenth Brumaire of Louis Bona-parte*: "The small peasants cannot represent themselves; they must be repre-sented. Their representative must appear simultaneously as their master, as an authority over them, as unrestricted governmental power that protects them from the other classes and sends them rain and sunshine from above."[18] Here the word is *Vertretung*, or political representation. However, as Gayatri Spivak points out, there is another German word, *Darstellung*, that also means "repre-sentation" but refers more precisely to a rhetorical re-presentation, or a signifi-cation as "trope." Spivak goes on to address the discontinuity and complicity of these two interrelated words as a critique of class formation and subject forma-tion in the Western political and philosophical traditions.[19]

In the case of China's Three Represents, the word *daibiao* is used liberally as an agent of, substitution for, or even identification with what it allegedly rep-resents—the advanced productive forces, the advanced culture, and the "inter-ests of the overwhelming majority of the Chinese people." Despite its obvious semantic slippage in this context, however, *daibiao* clearly does not refer to rep-resentation as an act of signification or discursive formation. That form of rep-resentation—*Darstellung*—is captured in the Chinese language either by the term *zaixian* (re-presentation) or the word *biaozheng* (signification-appearance) as in arts, literature, and philosophy. None of these Chinese words is used in Jiang Zemin's utterances about the Three Represents.

The theory or ideology of the Three Represents constitutes nothing more than an ideological representation-signification or *Darstellung*—a discursive, rhetorical formation of a trope. Jiang Zemin's logic retains obvious positivistic currents in that he equates and identifies the CCP with the "advanced productive forces" (new scientific and technological formations) and "advanced culture" (again referring to science and technology in addition to the "national spirit"). His re-presentation of the theoretical formulation, or the theory as trope, however, is steeped deeply in a system of signification that is decidedly Maoist and revolutionary. Not only do the syntactical structures of the political discourses on Three Represents reflect Maoist language, but the ideological justifications in the discourses bear a Maoist semantic foreclosure. Class struggle as a central theme in Maoist revolutionary discourse is completely rejected in the Three Represents, but to justify the admission of capitalists into the party, Jiang resorts to Maoist ideological markers that refer to "political position" and even "ethical attitudes" as a person's class identity rather than his or her economic status: "It is not advisable to judge a person's political integrity simply by whether one owns property and how much property he or she owns. Rather, we should judge him or her mainly by his or her political awareness, moral integrity, and performance."[20] It echoes Mao's (in)famous identification employed during the Cultural Revolution of the intellectuals and communist bureaucrats as "bourgeois representatives" based solely on their political stance.[21]

While the bulk of the theory of Three Represents tries to outline a charter of corporate culture in terms of management, organization, leadership, and performance capabilities, its representation of the CCP as a new corporate conglomerate, as it were, remains entangled in the old Maoist semiotic and logical matrix. The new CCP ruling elite is wrestling mightily with questions of how to identify itself with the advanced productive forces—new economic trends and strategies that promise efficiency and development—how to define the most subjective and idealistic notion of "advanced culture," and, above all, how to represent the interests of the broadest population without reifying class-based political distinctions. After all, the stakes are high: how the CCP can represent itself, both politically and symbolically, as it faces these vexing contradictions. Such is the Chinese version of globalism. As the ruling ideology, it can represent its own interests of maintaining a political and economic monopoly over the world's largest population only by exercising conceptual violence against its own ideological and political legacy, as well as by violating the fundamental interests of a disempowered, dispossessed multitude.

Notes

I want to thank Manfred B. Steger for inviting me to the Hawai'i conference, Ideological Dimensions of Globalization, in which an earlier version of this chapter was read and commented on by all participants. I feel grateful to all of them for their constructive criticism.

1. "Party Congress Concluded with New Central Committee Elected," *People's Daily News*, November 15, 2002, http://english.peopledaily.com.cn/200211/14/eng20021114_106807.shtml.

2. "Advancing Courageously along Orientation Charted by Party Congress," *People's Daily News*, November 15, 2002, http://english.peopledaily.com.cn/200211/15/eng20021115_106834.shtml.

3. Erik Eckholm, "China Set to Name New Party Chief as Jiang Steps Aside," *New York Times*, November 15, 2002.

4. For a critique of developmentalism in the capitalist world system, see Immanuel Wallerstein, *The Capitalist World Economy* (Cambridge: Cambridge University Press, 1979).

5. For discussions of Deng Xiaoping's deradicalization of Mao's revolutionary idealism, see Arif Dirlik and Maurice Meisner, eds., *Marxism and the Chinese Experience* (New York: Sharpe, 1989).

6. For a recent discussion of the ideological crisis, see Kalpana Misra, *From Post-Maoism to Post-Marxism: The Erosion of Official Ideology in Deng's China* (London: Routledge, 1998).

7. Zhao Ziping and Wang Zhegang, "'Sange daibia' de zhongyao lunshu shi zenyang tichu de?" (How was the 'Three Represents' discourse formulated?), *Remin ribao* (People's Daily), June 22, 2000.

8. John Pomfret, "New Deal for China's Capitalists; Businessmen Join Party but Run Their Own Show," *Washington Post,* July 3, 2001; and Craig Smith, "China's Leader Urges Opening Communist Party to Capitalists," *New York Times*, July 2, 2001, A9.

9. Jiang Zemin, "Report at the 16th National Congress of the Communist Party of China: Build a Well-off Society in an All-Round Way and Create a New Situation in Building Socialism with Chinese Characteristics," *People's Daily News,* November 18, 2002, http://english.peopledaily.com.cn/200211/18/eng20021118_106983.shtml.

10. For a comment from a neoliberal perspective, see Gao Xin's interview in *Duowei xinwen wang* (Chinese News Net). Gao Xin, "Jiang Zemin de wunai he Hu Jintao de jihui" (Jiang Zemin's frustration and Hu Jintao's opportunities), *Chinese News Net*, November 19, 2002, www2.chinesenewsnet.com/cgibin/newsfetch.MainNews/Opinion/Wed_Nov_2_0_13_35_10_2002.html; Gao Xin is a visiting fellow at Harvard and a political commentator for media in Taiwan and Hong Kong. For a New Left perspective, see the Huang Ping interview in Taiwan's newspaper, *China Times*. Huang Ping, "Zhongguo de xin zuopai he qu he cong" (Whither China's New Left), *Zhongguo shibao* (China Times), November 21, 2003. Huang Ping is a leading sociologist.

11. An assessment of the Three Represents theory by U.S. left academics is made by Barbara Foley, "Nationalism, Pseudo-Dialectics, and Capitalist Restoration: Some Comments on Jiang Zemin's Speech at the CCP 80th

Anniversary Gathering," unpublished manuscript, August 2001. Inquiries may be directed to bfoley@andromeda.rutgers.edu.

12. Treatises on corporate culture abound, for example, James W. Fairfield-Sonn, *Corporate Culture and the Quality Organization* (Westport, Conn: Quorum, 2001); Peg C. Neuhauser, Ray Bender, and Kirk L. Stromberg, *Culture.com: Building Corporate Culture in the Connected Workplace* (Toronto: Wiley Canada, 2000); Terrence E. Deal and Allan A. Kennedy, *Corporate Cultures: The Rites and Rituals of Corporate Life* (New York: Perseus, 2000).

13. See Michael Hardt and Antonio Negri, *Empire* (Cambridge: Harvard University Press, 2000).

14. I owe this point to Timothy Luke, whose incisive comments on my paper at the Hawai'i conference, along with many others, helped me restructure the arguments here.

15. Jiang Zemin, "Speech at the Meeting Celebrating the Eightieth Anniversary of the Founding of CCP," *China News and Report* [Information Office of the State Council, PRC], July 1, 2001, 8.

16. See Jiang Zemin, *Report at the 16th National Congress of the Communist Party of China*, sec. 6, "Cultural Development and Restructuring."

17. This appears as the first sentence of the preamble of the new CCP constitution. See "Zhongguo Gongchandang zhangcheng" (The constitution of the Chinese Communist party), *Renmin ribao* (People's Daily), November 19, 2002, A1.

18. Quoted from Gayatri Spivak, "Can Subalterns Speak?" in Cary Nelson and Lawrence Grossberg, eds., *Marxism and the Interpretation of Culture* (Urbana: University of Illinois Press, 1988), 277.

19. Spivak, "Can Subalterns Speak," 275–79.

20. Jiang Zemin, "Speech," 16.

21. For a discussion of Mao's idealistic categorization of classes during the Cultural Revolution, see Liu Kang, "Hegemony and Cultural Revolution," *New Literary History* 28 (1997): 69–86.

"ANTIGLOBALISM GLOBALIZATION" IN EAST ASIA: STATIST VERSUS SOCIETAL

Alvin Y. So

Globalism in this chapter refers to a neoliberal ideology of Anglo-American origin that endows the global project with certain norms and values, calls for certain policy prescriptions, and helps maintain and reproduce a certain economic, social, and political order. McMichael points to the following values, policy prescriptions, and emerging social order of globalism:[1]

- *Market liberalization and deregulation.* In order to enhance competitiveness in the world economy, developing countries must liberalize their market and eliminate inefficient regulations. Instead of erecting trade barriers to promote import substitution, developing countries should promote export-led growth and industrialization and welcome foreign investment.
- *The comparative advantage axiom.* The global project points to the world market rather than the domestic market for its stimulus. The assumption is that national prosperity derives from specialization in the forms of economic activities in which a country does best. Thus the slogan of the global project is to specialize and find your niche in the global marketplace.

- *Restructuring and democratization of the state.* In order to accomplish the neoliberal market prescriptions listed above, developing countries need to restructure their state: decentralize authority, downsize the bureaucracy, reduce state subsidies, and sell public enterprises. Also, in order to make the state more responsive to global market forces, developing countries must democratize and uphold human rights conditions.
- *Global governance.* Developing countries face a new world order in which global institutions (e.g., World Bank, IMF, G8 states, United Nations, and WTO) have assumed a more active governing role. The leverage of global governance includes debt and bailout, universal credit rating, human rights record, environmental safety regulation, national trade disputes, and military threats.

Although short-term agonies of the global project are many, its proponents believe that in the long run it will be highly beneficial to development. Thus Dittmer[2] remarks that the global project offers opportunities for generating both high profits for multinational corporations and rapid economic growth for host nations. This ideology of globalism, however, should be distinguished from the practice of *globalization*, which Manfred Steger refers to as a multidimensional set of objective processes characterized by an increasing exchanges of people, products, services, capital, and ideas across international borders.[3] Advances in technology, communication, and transportation have produced a global mobility at the end of the twentieth century that is unprecedented in speed, range, density, and accessibility. As a result, there is "an increase in interconnections, or interdependence, a rise in transnational flows, and an intensification of processes such that the world is, in some aspects, becoming a single place."[4]

In the north, the ideology of globalism and the objective process of globalization go hand in hand; globalism as ideology is a means to promote the globalization process, so the United States and American transnationals can continue their hegemonic domination of the world. However, the global project has led to poverty, inequality, racism, sexism, and poorer working conditions, as well as the destruction of global commons, indigenous culture and community, and environment. Consequently disillusioned citizens, unemployed and flexible workers, minorities, women, indigenous people, and religious groups have risen up to challenge the ideology of globalism, either to roll back or change the rules of "corporate globalization." Especially in the north, antiglobalism serves as a means to attack the dynamics of (neoliberal) globalization.

In East Asia the situation is different, since the East Asian antiglobalism movement is a means to promote, not roll back, the globalization process. The aim of this chapter is to show that "antiglobalism globalization" in East Asia has two different modes. First I first examine the antiglobalism of East Asian states and elites. Then I explore the antiglobalism of East Asian civil societies. At the end of this chapter, I discuss future prospects for the global project in East Asia.

Antiglobalism in Asia: The Statist Mode

Antiglobalism of East Asian States and Elites

East Asia's newly industrializing economies (NIes) are often taken as exemplars of the global project. For example, a World Bank publication entitled *The East Asian Miracle* described how Asian nations had since 1960 grown faster than all other regions of the world. However, despite embracing the global project at the surface, East Asian states and elites have actually initiated an "Asianization" movement to challenge the ideology of globalism. In my view, this Asianization movement has the following four elements:

Asian Confucian Values, Not Western Democratization

Since the 1980s, there has been a revival of Asian values in East Asia. The forerunners of Asian values include Lee Kuan Yew and Goh Chok Tong of Singapore and the supporters of the Singapore School in China, Japan, Korea, and Thailand.[5] The aim of the Singapore School is to articulate Confucianism across entire regions, such as East and Southeast Asia, or even across the entire Asian continent. The Singapore School argues that the East Asia's economic miracle owes much to its Confucian tradition. This is because Confucianism placed the family as the paramount institution within society, thus encouraging the emergence of family entrepreneurship in East Asia. Furthermore, it is argued, Confucianism shaped a new pattern of personal corporate management different from the West's rational, bureaucratic management.

In addition, the spokespersons of the Singapore School emphasize that Confucian paternalism has provided the needed political stability for rapid industrialization. The distaste for open criticism of authority, their fear of upsetting the unity of the community, and the knowledge that any violation of the community's rules of propriety easily lead to ostracism are said to have limited the appeal of Western democracy and social movements to the Asians. From this Confucian perspective, human rights and democracy are cast as luxuries that threaten social order and impede growth.[6]

Regional Integration, Not Comparative Advantages

The 1980s and 1990s witnessed a regionalization of production in East Asia as foreign investment from Japan, South Korea, and Taiwan became increasingly important in underwriting development in Southeast Asia. Dicken and Yeung point out that regionalizing strategies are significantly more powerful than globalizing strategies among Asian firms.[7] This is because the Asia-Pacific region has been a growth region since the late 1970s. Many countries in the region have either emerging markets or relatively low costs of production. The regional market and production location thus provide an opportunity for Asian firms to grow and establish their market position. In addition, there are substantial social, cultural, and political barriers to establishing a significant presence in North American and European markets. The Asian firms have yet to develop the capacity to compete with transnational corporations on their home turf.

A so-called flying geese ideology has been employed to justify the regionalizing developmental strategy of Asian firms. According to this view, Japanese firms have played the lead position in the East Asian region because Japan had the most advanced level of technological sophistication. Behind Japan follows a spreading "V formation" of decreasing levels of technical sophistication headed by the NIEs (Hong Kong, Singapore, South Korea, and Taiwan) and followed by the Southeast Asian states (Malaysia, Thailand, Indonesia, and the Philippines). The "geese" trailing behind Japan, it is alleged, will learn from the experience of the leader, move up in the product cycle, and eventually close the technological gap.

Network Capitalism, Not Marketization

Various proponents of the Asianization movement argue that the crux of East Asian development lies in network capitalism, not in liberalization of market or deregulation. For Lever-Tracy and Tracy,[8] for example, Chinese diaspora capitalism functions as the main motor of Asian economic development. The former is allegedly characterized by horizontal networks of mainly small- and medium-sized entrepreneurial family businesses linked transnationally through long-term personal relationships of reputation-based trust.

While Lever-Tracy and Tracy highlight the networks of small Chinese firms, Hamilton[9] highlights the distinctiveness of the large Japanese firms and networks. Japanese large business groups composed of several tiers of independent firms are more flexibly organized and more comprehensive than their American counterparts. According to this view, Japanese business groups created horizontal synergies by linking upstream firms that produce intermediate goods such as steel to downstream assembly firms that manufacture automobiles and other large-item consumer commodities. These firms are said to have created vertical synergies in each area of final production by developing *keiretsu*—vertically tiered hierarchies of firms that constitute "one-setism," the principle of self-sufficient production systems. To make these economic networks function as a self-sustaining system, they situated financial services, especially banking, insurance, and trading companies, at the center of each group.

Regional Cooperation, Not Global Governance

America was instrumental in setting up the APEC (Asia-Pacific Economic Cooperation) forum in order to promote its globalist project. Led by the United States, APEC includes non-Asian states such as Canada, Chile, Mexico, Australia, and New Zealand, as well as a number of Asian states (Japan, China, Hong Kong, Singapore, South Korea, Taiwan, Indonesia, Malaysia, the Philippines, Thailand, Papua New Guinea, and Brunei). The formation of APEC enabled the United States to address major economic issues and disputes in the Asia-Pacific region. In 1993 the United States spearheaded efforts to transform APEC into an Asia-Pacific economic community dedicated to fostering free trade and forging close trade and investment ties in the region.[10]

However, some Asian states have strong reservations regarding the transformation of APEC from a consultative forum to a regional trade bloc that would enhance the hegemonic position of the United States. Mahathir Mohamad, prime minister of Malaysia, was particularly vocal in his rejection: "We don't want APEC to become a structure community and we don't want it to become a trade bloc. We don't want APEC to overshadow ASEAN nor do we want to see APEC being dominated by powerful members. Everyone should be equal."[11]

The APEC forum meeting in Seattle in 1993, in fact, succeeded in forging a fledgling Asian identity reflected in sentiments of solidarity between China and ASEAN states to beat back the U.S. challenge. For example, there was support for the formation of the EAEC (East Asian Economic Caucus) as an alternative to an APEC dominated by American interests.

In short, the Asianization movement congeals around Confucian values (as against Western democratic values), the flying geese ideology of regional economic integration (as against comparative advantages and niche economy), Asian network capitalism based on disapora and trust (as against marketization and privatization), and Asian regional political cooperation (as against American global governance). What explains this pronounced antiglobalist stance of East Asian states and their elites? Why were various East Asian governments strong enough to challenge the Anglo-American globalist project? And precisely what are the goals of this Asianization resistance movement? In the remainder of this chapter, I will endeavor to provide some answers to these crucial questions.

What Explains the Antiglobalism of East Asian States?

After World War II, the United States replaced Great Britain as the hegemonic global power, which led to an unprecedented expansion of the capitalist world economy. In response to the threat of communism, the United States divided East Asia into two opposing spheres: (1) a communist bloc composed of China,

North Korea, and the Soviet Union and (2) an anticommunist bloc that included Japan, South Korea, and Taiwan. American patronage of its capitalist allies and assault on its communist foes in East Asia had a profound impact on economic and social development in this region.

For example, the Korean War, U.S. economic blockade, and forced withdrawal from the world economy in the 1950s influenced China to adopt the Leninist model of state building to better confront "imperialist enemies" from without and "counterrevolutionaries" from within. This Leninist party-state was extremely powerful as it extended both vertically and horizontally into every sphere of Chinese society. After 1978, however, while no longer committed to Leninist ideology, the Chinese Communist Party still had to deal with its strong Leninist state machinery to carry out its developmental polices.

In order to build a strong Japan to contain the spread of communism in East Asia, U.S. reforms imposed during the occupation period helped remove influential politicians, smash the military, dispossess landlords, and crush the labor movement. Then the Japanese state was empowered to formulate independent industrial and financial policies to promote economic development. In addition, the United States opened its huge domestic market for Japanese products and provided aids, loans, and other types of procurements. At the same time, for political reasons, the United States tolerated the closure of Japanese market to foreign enterprises, thus providing a crucial breathing space for Japanese corporations to recuperate from their World War II wounds.

Taiwan and South Korea were also blessed by the Cold War. Military tensions in the East Asian region seemed to justify the actions of the Taiwanese and Korean authoritarian states in building up the military, banning labor unions and strikes, and suspending democratic elections. American aid helped solve these countries' economic problems in the 1950s (e.g., alleviating huge government budget deficits, financing investment, and paying for imports), and foreign aid gave them powerful tools with which to intervene in the economy by, for example, enforcing compliance in the private sector and building up a strong defensive military. The United States was willing to open its own market to them while tolerating East Asia's continued discrimination against dollar exports.

Aided by these American Cold War policies, Japan quickly emerged as an economic power in the Asian region. China possessed a strong Leninist state ready to embark the Four Modernization programs, and by the late 1970s South Korea and Taiwan became successful NIEs engaging in export industrialization.

Under such conditions the global project arrived in East Asia. It was introduced during a period in which East Asian economies were at their upward phase, with exports expanding by leaps and bounds. Since the East Asian states had made it without adopting the policies of market liberalization, deregulation, democratization, and global governance, they would certainly look on the free market ideology of globalism with suspicion. Why should they adopt globalist policies if they could do without them in the first place? Moreover, as strong states, they had the capacity to deal with challenges of the global project, such as selectively introducing some measures (e.g., cutting tariffs) to satisfy transnational demands while firmly rejecting other measures that would harm their national interests.

The globalist project was introduced during a period in which the United States modified its anticommunist stand and adopted a mild policy of protectionism toward its former capitalist allies in East Asia. By the 1980s, the United States was no longer willing to trade access to the American market for foreign policy favors from the East Asian states. Asian states considered American globalist ideology highly hypocritical because this neoliberal project was introduced at the same time that the United States was closing off its previously open domestic market to the East Asian states.

Antiglobalism as a Means to Promote Asia-Centered Globalization

If the global(ist) project is a means for the United States to strengthen its hegemonic dominance of the world, then the Asianization project can be seen as a means for the East Asian states to strengthen their bargaining power against U.S. hegemony. The revival of Confucian values, for instance, can be seen as a mean to resist the imposition of U.S. democratic discursive onto East Asia.

The struggle for hegemonic domination was also evident at the beginning of the 1997 Asian financial crisis. At that time, the main donors for the initial financial adjustment package to rescue the Thai economy in late 1997 were Japan ($4 billion), South Korea and Taiwan ($2 billion), and China ($1 billion). These states were attempting to consolidate their regional position both economically and politically. The United States not only refused to support the Asian rescue package but also opposed regional calls to set up a Japanese-led $100 billion "Asian only" bailout. This generated considerable regional resentment against the United States, which in turn galvanized it and the IMF into strongly reasserting their position that adjustment funds not under the direct or indirect control of the IMF might not be properly used. Asian states may take, digest, and implement the IMF bailout package. However, the bailout package increasingly appears to be problematic to Asian states because it seems to provide the IMF with an opportunity to open East Asian economies, paving the way for globalization agencies to make inroads into the Asian banking sector and the Asian market.[12]

During the World Economic Forum East Asia economic summit held in Kuala Lumpur in October 2002, Prime Ministers Mahathir Mohamad of Malaysia, Thaksin Shinawatra of Thailand, and Goh Chok Tong of Singapore called for more and deeper integration and cooperation among East Asian nations on trade liberalization, human capital development, and regional security. They also pushed for establishing a common Asian currency, so that Asia would be less dependent on and less affected by the fluctuations of a major foreign currency such as the U.S. dollar. Greater economic integration in East Asia would put the region in a better position to respond to the formation of large economic blocs in Europe and the Americas.[13]

In this respect, the critique of antiglobalist ideology by East Asian states should not be taken as a gesture of their antiglobalization stand. Instead, antiglobalism should be seen as a strategy for East Asian states to attain upward mobility in the world economy so as to become the motive force and the epi-center of global capital accumulation. Instead of rolling back the globalization process, Asianization aims to shift the locus of globalization from an American-centered one to an Asian-centered one—in the attempt to make the twenty-first century the Asia-Pacific century.

Antiglobalism in East Asia: The Societal Mode

East Asian civil societies have voiced their own critique of Anglo-American globalism. Since the 1990s, East Asian NGOs organized many regional forums (e.g., the Asian social movements meeting) and several large-scale protest activities (like those against the Asian Developmental Bank's annual meeting and the People's Summit on APEC). Political activists want to advance civil society in East Asia because the interests of the people are different from those of the powerful state elites in East Asia.

Beyond the Statist Critique

In East Asia, the critique voiced by the civil societies is much more radical than that presented by their states. This societal critique has gone far beyond the call for Asian Confucianism, network capitalism, regional economic integration, and regional political cooperation. The Asian social movements meeting in Bangkok on August 10–12, 2002, for instance, issued the following strong statements:[14]

- *Opposing international financial institutions.* "The World Bank and the IMF continue to impose structural adjustment programs on vulnerable borrowing countries. Twenty years of structural adjustment have not produced growth or reduced poverty, but instead have enhanced the devastation of ordinary people's lives through increased alienation of the majority from public services, jobs and food security; deteriorating labor standards; the dismantling of public protections for the poor and vulnerable; and the destruction of local agriculture and industries. We call for a region-wide campaign to get the IMF, the World Bank, and the Asian Development Bank out of Asia and the Pacific. We demand a complete end to all structural adjustment programs."

- *Opposing militarism.* "Neoliberalism operates alongside militarism, globalized war and dictatorship. We demand an end to all U.S. military presence and intervention in Asia, especially in Afghanistan, Korea, Japan, Philippines, and Uzbekistan. We condemn U.S. and British threats to invade Iraq."

- *Promoting political and cultural identity.* "Neoliberalism and global capitalism go hand-in-hand with the political exclusion of certain classes, ethnic, and religious groups, and marginalize the notions of solidarity within the rich diversity of Asian societies. We resolve to support the rights of minority groups, class struggles, and the struggles of all peoples towards self-determination."

- *Promoting food sovereignty, agriculture, and trade.* "Strategies to increase food security must be based on a rights-based approach and the concept of food sovereignty. We resolve to support peasant, fisher, and indigenous people's movements in their struggles for food sovereignty, and for just systems of community control over food production and the communes. We demand that the removal of the WTO and the transnational corporations from food and agriculture."

In this respect, the societal mode of antiglobalism in East Asia shares common ground with northern antiglobalist movements in that both criticize the multinationals and global capital as well as call for citizens to play a stronger role in curbing the rules of the market and trade in the global order.

Beyond the Critique of Northern NGOs

East Asian antiglobalism differs in some crucial ways from its northern counterpart. For example, on the labor question, East Asian NGOs are very critical of the way U.S. and European trade unions have argued that the WTO would be strengthened if it took up tariffs and labor rights. In the view of East Asian NGOs, the North's unions should not be calling for a more powerful WTO because (beneath the surface rhetoric about human rights in the south) this is essentially a protectionist movement aimed at safeguarding jobs in the north at the expense of the workers in the south.[15]

Having experienced authoritarian rule directly, East Asian civil societies pay more attention to the issues of human rights and democratization than their counterparts in the north. In the People's Summit on APEC in 1997, for example, the human rights forum used dramatic theater and moderated discussion to explore concrete instances of human rights violations in such APEC countries as East Timor, China, and Indonesia. In a mock trial, eighteen APEC leaders for were tried for crimes against humanity. The Singaporean state, for instance, is seen as ruled by a party dictatorship bent on staying in power through the efficient manipulation of the police, judiciary, press, and social engineering. For political activists, the critical issues facing East Asia include how to formulate a strategy of effective democratic change in authoritarian politics, how to make the authoritarian state accountable, effective, clean, and democratic, and how to participate in elite-dominated parliamentary politics when a formal democracy has been set up.

Globalization as a Strategy of Antiglobalism

In their efforts to promote antiglobalism, many East Asian civil societies have pursued globalization strategies. First, their activities possess a firm global focus. As Walden Bello[16] explains, his organization, Focus on the Global South, aims to "look at Asian economic, political, and ecological issues, linking them into the broader picture. . . . Whether it was a question of opposing the U.S. military, or the World Bank or IMF, or multinational corporations, it was crucial to begin creating cross-regional links. . . . National movements, important as they are, have to combine with the creation of regional and global movement."

Second, East Asian NGOs work toward a global recruitment of their members, supporters, and allies. Focus on the Global South, for example, is Bangkok based and largely composed of Thai scholars. Its two directors, however, are from the Philippines and India. In addition, the organization appears to be out of touch with Korean and Japanese movements. On the other hand, Focus on the Global South works assiduously to bring together the global movements of the two hemispheres, particularly the peace movements and the anticorporate globalization campaigns.

The power of global networking was also demonstrated when the NGO Forum protested against the Asia Development Bank on May 9, 2002. A letter from the forum was signed by Freedom from Debt Coalition (Philippines), Society for Environment and Human Development (Bangladesh), Bank Information Center (Sri Lanka), Towards Ecological Recovery and Regional Alliance (Thailand), INFID (Indonesia), China Green Student Forum (China), Mekong Watch (Japan), Oxfam Community Aid Abroad (Australia), Rockefeller Brothers Fund (USA), and Friends of the Earth International (Amsterdam).

Third, East Asian NGOs largely rely on funding from global organizations. Focus on the Global South has more than twenty major funders, including European NGOs such as NOVIB, Oxfam, Inter Pares, and Development and Peace in Canada. It also receives money from the Ford Foundation and other corporate outfits on a project-by-project basis. East Asian civil society is similar to East Asian states in pursuing a strategy of what can be called an antiglobalism globalization: engaging in activities with a global focus, recruiting members, supporters, and allies on a global scale, and drawing on global funding.

Conclusion: The Two Modes of Antiglobalism in East Asia

East Asian states have initiated an "Asianization" movement to challenge the basic tenets of neoliberal market globalism, legitimate the interests of authoritarian states, and promote the upward mobility of Asian states in the world economy. Thus Asianization should not be taken as antiglobalization in the northern sense of the concept. Instead, it should be seen as a strategy for East Asian states to shift the globalization process from an American-centered one to an Asian-centered one, so that Asia may become the principal force of global capital accumulation in the twenty-first century.

Compared to the statist mode, the civil society mode appears to be far more radical in its antiglobalist critique. East Asian civil societies condemn neoliberal globalization for cutting back wages, jobs, and government social services, for creating widespread poverty and inequality, and for endorsing the exploitation and polluting of the environment by transnational corporations. Unlike its Anglo-American counterpart, East Asian antiglobalism makes authoritarian states its chief targets, issuing strong calls for the protection of human rights and other liberalization measures. To promote their brand of antiglobalism, East Asian civil societies transnationalize their local and national struggles, seek funding from global agencies, and develop networks with global NGOs.

What is the future prospect for these two modes of antiglobalism project in East Asia? There are three possible scenarios. The first is the triumph of the statist mode of antiglobalism. Asianization may continue unabated in the early twentieth-first century after East Asia recovers from its economic downturn. Asian business networks may play a more prominent role in promoting regional economic integration, and Asian states may work more closely with one another in designing a collective approach to solve emergent problems in the region. If East Asian economic development continues, antiglobalism globalization may become the model of development for the states in the south.

The second is the triumph of the societal mode of antiglobalism. On the one hand, the statist mode may fail because other Asian states view the rise of Japan to regional power with alarm; because China and Taiwan do not reach a common ground to solve national reunification issues; and because China fails to develop close economic and political ties with Japan. In addition, regional ties linking the East Asian region may remain largely commercial, with very little institutionalization of political authority. On the other hand, the societal mode seems to be gaining strength among the political activists in East Asia. If they succeed in overthrowing the East Asian authoritarian regimes, they may join forces with political activists in the north and the south, thus posing a robust challenge to Anglo-American globalism.

The third possible scenario is the triumph of globalism in East Asia. The East Asian states may be too weak and too half-hearted to challenge the global project, and East Asian civil societies may prove to be no match for the hegemonic domination of the Anglo-American states and transnationals. Then the center of antiglobalism movement would be based in either the north or the south but not in East Asia.

Which scenario will come true? As of this writing in 2003, it is too early to tell the outcome, given the short history of the two modes of antiglobalism in movements in East Asia and the general sense of uncertainty brought on by the events of 9/11. At any rate, in this chapter I have shown that although in the north globalist ideology and the process of the global project generally go hand and hand, East Asian antiglobalism is typically a strategy to promote globalization, and vice versa. East Asian states use antiglobalism to propel Asia to the center of global capital accumulation, and East Asian civil societies use globalization as a strategy to promote antiglobalism. I have also shown that antiglobalism pursued at the top by states is quite different from antiglobalism at the bottom promoted by political activists in the civil society. It is therefore important to consider regional factors (East Asia versus Anglo-American) and social divisions (states versus civil societies) in the study of both globalism and globalization.

Notes

1. Philip McMichael, *Development and Social Change* (Thousand Oaks, Calif.: Pine Forge, 1996), 148–76.

2. Lowell Dittmer, "Globalization and the Asian Financial Crisis," *Asian Perspective* 23 (1999): 46.

3. Manfred Steger, *Globalism: The New Market Ideology* (Lanham, Md.: Rowman & Littlefield, 2002).

4. James H. Mittelman, *The Globalization Syndrome: Transformation and Resistance* (Princeton: Princeton University Press, 2000), 5.

5. Sang-In Jun, "No (Logical) Place for Asian Values in East Asia's Economic Development," *Development and Society* 28, no. 2 (1999): 191–204.

6. William H. Thornton, "After the Fall: A Response to Dirlik and Jun," *Development and Society* 29, no. 1 (1999): 111–21.

7. Peter Dicken and Henry Wai-Chung Yeung, "Investing in the Future: East and Southeast Asian Firms in the Global Economy," in *Globalization and the Asia-Pacific*, ed. Kris Olds, Peter Dicken, Philip F. Kelly, Lily Kong, and Henry W. C. Yeung (London: Routledge, 1999), 117.

8. Constance Lever-Tracy and Noel Tracy, "The Three Faces of Capitalism and the Asian Crisis," *Bulletin of Concerned Asian Scholars* 31, no. 3 (1999): 5.

9. Gary Hamilton, "Asian Business Network in Transition," in *The Politics of the Asian Economic Crisis*, ed. T. J. Pempel (Ithaca, N.Y.: Cornell University Press, 1999).

10. James Mittelman at the Hawai'i conference on "The Ideological Dimensions of Globalization" argued that regional organization can be seen as a tool for promoting globalization, for example, APEC can be seen as an instrument for the United States to promote its global interests in Asia. While this observation is to a certain extent correct, researchers need to examine the precise nature and the goals of regional organizations before determining whether they are pro- or antiglobalization. For example, APEC could be transformed into an arena through which Asian states resist the U.S.-led globalization process. Thus Asian states did not want APEC to become a free trade area but wanted it to be a consultative forum only. They are also planning to set up an alternative regional organization (e.g., the East Asian Economic Caucus, which excludes the United States) to undermine the power of the APEC.

11. *Australian*, September 19, 1994, 2.

12. Richard Higgott, "The Political Economy of Globalisation in East Asia: The Salience of Region Building," in *Globalization and the Asia-Pacific*, ed. Kris Olds, Peter Dicken, Philip F. Kelly, Lily Kong, and Henry W. C. Yeung (London: Routledge, 1999), 103–4.

13. *South China Morning Post*, October 25, 2002, 16.

14. Asian Social Movement Meeting, "Another World Is Possible! Mobilise against Neoliberalism," www.focusweb.org/publications/2002/Statement-of-asian-social-movements-meeting -2002.html (April 22, 2003).

15. Walden Bello, "Pacific Panopticon." *New Left Review* 16 (2002): 7. Also available at the website: www.focusweb.org/publications/2002/New-Left-review-16.htm.

16. Bello, "Pacific Panopticon," 4.

KOZO KAIKAKU: THE EMERGENCE OF NEOLIBERAL GLOBALIZATION DISCOURSE IN JAPAN

Fumio Iida

There is no denying that the neoliberal globalization discourse is spreading around the world, and contemporary Japanese society is no exception to the rule. However, there are many different ways in which neoliberal globalization discourse is contextualized in different regions or localities. In this chapter, I want to sketch some of the ways in which neoliberal globalist ideas emerged in contemporary Japanese political discourse. To do so, I will critically examine some dimensions of the recent Japanese political discourse labeled *kozo kaikaku*, "structural reform."

The current argument for *kozo kaikaku* was initiated in the 1980s by a group of conservatives and became a very fashionable topic in Japanese political arguments during the 1990s.[1] Although the concrete meaning of the notion of *kozo kaikaku* differs from theorist to theorist, central claims are common in most of the theories. First, proponents of *kozo kaikaku* argue that postwar Japanese society is characterized by its unique *kozo* (structure), which distinguishes it from the rest of the world. Second, they warn that the contemporary Japanese market system is experiencing paralysis because of this unique *kozo*. Finally, *kozo kaikaku* proponents conclude that this unique Japanese social structure should be totally revised to revitalize the free and proper functioning of the Japanese market.

So far as *kozo kaikaku* represents an attempt to reform Japanese society along free market models, there is good reason to believe that *kozo kaikaku* is one particular variation of the neoliberal globalist discourse that exists in the West. From a comparative perspective, however, there is one significant difference between the Western globalist discourse and the Japanese *kozo kaikaku* movement. Whereas Western globalist movements face strong opposition from both right and left, Japanese *kozo kaikaku* discourse has so far kept serious challenges from potential opponents to a minimum.

One good indication of the exceptional hegemony of *kozo kaikaku* discourse is exemplified by the rise of the Koizumi LDP (Liberal Democratic Party, i.e., Conservative) cabinet in 2001. Prime Minister Junnichiro Koizumi had enthusiastically advocated *kozo kaikaku* since the 1980s and was elected prime minister primarily because of his wholehearted commitment to *kozo kaikaku*. For a year following his accession to power in the spring of 2001, most opinion polls showed support for Koizumi running at nearly 80 percent, which was quite an astonishing figure in postwar Japanese history. Although the ratings have fluctuated between 70 percent and 40 percent since the beginning of 2002, they remain far higher than those of most other Japanese prime ministers in modern history.[2]

Koizumi faced no effective opposition or challenge, since people on his political right and left expressed support for the *kozo kaikaku* movement. For example, Yukio Hatoyama, a former leader of the Democratic Party (i.e., Egalitarian Liberal plus Liberal Socialist), once confessed in an official statement in the Diet that his party would remain friendly to Koizumi as long as he stuck to *kozo kaikaku*. Since this statement was made by the head of the largest party in opposition, most Japanese politicians took it as signifying hegemonic predominance of *kozo kaikaku* discourse.

In the rest of this chapter I will address the following questions: What is the ideological origin of current *kozo kaikaku* discourse? What is the central claim of *kozo kaikaku*, and how does it differ from Western neoliberal globalist discourse? Why are forces outside the neoliberal camp unable to organize an effective challenge to *kozo kaikaku*? What is the ideological impact of this exceptional hegemony of *kozo kaikaku*, especially on the formation of egalitarian social visions under current Japanese conditions?

This chapter challenges the prevalent view that current *kozo kaikaku* discourse is about the superficial adjustment of economic arrangements to cope with temporary economic conditions.[3] I argue that *kozo kaikaku* discourse involves a more profound struggle between old and new conservatives who have attempted to provide comprehensive social visions suitable to the cultural and political conditions of our time. I also intend to show that this conservative struggle contains an element of nationalism in the sense that both old and new conservatives compete for the nationalistic sentiments of the citizenry by manipulating dominant social symbols that define the Japanese position within the global market and community. In short, this chapter attempts to interpret *kozo kaikaku* as a conservative ideological movement that seeks to stabilize hierarchical social order through neoliberal institutional arrangements.

Given the exceptional hegemony of *kozo kaikaku* discourse, it is not accurate to reduce the issue of *kozo kaikaku* to the adjustment of economic arrangements. If *kozo kaikaku* were merely about the choice of economic arrangements, it would be quite unreasonable for the egalitarian liberals or socialists to support *kozo kaikaku*, however weak or reluctant their support may be. Therefore, it is crucial to note that *kozo kaikaku* theorists also provided an interesting analysis concerning the cultural and political conditions that made neoliberal globalization inevitable. It was not the neoliberal economic arrangements per se, but this underlying social analysis that secured some of the claims of the egalitarians and even those further left.

On the other hand, there is good reason to interpret the dynamics of *kozo kaikaku* discourse from the standpoint of manipulating dominant national symbols and identities. Indeed, features of *kozo kaikaku* can be best understood when analyzed as a variation of a nationalist movement. Many key notions or proposals of *kozo kaikaku* are vaguely defined in order to attract as many constituencies as possible, as is often the case with nationalist slogans. Moreover, like most other discursive nationalist formations, *kozo kaikaku* rests heavily on the emotional uses of political images and symbols in TV news shows or Internet broadcasting, rather than rational exchanges of words and ideas. Finally, and most importantly, as I will show in more detail in a later section of this chapter, some variations of *kozo kaikaku* discourse point to a more direct connection between their neoliberal social visions and nationalist features like militaristic expansion or discriminatory measures against foreign nationalities.[4]

Since *kozo kaikaku* constitutes a movement that blends neoliberal globalism with a nationalist discourse in a tactical way, I want to begin my argument with an analysis of the dominant conservative understanding of Japanese national identity that was prevalent in the 1960s and 1970s. A proper understanding of this old conservative discourse is necessary because, first and foremost, most arguments from the conservative camp concerning *kozo kaikaku* have aimed at a self-critique of this old conservative ideology. This old conservative discourse is also important because recent arguments from egalitarians and leftists attempt to refute some of its most important premises.

The Japanese Miracle and the Hegemony of
Old Conservative Ideology in the 1970s

Just before *kozo kaikaku* discourse began to take shape at the beginning of the 1980s, Japanese society as a whole enjoyed what it had achieved in its postwar recovery. At that time, the major role of the conservatives was to justify their hegemony by explaining the inevitability of this exceptional success. While Japan became one of the most important economic powers in the world market, there emerged a conservative nationalist discourse that attributed postwar prosperity to their rule.

Although each conservative theorist worked on several different concrete subjects, they all shared some common ideological ground. The first feature of this old conservative discourse was that it took the postwar pacifist constitution and the subsequent political reforms by the U.S. Occupation Forces as a given precondition for postwar conservative thinking. Ironically enough, the postwar constitution and subsequent democratization, which were totally hostile to the original orientation of the conservatives, made an indispensable contribution to the development of old conservative ideologies in two respects.

First, the pacifist constitution and its subsequent reforms made it possible for the conservatives to concentrate on postwar economic recovery. Even though their natural inclination was to opt for rearmament, postwar conservatives refrained from allocating too many resources for military expenditures due to the extremely pacifist constitution. In lieu of giving up their military aspirations, postwar Japanese conservatives relied primarily on U.S. defense power and concentrated their attention on economic recovery.[5] Second, Japanese conservatives at this early period used the postwar Japanese constitution as an arena for their postwar nationalist struggles. Conservatives highlighted the fact that the new constitution was "imposed" by the United States. Denouncing the status of Japan as a semisovereign nation until it could freely amend its constitution, conservatives succeeded in stirring up nationalist sentiments that had been embedded latently in the minds of many ordinary Japanese citizens.[6]

The second feature of the old conservative narrative was its preference for a statist cooperative relationship over competitive market mechanisms as the main social device for postwar recovery. There were several justifications for this preference among postwar Japanese conservatives. For one, due to the enormous scarcity of social resources in the recovery process, conservatives maintained that those resources should be allocated strategically by governmental guidance for the sake of efficiency. Moreover, conservatives embraced the Confucian tradition of regarding the public sphere as the ideal place for gifted people to show their abilities. Thus old conservatives were far more confident of the efficacy of public control than new conservatives are under the *kozo kaikaku* framework.[7]

In the process of implementing their statist political visions, old postwar conservatives devised a technique to accommodate their statist preference to the postwar democratic environment. Postwar conservatives needed to ensure that their emphasis on the state would not revive prewar Japanese authoritarian rule, which contained strong administrative prerogatives in its formal legal dimension. To do so, they developed an informal technique of statist control labeled "administrative guidance." They argued that governmental control over private spheres would not infringe on democratic principles so long as the private sector followed the intention of the government by anticipating its intent. Thus the conservative ruling class revealed its policy intentions through informal guidance and suggestions, not formal law or orders. While this technique helped accommodate conservative aspirations in the postwar democratic environment, it made postwar conservative rule susceptible to corruption because it let the politicians exert an arbitrary influence on administration under informal settings.[8]

The third and final feature of the old postwar conservative discourse was that it justified conservative dominance based on its quasi-egalitarian distributive effects. Even though the conservative LDP had monopolized power for more than three decades, they occasionally went along with some egalitarian claims that were initially raised by socialists and other opposition voices. Therefore, the LDP was once regarded as a most typical example of what party theory labeled "a catch-all party." Although the ultimate goal of old conservatives was to maintain hierarchical distribution, they also realized that a decent degree of parity among different social sectors was required to stabilize postwar democracy in the long run.[9]

According to the old conservative discourse, then, these quasi-egalitarian distributive tendencies resulted in one particularly important ideological and moral consequence—a peculiar ethic called *Ie* (Household) that developed under postwar conservative rule; it was in sharp contrast to a Western ethic of individualism. According to the ethics of *Ie*, most Japanese social institutions, from companies to government, are organized along the most cooperative and harmonious relationships within an idealized household. In Japanese social institutions, it was customary for the leaders to take some interests of the ordinary members into account even without the ordinary members' expressed demand, just as the patriarchical father is supposed to act on behalf of the family even when family members do not ask him to do so explicitly. By relying on this obvious Confucian image of the idealized household, old conservatives justified their postwar rule as reflecting at least a certain degree of interest on the part of social losers who for more than three decades did not have a chance to be in power.[10]

As should be clear from my analysis so far, the old conservative ideology contrasts with *kozo kaikaku* discourse in many significant respects. In addition to being a statist discourse, the old conservative discourse differs from *kozo kaikaku* in its isolationist and exceptionalist features. Indeed, three features I mentioned above point to some aspect of postwar Japanese social life that allegedly distinguishes it from the rest of the world. At times, conservatives requested that Japan be exempt from universal duties and obligations due to the serious social damages caused by the war. At other times, conservatives highlighted the Confucian tradition or collectivist ethics as a reason for special consideration.

Whatever the concrete arguments may have been, the old conservative discourse was an attempt to implement statist capitalism in a society where some special conditions applied. Luckily for the postwar conservatives, actual historical development seemed to prove their thesis of exceptionalism. Referring to the overwhelming economic growth, postwar conservatives could easily argue that their unique social vision was quite efficient and therefore worth holding on to.[11] In addition, old conservatives succeeded in discrediting postwar oppositional theorizing by pointing to the latter's inflexibility toward postwar Japanese conditions. According to old conservative discourse, oppositional arguments—like those made by socialists—did not pay enough attention to the particular needs and conditions of postwar Japan, and they remained too abstract and universalistic.

Kozo Kaikaku after the 1980s: Three Versions

So long as the postwar conservative ruling class succeeded in distributing at least some of the economic gains, most Japanese refrained from probing the limits of the old conservative discourse. However, when Japan experienced significant economic decline beginning in the 1980s suddenly there were good reasons for ordinary Japanese people to question some of the fundamental premises they used to accept without serious reservations.

LDP Prime Minister Yasuhiro Nakasone first presented a prototype argument of *kozo kaikaku* in the mid-1980s. A good friend of Margaret Thatcher and Ronald Reagan, Nakasone proposed privatization of major public sectors such as the national railway or telecommunication networks. In other words, he sought to introduce laissez-faire neoliberal elements into Japanese society.[12] Around the same time, the government's official reports concerning trade imbalances started referring to its neoliberal globalization discourse as *kozo kaikaku*. Since then, the notion of *kozo kaikaku* has received wide public recognition.

As *kozo kaikaku* discourse strengthened over time, it collected a number of serious ambiguities and conflicts. Using the label *kozo kaikaku*, different people have made different claims. Next, I divide these claims into three major variants. These three versions of *kozo kaikaku* discourse differ significantly from the old conservative ideology and offer a different justification for their neoliberal solutions.

The first version of *kozo kaikaku* discourse finds the major problem of old conservative rule to be its declining productivity and economic performance under new social circumstances. According to this variant, Japanese social structure should be reformed primarily because it prevents the Japanese mar-

210

ket from maintaining the same level of economic performance any longer. This is the view that is most commonly held by major economists who work for government or private think tanks.[13]

One important feature of this version of the *kozo kaikaku* argument is that its primary concern lies in improving economic performance. This means that there is no logical connection between achieving the final goal of this variation and adopting laissez-faire neoliberal economic arrangements. Proponents of this variation might even opt for statist policies that were endorsed by the old conservatives—at least as a temporal measure—if they contributed to the improvement of Japanese economic performance.

But even if proponents of this variant chose to endorse statist policies, they would still differ significantly from the old conservatives' policies in that they support different industrial sectors. Whereas the old conservatives focused on traditional heavy industries, the champions of *kozo kaikaku* support new industries such as information technology and biotechnology. As one commentator correctly pointed out, there is a good possibility that, under different technological constellations, *kozo kaikaku* might result in stronger state control of the market.[14]

Another important difference between this variation and the old conservative discourse lies in its distributive consequences. Whereas old conservatives highlighted the quasi-egalitarian distributive effects of their policies, champions of this *kozo kaikaku* variation tend to be silent about this topic. Some have even denounced egalitarianism as one of the "worst features" of the old conservative discourse. Given the fact that Western globalization discourse often makes the claim that "globalism benefits everyone," this retreat from egalitarianism is one of the most important features of Japanese *kozo kaikaku* discourse from a comparative perspective.[15]

The second variant of *kozo kaikaku* discourse recommends structural reform primarily because old conservative rule lacked democratic accountability. The proponents of this version strongly denounce the corruptive tendencies of old conservative politics and its underlying ethics of "the household" and attempt to revise them along lines that satisfy legalistic and individualistic accountability requirements to secure the preconditions for fair competition.

When *kozo kaikaku* discourse emerged in the 1980s, the major proponents of this version were foreign critics of Japanese society and Japanese business culture who denounced Japan for its excessively complicated customs system or other nonlegal barriers.[16] As the *kozo kaikaku* debate unfolded, however, a significant number of Japanese proponents of this view emerged. First developed by foreigners, this variant contained an element of cultural comparison calling into question the antidemocratic sociopolitical culture of postwar Japan and its underlying collectivist ethics. Indeed, in order to highlight the bias that is latent within its own culture, postwar Japanese society required critical voices from outside.

Another important feature of this version is that it best explains the reasons why egalitarians, as well as conservatives, support *kozo kaikaku* discourse. Indeed, some of the policies recommended by this variation have positive potential for the development of egalitarian politics under contemporary Japanese conditions. For example, one of the policies endorsed by this variant is information disclosure in government and the abolition of informal administration. Likewise, strengthened judicial review and equal opportunity for women were policy issues implemented by the proponents of this variant— policies long awaited by egalitarians. In addition, the implementation of these concrete policy proposals bolstered the standing of some egalitarian professionals whose specialist knowledge was indispensable in implementing these reform policies.[17]

The third version endorses *kozo kaikaku* discourse because of its moral effect in maintaining the nationalist aspirations of the Japanese people. This variant shares some common ground with the first version in starting with the diagnosis that the Japanese economy has been declining since the 1980s. However, whereas the first variant highlights only the economic consequences of recent changes, this variation emphasizes their political and cultural effects. The major concern of this version is to maintain Japanese national status and reputation in international society under the new circumstance of economic uncertainty.[18]

In order to satisfy their nationalistic aspirations, proponents of this version developed a sort of dualistic standard in terms of their foreign policy. In regard to Western industrial countries, the proponents of the third variant revise these policies along the lines of universal norms and standards. They concede that the rules and social customs unique to postwar Japanese society should be significantly revised as universalized norms and standards suggest.

This version rejects seeing most other Asian countries as equal partners with whom Japanese share universal norms and standards. Examples of this include Prime Minister Koizumi's official visit to Yasukuni Shinto shrine and the military actions of the Japanese Defense Force after September 11—in spite of strong opposition from Korea and China. In addition, a group of *kozo kaikaku* nationalists sought to justify Japanese World War II invasions in history textbooks. Finally, Japanese immigration policy toward Asian neighboring countries still remains far stricter compared with those of other major advanced countries.[19]

In order to justify these nationalistic policies toward Asian countries, the proponents of this variant refer to the significant changes in their attitudes toward Western societies. They argue that what made postwar Japanese conservatives relatively apologetic to Asian countries was the fact that postwar Japanese society remained a sort of semisovereign state that was exempt from universal regulations and obligations under the guardianship of the United States. Now that Japanese society has recovered full sovereignty by accepting universalized rules, there is no reason for Japanese conservatives to maintain self-restraint in terms of their nationalistic urges.[20]

As already noted, current Japanese discourse on *kozo kaikaku* is a mixture of mutually conflicting political visions. At times, each variant shares some common claims and endorses similar policies. However, this does not mean that the three versions are making the same claims at all times. In some important cases, they highlight different aspects of the new Japanese environment and suggest different conflicting policies.

What is important to note here is that the current popularity of *kozo kaikaku* discourse stems from the fact that the new conservatives are tactically conflating these many different faces of *kozo kaikaku* under one political label. Although the notion of *kozo kaikaku* contains many conflicting political claims, the current conservative ruling class is calculating enough to use the ambiguity in its favor. The new conservatives are gaining majority support by shifting popular attention from one aspect of *kozo kaikaku* to another. In particular, the fluctuating international situation after September 11 provides new conservatives a good opportunity to turn people's attention from the economic crisis to foreign affairs and the resurgence of nationalism.

Conclusion: Toward More Egalitarian Political Visions in the Age of Globalization?

I conclude by summarizing the features of *kozo kaikaku* discourse from a comparative perspective. There are a number of features that distinguish *kozo kaikaku* discourse from Western neoliberal globalist discourse. One feature that is entirely missing from Japanese *kozo kaikaku* discourse is the ideological claim that globalism benefits everyone. So long as *kozo kaikaku* is an attempt to retreat from old conservative quasi-egalitarianism, there is little reason for the *kozo kaikaku* proponents to justify their political visions from the standpoint of benefiting people.

The most distinctive feature of *kozo kaikaku* discourse is its strange marriage of nationalism and globalism. Whereas Western nationalists offer major criticisms of the neoliberal globalist discourse, Japanese nationalism often unfolds hand in hand with globalism.[21] In the process of justifying the alliance between these strange bedfellows, Japanese conservatives developed a dualist approach applying different standards to Asian and Western countries.

My emphasis on the nationalistic elements in *kozo kaikaku* discourse is important not only from a comparative perspective but also in showing what a possible Japanese egalitarian struggle might look like. So far as *kozo kaikaku* is a variation of nationalist discourse that contains contradictory claims under vague vocabulary, egalitarian critics can take advantage of many potential openings.

Such an egalitarian critique must begin with differentiating the many claims of *kozo kaikaku* and culminate in pointing to the internal contradictions and inconsistencies in conservative discourse. Specifically, egalitarians need to clarify that nationalist claims always hamper egalitarian concerns, whereas accountability claims serve egalitarian political purposes.

The conservative policies after September 11 tend toward the nationalist direction because many Western countries have requested a Japanese commitment to militarization and hence nationalism. Therefore, there is an urgent need for egalitarians to envision alternative policies. To be sure, growing numbers of Japanese citizens participate in single-issue protests such as antiwar demonstrations. However, the most pressing task for egalitarians is to provide an alternative political vision that helps convert these ad hoc frustrations into a more comprehensive, systematic critique of the *kozo kaikaku* globalization discourse.

Notes

I want to thank Mitsutoshi Ito, Ikuo Kume, and Jon Simons for their useful comments on earlier versions of this chapter.

1. For a more systematic account of what the Japanese government means by *kozo kaikaku*, see Economic Planning Agency, ed., *Kozo kaikaku no tameno keizai shakai keikaku: Katsuryoku aru keizai, annshinn dekiru kurashi* (Socioeconomic planning for *kozo kaikaku*: Towards an active economy and decent life) (Tokyo: Ministry of Finance Printing Bureau, 1995).

2. For an analysis of the exceptional support that the Koizumi cabinet received at the beginning of his rule, see Heisei Seron Kenkyu Kai and Ikuo Kabashima, "Hitsudoku no toshi yukensha chosa" (Must-see data survey among city voters), *Ronza*, July 2001, 40–59.

3. For a typical example that explains the emergence of *kozo kaikaku* discourse from the standpoint of the transition of the economic environment of Japanese society, see Yoshiyuki Mita, *Nihon keizai no kozo kaikaku: Jitsugen suru 21 seiki voluntary shakai* (Kozo kaikaku of Japanese economy: The realization of a voluntary society in the 21st century) (Tokyo: Chuou Keizai Sha, 2000), 1–45.

4. For an analysis of the symbolic manipulation of the Koizumi government, see Atushi Kusano, "'Makiko boom' to iu kiken na kasou genjistu" ('Makiko boom' as a dangerous virtual reality), *Ronza*, August 2001, 28–35.

5. A typical conservative understanding concerning the relationship between postwar Japanese pacifism, economic progress, and nationalism is elaborated in Junich Kyogoku, *Nihon no seiji* (Japanese politics) (Tokyo: University of Tokyo Press, 1983), 44–59.

6. It is often pointed out that the LDP never put forth a serious proposal for constitutional amendment during more than thirty years in power. This means

that postwar conservatives attempted to use the symbolic effect of claims for constitutional amendment.

7. The following literature best exemplifies these features of postwar Japanese bureaucracy. Kiyoaki Tsuji, *Shin pan: Nihon kanryo sei no kenkyu* (Studies on Japanese bureaucracy, new ed.) (Tokyo: University of Tokyo Press, 1969), 187–205.

8. For an analysis of Japanese informal administrative methodology from a comparative perspective, see Takehisa Nakagawa, "Administrative Guidance: A Tentative Model of How Japanese Lawyers Understand It," *Kobe University Law Review* 14 (1998): 1–20.

9. Seizaburo Sato and Tetsuhisa Matsuzaki, *Jiminto seiken* (Liberal Democratic Party government) (Tokyo: Chuo Koron, 1986), chaps. 1, 5.

10. Yasusuke Murakami et al., *Bunmei to shite no ie shakai* (Household society as a civilization) (Tokyo: Chuo Koron, 1979). The following best exemplifies the relation between the collectivist ethics and success of postwar Japan: Eshun Hamaguchi and Shumpei Kumon, eds., *Nihono teki shudan shugi* (Collectivism in a Japanese style) (Tokyo: Yuhikaku, 1982).

11. For a classical explanation of the postwar Japanese success from exceptionalist perspectives, see Chalmers Johnson, *The MITI and the Japanese Miracle* (Stanford: Stanford University Press, 1982).

12. The following provides detailed analysis of the privatization project of the Nakasone cabinet and its ideological background: Jun Iio, *Mineika no seiji katei: Rincho gata kaikaku no seika to genkai* (Political process of privatization: The promises and limits of committee politics) (Tokyo: University of Tokyo Press, 1993), 222–98.

13. The following best exemplifies the productivity variation of the *kozo kaikaku* argument: Kazuo Yoshida, *Hatan suru nihon zaisei: Naze zaisei kozo kaikaku ga hitsuyou ka?* (Japanese fiscal system in crisis: Why is *kozo kaikaku* inevitable?) (Tokyo: Ookura Zaimu Kyokai, 1997).

14. Yukio Yanbe, *"Kozo kaikaku" to iu gensou: Keizai kiki kara dou dasshutsu suruka* (A phantom "kozo kaikaku": How to escape from the economic crisis) (Tokyo: Iwanami, 2001).

15. See Manfred B. Steger, *Globalism: The New Market Ideology* (Lanham, Md.: Rowman & Littlefield, 2002), chap. 3.

16. Although the following does not resort to the notion of *kozo kaikaku*, it proposes drastic reform along the lines suggested by the accountability argument: Karl von Wolferen, *The Enigma of Japanese Power: People and Politics in a Stateless Nation* (New York: Vintage, 1990).

17. A representative figure who is committed to *kozo kaiakaku* from an egalitarian perspective is Kohei Nakabou, a former president of the Japan Bar Association. For the role of Nakabou and other egalitarians in the *kozo kaikaku* movement, see Akira Amakawa and Toshiki Odanaka, *Chiho jichi/shiho kaikaku* (Local autonomy/legal reform) (Tokyo: Shogakkan, 2001).

18. For a typical expression of this variation, see Eisuke Sakakibara, *Shin seiki heno kozo kaikaku: Shinpo kara kyousei he* (*Kozo kaikaku* toward the new century: From progress to coexistence) (Tokyo: Yomiuri Newspaper Publishers, 1997).

19. For a reactionary proposal that aims to maintain restrictive immigration policy in spite of globalization and the declining Japanese birth rate, see Nishio Kanji, *Shiso no shutsugen* (The emergence of thoughts) (Tokyo: Toyo Keizai Shinpo, 1994), 60–100. Nishio is also committed to another extremist movement aiming to publish a school textbook that denies the existence of Japanese genocide in China during World War II. Kanji Nishio, *Atarashii rekishi kyoukasho* (New textbook of Japanese history) (Tokyo: Fusou, 2001).

20. See Norihiro Kato, *Haisengo ron* (Thoughts after the defeat in war) (Tokyo: Kodansha, 1997).

21. For the relationship between nationalism and globalism in the West, see Steger, *Globalism*, 86–104.

GLOBAL ORDER AND THE HISTORICAL STRUCTURES OF *DAR AL-ISLAM*

MOHAMMED A. BAMYEH

As a universalist religion, Islam is already part of a very old formula of globalization. Many commentators have sought to outline how global processes were fostered historically through precepts of the faith, religious affiliations, and political systems brought about by Islam.[1] My aim in this chapter is not to argue again that Islam historically encouraged expansive processes with strong affinities to contemporary globalization, nor to suggest, as many have, that contemporary Islamic resurgence, in its various forms, is promoted by the globalization of economic, political, and cultural networks. These are valid points, but what is sorely missing from much of the discussion on Islam in the global order is an answer to the question of whether the historical experience of the former informs the latter. In other words, does the historical career of the *dar al-Islam* teach us something about basic structures that any humane global system would be expected to adopt as its operational logic?

The Muslim world, or *dar al-Islam* as it was historically known to Muslims, could function *as a unit* only to the extent that it adhered to three fundamental principles, one political, the other social, and the third cultural—partial control, free movement, and cultural heteroglossia—which I will comment on shortly. The further argument is that these principles are not strictly "historical,"

217

that is, they represent features of an antiquated system and basic norms with which *any* global system could function with maximal systematization and minimal interruption. Thus it is not too surprising to see that these principles are analogous in spirit to some emerging conceptions today regarding how to construct a *modern* global system characterized by maximal systematization and minimal interruption, while at the same time remaining nonimperialistic. In its general patterns, globalization today can be regarded as an attempt, so far inconclusive, to *return* from the age of nation-states and colonial power politics to older political, social, and cultural concepts that once regulated and humanized a well-connected global life. In this sense globalization is a very old story that is yet to be fully remembered.

The three principles listed above persisted remarkably well throughout Islamic history, with many occasional interruptions, the latest and most enduring of which occasion the modern colonial epoch and the formation of modern states. The vitality and remarkable career of these principles had, as I hope will become apparent, little to do with the "benevolence" or conscious strategies of any particular government or sovereign in Islamic history. Frequently they persisted *against* the expressed wishes of governments, which until the modern period had no means by which to establish total control, prohibit population movements, or impose common cultural orthodoxies.

During the epoch of colonialism and then the nation-state systematic attempts were made to replace these principles, which had provided global Islam historically with its convivial nature.[2] Yet only well-organized conviviality, conducive to global commerce and predictability, was replaced, with nervous systems that relied on violence and power as primary guaranteeing mechanisms of predictability. Those mechanisms, costly as they are, were not as efficient in reaching their goal as much as older patterns that seem loaded with medieval features of social organization. In what follows, I elaborate on how each of the three principles operated historically and conclude by suggesting how each may be in the process of being reinvoked today as a pillar of global life.

Partial Control

Until the reforms of Mohammad Ali in early-nineteenth-century Egypt, which were intended to strengthen the state in the face of European incursions, the Egyptian state exemplified a pattern of partial control that had typified Muslim polities throughout history and distinguished them from European city- and then nation-states. Unlike European states, which especially since the nineteenth century came to be seen as ultimate organizing embodiments of society, the Islamic state was historically regarded (by constituents and rulers alike) as only *one* among several sources of legitimate authority in society. Its control was territorially limited to major cities. Beyond the cities but sometimes even within them control had to be shared with other networks of religious authorities, tribal notables, merchant guilds, Sufi orders, and vast networks of extended families.[3]

Even in Egypt, the process of *étatisation* of society was never fully successful, as many recent studies reveal,[4] in spite of the major inroads and massive investment in and by state institutions since the Nasser period. Elsewhere the state record in its attempt to impose control involves a variety of untenable or unsuccessful experiments. In places like Saudi Arabia and Iraq, for example, the state expanded into society through a mixture of extreme repression and patronage, both facilitated by an accidental advantage accruing to state elites (such as oil revenue). This has led to a highly contested state whose parasitic nature over society could only be confirmed by its behavior, governed as it was more by conspiratorial than strategic thinking. In other places, where state elites did not have the unique advantage of sudden income, to various degrees the historical pattern of partial control holds: the state is regarded as one actor among many in society, and the state knows that fact even as it must claim otherwise.[5] States that accept this feature, such as Yemen, survive, and those that do not, such as Somalia under Ziad Berri or Afghanistan under Hafizullah Amin, do not.

Historically, the principle of partial control involves predictable structures, many of which are considered by some prominent sociologists to be antithetical to modernity.[6] Although they were not expected to survive modernity, they did, albeit in truncated, less organized, and unpredictable—*less civic*—forms. One of the most sustained explorations of the principle of partial control is Roy Mottahedeh's study of the Buyid dynasty. Under the nominal tutelage of declining 'Abbasids, it assumed control of Persia and Iraq during the tenth and eleventh centuries. The image of that society provided by Mottahedeh is one of natural fragmentation into status, occupational, clan, and other groups. Such a society strove for the kind of governance that provided a semblance of general order and legitimate arbitration, not unity.

As a rule, the preeminent requirement of governance was to ensure a particular notion of law and order or, as its constituents understood it, "justice." This notion, in turn, had a meaning appropriate for a society accustomed to partial rather than total controls. As Mottahedeh explains it, "justice" then meant not so much applying the "law" as *balancing* various interests, so that no one of them would impose itself on the others. This conception of justice is significant because it supposes a specific nature of governing. Far from embodying society or representing its collective mission, as it would under nationalism, for example, the Buyid state could in effect only be ruled over by *outsiders*. In a fragmented society that saw its fragmentation as natural and necessary rather than an obstacle to be overcome, the necessary balancing could only be performed by an impartial arbitrator who, by definition, could only be an outsider to all concerned groups.

This process of forming "society" through the influence of outsiders has

typified practically the entirety of Islamic history. In the first real Islamic community—Medina under Muhammad—we could already see this dynamic of a
transtribal *umma* being formed by an outsider. Muhammad succeeded bril-
liantly in Medina, where the conflictual tribes, needing common adjudication,
all expressed faith in Islam before even seeing the prophet, who at that point
had absolutely no more prospects in his hometown of Mecca. In other words,
a transtribal society could be built only by someone with an ideology transcending the particularities of any specific tribes.

The success of early Islam consisted to a great extent in its ability to graft a
common spiritual language on all transtribal, voluntary public spaces of the
pre-Islamic era in Arabia. All pre-Islamic institutions of peace, trade, and civic
life that had been organized above the level of the tribe, such as the *haram* of
Mecca, the pilgrimage, and the sacred months, were simply absorbed into
Islam. Even more remarkably, Islam incorporated such common spaces without elaborating a clear doctrine of a *common state*. In a way, this combination—
unifying the institutions of public life under a common religious discourse but
leaving the question of government open—corresponded to a society that was
familiar with the principle of partial control, had already developed an institutional life corresponding to it, and needed only a mechanism of impartial arbitration to guarantee its functioning. Beyond that, there is no evidence anywhere in early Islamic history that a "state" as such or total control of society
and panoramic supervision of social life was anyone's intention.

Even as it developed later, the Islamic state violated the principle of partial
control at its own peril. It found itself sharing control over society with diverse
groups, each with its own distinctive organizational mode and operational logic.
These groups consisted of cross-cleavages of various interests, each with a def-
inite type of social experience and mode of social organization, and a specific
type of relation to other types of groups in public life. Until the modern period,
significant social categories that ameliorated the possibilities of total control
over society by a central state included tribes, millets, families, urban notables
(*a'yan*), merchants, professional guilds, and the learned networks (*'ulama*).
Indeed, it was out of the first attempt by an imperial Islamic state, the 'Abbasids,
to establish total control by imposing a single orthodoxy (833–848 A.D.) that
the state learned its limits.[7] It scarcely repeated that error thereafter because it
did not wish to hear again that the true heirs to the prophet could be nonstate
social categories (e.g., the learned men, *'ulama*, who indeed made that claim)—
and by implication denying a monopoly over that honorific to the caliph.

Free Movement

Corollary to the principle of partial control was a principle of free movement
of pilgrims, adventurers, merchants, and various communities throughout the

massive *dar al-Islam*, although the Islamic world was divided between various political centers of power for most of its history. Travel eased demographic pressures (thereby alleviating social troubles), offered vital channels of communication among intellectual communities, provided for a distinct global civil society forged across the great urban centers (nominally under the jurisdiction of different sovereigns), and endowed especially the cities with a vibrant multicultural fabric. The great literary product of this principle can be appreciated in the *Thousand and One Nights*, in which the protagonists are more often on the road to one destination or another than at home.

The principle of free movement ignored "borders," which may have meant a great deal to sovereigns but were given as little attention as possible by the populations on the move. A *strong* idea of "borders," as would be attempted by nation-states, was not compatible with the notion of a global *umma* whose domain was defined more by ideational than political expansion. The latter of course usually helped the former, but even in that case, conquests were rarely conducted "in the name of the king (or queen)," as they would be for Europeans, but exclusively in the name of Islam and of God.

Like the principle of partial control, the principle of free movement originated in dynamics having little to do with the foresight or planning of governments and sovereigns. The Muslim world in effect inherited the territorial space of older world systems. Conversion to Islam in many places, most obviously in central Africa and Southeast Asia, resulted from an exogenous expansion of trade and an indigenous desire to surround connections with global trade partners with a binding ethical cosmos. Islam was primarily an urban religion appealing most immediately, although not exclusively, to the classes involved in long-distance trade (Muhammad was a merchant before becoming a prophet).

Apart from these preconstitutive factors, the principle of free movement by its nature fostered the further evolution of networks engraved in the fabric of deep reality. One of these was common educational and mannerist expectations, which allowed for the easy circulation of at least the elites. Thus Ibn Battuta, one of the most famous of travelers in Islamic history, could be trained as a judge in Morocco and find employment as far away as India. The principle of free movement mixed elements of social experience, so that a traveler could in the same voyage act as a merchant, at another time as a pilgrim, an adventurer, or a paramour.

The ultimate outcome was the creation of a global civil society maintained through various networks connecting the great urban centers of the Islamic world. Many such networks forged together the learned communities,[8] establishing global spaces for the dissemination of discourses and debates in philosophy, the sciences, mathematics, ethics, legal rules, and theology. Another type of network connected merchant cultures in ways that were both extraordinarily complex and predictable. Several prominent historians, such as S. D. Goitein,

Janet Abu-Lughod, Bishara Doumani, Soraiya Faroqhi, and Leila Tarazi Fawaz, have sought to uncover various patterns and structures of these networks. Through these efforts more is being learned about the patterns of connection among at least merchant communities in the Islamic world. Some of these studies focus on macroprocesses and structures, while others attempt to uncover larger dynamics of connectivity out of a detailed focus on a specific local setting. It is impossible to summarize the rich range of these works here, but what is evident is that global merchant networks throughout the Islamic world were facilitated by a number of regular institutions—caravans,[9] caravanseries, credit arrangements, agents. The rules of these institutions were well-known to all participants, and their regularity presupposed movement that was not only free but regulated by collective institutions designed to protect from or ensure against the perils of road and sea.

What is obvious insofar as the political tutelage over trade routes throughout the Islamic world is concerned is that such routes defined, as well as lent legitimacy to, imperial systems, even though they did not depend on the imperial system safeguarding them possessing *any feature other than willingness to respect free movement*. The practical inescapability of the principle of free movement in an urban-centered Islamic world whose wealth was derived substantially from trade ensured the demise of any political system that sought to suffocate it.[10] In the same way that Islamic empires inherited older global trade routes, Mongols did the same from the Muslims for a while, and the eventual Portuguese, Dutch, and English powers grafted themselves on older routes while nourishing new ones.

There was nothing specifically "Islamic" about trade and its routes, only the addition of a common ethical and ideational cosmos to an already very old conception of free movement. The later European idea of "free trade" registered a *retreat* from that richer notion of free movement. In the notion of "free trade," as opposed to "free movement," the primary impulse is given to self-interest and avarice, and those were placed on the same ethical plane that had hitherto been allocated to a notion of free movement safeguarded by common ethical identity and, when this was not available, common mannerist expectations of civilized life and common nonstate institutions.

Heteroglossia

Since its origins, Islam has stereotypically been understood (by both its defenders and detractors) as a house of harmony and perfect social order.[11] However, Islam operated in the spiritual, legal, moral, and political realms as a highly hybrid and varied practice.[12] The overemphasized Sunni "orthodoxy" of mainstream Islam lived at peace with a more "customary" Islam,[13] in which various folk traditions were intermingled. It also lived with a diversity of schools and interpretive juridical modes that spawned various novel supplements to the "tradition" under the practice of *ijtihad*.

This crucial property of Islam requires clarification. The term "heteroglossia" was coined in the 1930s by the Russian literary scholar Mikhail Bakhtin, which he used to analyze how the same literary work (usually a realist novel) habituated a multiplicity of voices representing various social standpoints. There are two interrelated ways in which this formulation could be expanded to account for larger discourses, such as religion. The first concerns a distinction between "heteroglossia" and "diversity," the second the social unconscious of religion.

Heteroglossia is not simple diversity in the sense that the community of believers does not regard itself as diverse as it may objectively be. As Bakhtin outlines it, voices in the novel inhabit the same narrative space when they emanate from a diversity of social locations and interests. "Diversity," the term we are more used to, would in this case describe a condition in which a variety of narratives compete to tell their own story, whereas "heteroglossia" describes a condition in which a single narrative imposes order, *but not unity*, on the variety of voices within it. Heteroglossia is unity imagined, diversity is disunity proclaimed. The former allows particular voices to express themselves as if they were the voices of all; the latter allows particular voices to express themselves largely to those that are alike. Each is a different game of social communication, but the basic difference is that while diversity is recognizable at the borderlines of communities, heteroglossia is the unrecognized, and thus *unconscious*, property of the community. It is due to these properties that heteroglossia, unlike diversity, is better equipped to escape repression or censorship. Likewise, it is also due to these properties that heteroglossia is better equipped to advance toward universalism—*its only cause*.

Islam is not the only belief system with heteroglossic properties. What concerns us here is how these properties evolved to become indispensable for the social life of the faith. No ideology that hopes to become universal can escape heteroglossia. Already at its founding phase, during Muhammad's own lifetime, Islam transformed from a local, Mecca-centered tradition into a universal belief system incorporating the interests and viewpoints of various social groups, classes, tribes, and styles of life.[14] The point of departure was identified with Muhammad's *Hijra* into Medina—in effect abandoning his hometown, Mecca, which had resolutely rejected his prophetic claims, for a larger world. That event commenced not only a transformation in the social *composition* of the Muslim community, but also in the Qur'anic text itself, which in its Medinian phase becomes far more elaborate in expounding legal and ethical rules in response to a *variety* of new social situations, issues, and problems. The early classic Muslim commentaries were well aware of this multiple situatedness of the holy text, and the fact that Islam began its global career in Medina rather than Mecca is indicated by Muslims everywhere in the commencement of the Islamic calendar with Muhammad's *migration*, rather than, say, his birth or even his first revelations.

That a *variety* of social forces and interests imagined themselves to be the addressees of a single divine message meant that the further expansion of Islam worldwide could only do more of the same. Thus Islam in its long history could simultaneously be used to justify revolutions advocating communist equality; others defending inequalities of wealth. Movements opposed any political authority not explicitly consented to by the *umma*; others praised the virtues of despotic rule. Practices oriented toward mystical Sufism; opposing doctrines required rational theological sobriety. Gender inequality was defended, *as well as* gender equality. Economic doctrines oriented toward the interests of the merchant class; others highlighted the needs of the poor. Sayings, all attributed to the prophet, praised austerity and modesty; others, likewise attributed to the prophet, defended the rights of the wealthy to live ostentatiously. And so on.

The point is that this variety of points of stress, standpoints, and special interests do not devolve into a sense of infinite chaos, regardless of how seemingly infinite the range of possibilities may be. It is indeed a remarkable property of heteroglossic systems to ensure precisely against this possibility, at the same time as they advance further and further along the path of universal recruitment of souls and establish themselves deeper and deeper into the fabric of deep history with every passing century of their existence. Thus religion appears much older and much vaster than any soul that is implicated in it. So much so that the soul has less of an incentive to see itself imprisoned by a vast time-space horizon, than to realize the practical advantage it could accrue by drawing on the heteroglossic resources already at its disposal. In doing so, whether its course takes it to where it wishes to be or allows it to resist impositions or persist in their face, that soul only *adds more* to an already inexhaustible reservoir of heteroglossia.

Just like the two previous principles—partial control and free movement—heteroglossia thrives best when existing authorities do not have sufficient power to impose orthodoxies, whether against avowed heterodoxies or hidden ones, as attempted by the Inquisition (which has no real parallel in Islamic history, apart from the *Mihna* of 833–848). It is a propensity of all large global systems to give at least an occasional rise to calls for strong ruling authority. However, the universalist potentials of the system, which are possible only through heteroglossia rather than force, survive best when the system itself includes the possibilities of strong egalitarian claims. This was one of the great features of historical as well as contemporary Islam, in which a central tenet highlights the *equality* of the believers and, as an extension of this principle, rejects excessive authority claims to religious or political authorities. The fact that such authorities seek to subvert that principle is attributable more to the nature of state-

or empire-centered political life than to the universalist properties of the faith. It is those and *not state politics* that are heteroglossic *by necessity*.

Conclusion

There are two points to be made in conclusion. One concerns what happened or is happening in the Islamic world since these principles were violated in modern history. The second concerns larger questions of globalization today in light of the historical experience of *dar al-Islam*. Whether something analogous to the three structures outlined here could emerge in order to foster a humane style of global order—which of course would not use the term "Islam"—in the final analysis it is the *structures* that matter, not their name.

In much of the Muslim world, the three principles identified here mutually reinforced each other through a delicate yet remarkably stable balance for several centuries. When they were violated in modernity, no subsequent system managed to replace the sense of systematization, certitudes, predictability, and conviviality they once provided. Rather, the colonial epoch was generally followed, especially in the Middle East, with an unusual period of almost uniform authoritarianism of a new and highly intrusive kind. It is possible that this period is coming to an end currently, but the dynamics involved in nourishing authoritarianism are all implicated in the direct challenge posed to the three fundamental principles of *dar al-Islam* since and after colonialism. Some commentators, like Richard Bulliett, argue that authoritarian states in the Middle East became possible only after Islam was *weakened* by colonialism. "Islam" functioned historically as an equivalent to the concept of "the people" in the West—the discourse most appropriate for limiting the tyrannical tendencies of the state.[15]

It is far from obvious that contemporary Islamic social movements are capable of restoring these principles. Invariably, however, they address themselves to the failures of the postcolonial state, and their increased popularity points to a widespread sense that society will resolve its manifold modern problems only if it reverts to some sense of "authenticity." This is not the same as anti-modernity, but in effect the opposite.[16] It is an attempt to introduce modernity in ways that do not seem coercive or imposed by illegitimate, unaccountable, or outside forces whose expressions of concern for the well-being of the *umma* are unlikely to be believed. Unlikely, that is, not out of some "traditional" intractability; it is just that the track record of imperialism *demonstrating* its care for those it invades is simply not there.

Humane facets of globalization today could only be expected to mimic in some way the same historical principles of *dar al-Islam* outlined here. Mimic, that is, because I suspect that the Islamic experience was not unique in foster-

ing global systems fashioned by basic and therefore historically recurrent principles for the social organization of global life. First, the principle of partial control points to a present possibility, namely, a global system run by a multiplicity of centers, which include states, suprastate institutions, transnational
bureaucracies, and civil society groups in their various permutations. The principle of partial control indicates two facts that are already creeping into the
scene: first, no one actor controls the system as a whole. Second, within existing domains of "sovereignty" (i.e., states) other forces are being accepted as
alternatives or partners to the state, and these include both internal nonstate
actors as well as transnational institutions.

The principle of free movement is also part of this emerging picture,
although in an even less developed form than the principle of partial control.
So far the principle is being applied to the "free movement" of capital, goods,
and even services, far more than to people. In some places, however, such as
the European Union, the logic of free movement is reaching a fuller maturity:
the free movement of people is a natural corollary to the free movement of
things in general. Saskia Sassen has long argued that people simply follow in
their own movement pathways already opened up by the movement of capital.
The fact that we speak of immigration as a "problem" indicates that our analysis of global realities lags behind its realities: if a global economy invites the
free movement of things and further ensconces that freedom as its primary act
of faith, it will be impossible to separate people from their things. When this
movement is made illegal, it will violate legality and go on. Global order, after
all, does not consist only of that which is allowed.

Finally, it is already apparent that something we may call "global culture" is
beginning to take shape, and much has already been written about it. Whether
it will take a large heteroglossic form as in the case of Islam cannot be definitely
answered here, but what is clear is that we are already beginning to see global
social movements combining very different attitudes under the mantle of overarching, intercommunicative discourses, for example, global feminism, global
human rights approaches, or global peace movements. But even more remarkably, we still have the very old forces of religious faith now arguing for an appropriately larger expansion of the old heteroglossic field. For example, Muhammad Shahrur argues that Islam must now be considered simply another name
for universal humanism, so that even those who do not identify as Muslims can
be regarded as such if they subscribe to a basic, undemanding, and uncompli-
cated moral code. Farid Esack identifies as a central quest of our times the battle within every society of the forces of materialism against the forces of spiritu-
ality, not the battle of East versus West.

Can we have a different style of global order? Certainly, and currently there
is an attempt to articulate a very different world order, which is also informed,
or claims to be informed, by history. It is called imperialism. Living in Wash-

ington as I write this, I find it remarkable that advocates of this imperialism actually use this term with no apparent sense of impropriety. The idea is of course very old, and so is the logic. From an imperial perspective, global systems require central control, which could be accomplished unilaterally rather than through the consent of the world being controlled. It is in the nature of this imperialism to be immune to the argument that the world could be organized differently. The reason for this deafness is simple: no global power that feels a sense of unique supremacy has ever resisted the temptation to regard the world at large as its proper object of control.

This imperial logic likewise negates the two other principles. It is only a small step from the illusion that total control is possible to the illusion that movement of people and things can be policed through, as it is now called with no apparent sense of Orwellian irony, a "total information awareness" system. The notion that the system can be fully supervised is a logical extension of the notion that it can with unilateral effectiveness dictate what is allowed and what is not. If an imperial system is already prefigured in its perception of success against older imperial adversaries, it is unlikely to be impressed by the failures of control, failures that it is more likely to regard as licenses for amassing more power than as opportunities for adjusting to reality. For example, its conviction of the possibility of total control deludes it into sincerely believing that a policy of "zero tolerance" to narcotics is both viable and essential—in the face of decades of evidence that the demand for narcotics is irrepressible. In this sense a "zero tolerance" stance illustrates not how a great power deals with one isolated problem. It is rather an epigraph for power insatiable with any limit. Insatiable, because it sincerely believes that the world cannot be run otherwise.

The same also holds in regard to global culture. Former empires, including Islamic ones, sought, whenever they felt they had the power to do it, to impose orthodoxy or inspect the inner beliefs of people. Even so, we see underpinning imperial behavior a sense that global order must reach a certain cultural finality. In recent times, many American commentators were puzzled by public opinion polls in Islamic counties showing majorities opposing U.S. policies while at the same time being relatively friendly or nonchalant toward what is called "American culture."[17] The puzzlement had to do with the interpretive logic of imperialism. From its point of view, global culture lends credence to global power, and therefore such a culture, to the extent it is needed, leads to an identification with its politics rather than to heteroglossia.

At this stage we seem to have one of two choices, and it is time that we indicate clearly that they are not the same: imperialism or globalization. It is time we finally recognize clearly that the latter does not presume the former. I have elsewhere highlighted the difference between the two.[18] Imperialism may at certain historical junctures act as a "rational" force, when its work is in tandem with larger voluntaristic processes in the economy and culture, but it can also be "irrational," that is, when its behavior is determined more by a sense of absolute power and is less anchored in larger economic and cultural processes. The lessons from the historical structures of the Islamic world I sought to outline here suggest how a world civilizational order might be possible. In all likelihood such an order would be far more humane and negotiable than is the case when sovereigns think that they have the power to actually attempt what Hegel only imagined. He did not call it "imperialism" then, nor did his more contemporary students. But it is possible to call it that, because if we consider how global orders existed before, we realize that history does not end with global order. Only an imperial vision can fantasize about such an impossible prospect. It is perhaps in the nature of empires, after all, to imagine that history ends with them. But as we know, history cannot end because it really exists only to carry out a very simply task: to ensure that in due time all are buried, the great and the small.

Notes

1. For a conceptual summary, see Mohammed A. Bamyeh, *The Ends of Globalization* (Minneapolis: University of Minnesota Press, 2000).

2. For a justification of the term "convivial Islam," see Olivier Roy, *The Failure of Political Islam* (Cambridge: Harvard University Press, 1994).

3. Afghanistan was the last remaining example of this kind of state in recent history. It was finally unsettled by the overthrow of the king and subsequent turmoil in the 1970s. The carnage brought about by the attempt at full control was magnified to cataclysmic proportions as the country became a battle ground of superpowers and other outside powers.

4. For recent studies, see Diane Singerman, *Avenues of Participation: Family, Politics, and Networks in Urban Quarters of Cairo* (Princeton: Princeton University Press, 1995); Lisa Anderson, *The State and Social Transformation in Tunisia and Libya, 1830–1980* (Princeton: Princeton University Press, 1986).

5. During a 2002 visit to Georgetown University, former prime minister of Yemen Abdolkarim Al-Eryani freely acknowledged that on frequent occasions tribes regard the Yemeni state as just another tribe, albeit one with more resources, but nonetheless one with which they negotiate in the same reciprocal way tribes negotiate with each other.

6. This view is quite preponderant in the literature. For a good example, see Anthony Giddens, *The Consequences of Modernity* (Stanford: Stanford University Press, 1990).

7. For an elaboration of this episode, see John Kelsay, "Civil Society and Government in Islam," in *Islamic Political Ethics: Civil Society, Pluralism, and Conflict*, ed. Sohail Hashmi (Princeton: Princeton University Press, 2002); Dale F. Eickel-

man and Jon W. Anderson, "Redefining Muslim Publics," in *New Media in the Muslim World: The Emerging Public Sphere*, ed. Dale F. Eickelman and Jon W. Anderson (Bloomington: Indiana University Press, 1999).

8. Some recent attempts are being made to chart out such network. For example, see John Voll, "Islam as a Special World-System," *Journal of World History* 5, no. 2 (1994): 213–26.

9. Some historians like Faroqhi emphasize the role of imperial governments in organizing such collective ventures as the pilgrimage caravans. This does not, however, contradict the fact that free movement was organized by voluntary associations in other cases, nor does it suggest that they would have been impossible without governmental effort. Particularly in the case of pilgrimage caravans, governments obviously sought legitimacy out of supporting the venture.

10. The comments of Ibn Battuta on the Mongol invasion are significant here because they depart from the usual pattern of supporting Muslim rulers fighting infidels. Rather, Ibn Battuta blames the invasion directly on efforts by Muslim rulers in Iraq and Persia to disrupt trade routes. See Ibn Battuta, *Voyages d'ibn Battuta* (1325–1353; Paris: Éditions Anthropos, 1969), 3:23–24.

11. For a good example of the defensive attitude, see William Montgomery Watt, *Islam and the Integration of Society* (Evanston: Northwestern University Press, 1961).

12. For a portrayal of how Islam succeeded as a social movement at its point of inception precisely because it could accommodate that diversity, see Bamyeh, *The Social Origins of Islam* (Minneapolis: University of Minnesota Press, 1999).

13. For a justification of the term "customary Islam," see Charles Kurzman's introduction to *Liberal Islam* (New York: Oxford University Press, 1998).

14. For a detailed exposition of this process, see Bamyeh, *Social Origins of Islam*.

15. Richard Bulliet, "Twenty Years of Islamic Politics," *Middle East Journal*, Spring 1999.

16. For an explication of this point, see Mohammed A. Bamyeh, "Dialectics of Islam and Global Modernity," *Social Analysis* 43, no. 3 (2002).

17. See numbers and analysis in the reports by James J. Zogby, *What Arabs Think: Values, Beliefs, and Concerns* (Utica, N.Y.: Zogby International, 2002); John Zogby, *The 10 Nation "Impressions of America" Poll Report* (Utica, N.Y.: Zogby International, 2002).

18. See Bamyeh, *Ends of Globalization*, chap. 2.

THE EMPEROR'S MAP: LATIN AMERICAN CRITIQUES OF GLOBALISM

Eduardo Mendieta

Much of what ideologies say is true, and would be ineffectual if it were not, but ideologies also contain a good many propositions which are flagrantly false, and do so less because of some inherent quality than because of the distortions into which they are commonly forced in their attempts to ratify and legitimate unjust, oppressive political systems.[1]

There are many globalizations, all of which are not always in accord at any given time. Sometimes, some globalizations work against others. Generally, some globalizations are not simultaneous with others. Globalization is not global at once and all over. This internal heterogeneity breeds conflict, as well as other perspectives on globalization. A way to deal with this internal heterogeneity of globalization has been to introduce lexical markers: globalization, globalism, planetarization, mundalization, and so on.[2] The globalization of globalization is a result of a conflict over who gets to define which globalization is assumed to be both inevitable and desirable. Some of the issues about which globalization gets to be globalized have been addressed in terms of globalization's relationship to modernity, postmodernity, postcolonialism, and most recently post-occidentalism.[3]

What is common to all of these geopolitical macrotemporal markers (modernity, postmodernity, postcolonialism, etc.) is that like Foucault's panopticon they seek to survey, monitor, and ultimately regiment the world in accordance with a *chronotope* that is immune to questioning and unassailable by historization.[4] To avoid perpetuating the imperial designs and fantasies that underwrite these chronotopologies, it is necessary to make explicit how this new chronotopological (or what I call geopolitical metatemporal) marker relates to a "civilizational" mission that has come to define the West and its others. Unveiling the relationship between globalization and the West's millennial civilizational mission may proceed by way of addressing the following questions: So long as there are many globalizations and not all of them are global simultaneously, what globalization is imagined? Who imagines it? In what image, metaphor, or trope is this imagined globalization imagined? And where, in geopolitical space-time, is located this imagining agent imaging his or her imagined globalization?

Following up on Edward Said's incursion into these questions,[5] I argue in this chapter that within the logic of globalization—to which belongs the simultaneous westernization and orientalization of the world—the West has had to imagine itself as it never was. In other words, within the logic of globalization—within the contestation and drawing of battle lines, in which the goal is to globalize a certain globalization—the West has never been Western, although the West has been undergoing westernization. In other words, the struggle about globalization is a struggle about what the West will be, about what type of westernization to which we should submit not just the "others" of the West, but also the West itself.

In order to approach my subject, I will focus most specifically on the way in which the United States has become the main agent and vendor of a certain type of globalization, which it peddles in and imposes over the world, while arguing that this is both the health and future of the West and the best the West has to bequeath itself and humanity. More concretely still, I will focus on the relationship between the United State and Latin America in order to approach the way in which the United States has positioned itself as, and at the vanguard of, the movement to save the West.[6] In order to this discuss this relationship between the United States and Latin America, I will profile four types of Latinamericanisms, which in turn have become a register of that familial but fractious relationship. I will close with an overview of what I take to be two virtues of the Latinamericanist approach to globalization and globalisms.

Latinamericanisms

Latinamericanism is the name for forms of knowledge, ideological attitudes, and spectral mirrors. Latinamericanism as a form of knowledge has assumed different forms, as we will see, hence the plural in the title of this section. Analogously, Latinamericanism is plural because it has been about how Latin America has been portrayed by at least four major agents of imagination: Latin America itself, the United States, Europe, and most recently Latinos. There are many

Latin Americas, and not solely because of the waxing and waning of its boundaries and shifting place in the Western imaginary, as Arturo Ardao has documented so excellently,[7] but also because it has been imagined differently by different social actors. Finally, Latinamericanism has to do with the specters that haunt the rise of the West to global dominance, and because in it (the imagined Latin America) we also find reflected the dreams of an alternate "America" and possibly a different West. In the following, I will differentiate among four types of Latinamericanism that register not just a particular chronology but also the shifting of the location, or geopolitical place, of the imaging agent.

The *first* type of Latinamericanism to emerge did so in part as a response to both 1848 and 1898.[8] This Latinamericanism juxtaposed the United States to Latin America in terms of their distinctive and opposite cultural and spiritual outlooks. One is crass, materialistic, utilitarian, soulless, and lacking cultural roots, while the other is the true inheritor of the European spirit of culture, civilization, and idealistic principles grounded in love and tradition. These distinctions are made in the work of José Enrique Rodó[9] but are also found in the work of José Martí.[10] This opposition was influential for generations of thinkers in Latin America, even those who did not share the original set of terms or animus. In the work of some Mexican thinkers like José Vasconcelos, Leopoldo Zea, and even Octavio Paz, we find these kinds of differentiations.

Another source of this type of Latinamericanism was the Latin American affirmation of its identity vis-à-vis Europe for similar reasons that Latin America sought to differentiate itself from the United States, namely, imperialism, war, and its putative patrician cultures of disdain for the colonized and the racially mixed. Yet not all intellectuals rejected unequivocally Latin America's relationship to Europe.[11] For some, the problem was that Latin America was not enough like Europe. This is a view that we find expressed in the work of Domingo Sarmiento, who basically established a whole school of thought based on the opposition "civilization and barbarism."[12]

This first type of Latinamericanism descended from the era of U.S. colonial and imperialistic expansion and Latin America's affirmation of its distinctive cultural traditions. This Latinamericanism was based on a geopolitics of culture and may therefore be correctly characterized as a "Kulturkampf Latinamericanism," one that juxtaposed the spirit of an imperialistic modernity to the promise of a humanistic and pluralistic form of modernization that in the words of Pedro Henriquez Ureña was embodied in the idea of America as the fatherland of justice.[13]

We will linger briefly over the emergence of this Kulturkampf Latinamericanism, for it emerges at the very moment when a semantic shift is taking place in Europe. Latin America, as the name for the nations and lands in South America formerly controlled by Spain, makes its appearance in the lexicon of geopolitics at the moment when Europe is ceasing to talk about Romania and Germania, the

Gales and the Franks, and begins to talk about the Anglo-Saxons and the Latins, or the mixture of Gales and Franks that made up the western Holy Roman Empire. These shifts are registered over a span of about half a century, five decades in which England consolidates its power over the East, just as the United States begins to consolidate its power over the West. There is a division of labor: the United Kingdom conquers the East and Africa, while the United States launches itself over the American continent. As a counterstrategy, France seeks to consolidate a cultural homogeneity between the Franks and Gales to form a unified front against the "Anglo-Saxons." These geopolitical struggles, waged in terms of the invention of cultural traditions that fractured irretrievably with the Reformation and the discovery of the New World, left their trace in terms of names that conjure up fictions by fiat (notwithstanding Leopold von Ranke's attempt to see the histories of the Latin and Teutonic nations in terms of a series of common processes that included migrations (*Völkerwanderungen*), the Crusades, and the discovery of the New World.[14] The struggle for the heartland, the soul, the inheritance of the West, of Western culture, of Greco-Roman culture, was mirrored in this first type of Latinamericanism, which struggled against the crass utilitarianism and hedonistic individualism of Anglo-Saxon culture.

The second type of Latinamericanism emerged after World War II and the onset of the Cold War in the United States, more precisely, with the National Defense Education Act of 1958, which determined that investing in educational programs that could contribute to the defense of the nation was a national security priority.[15] Guided by national security and defense goals, area studies programs were developed that sought to parcel the world in terms of areas of strategic interest. Clearly Latin America was a major area of geopolitical strategic interest, and thus arose what I call "area studies Latinamericanism." Its goal was to gather and disseminate knowledge about so-called Third World countries. This Latinamericanism treated Latin America like any other foreign land, although there was from the inception an ambiguity about treating Latin America like Asia and Africa. There were some fascinating debates, the Eugene Bolton debates for instance, which argued that Latin America should be studied in the same way that the United States and Canada should be studied. Nonetheless, Cold War knowledge interests dictated the research model that sought to learn as much as possible about other cultures in terms of their vulnerability and potentiality for becoming germinals of sedition.

The epistemological matrix undergirding this research is determined by the idea of First, Second, and Third Worlds, a sequence that is underwritten by the teleology of modernity.[16] Area studies was a major tool for geopolitical gerrymandering as well as epistemic surveillance. As it pertained to Latin America, area studies always imposed an analytical template that blinded its researchers to the very unique problems of Latin America—hybridization, mestizaje, century-old inequities between the countryside and the city, as well as deeply

234

entrenched traditions of caciqueism (or neopotism), on the one hand, and on the other, ideas about the common good that always conspired to promote social revolutions.

This type of Latinamericanism, then, was a way to think or represent Latin America from the standpoint of the North American academy, albeit explicitly at the service of the American Cold War project. But to be fair, what I am calling "area studies Latinamericanism" has two foci: a Latinamericanism of Latin America as the land of underdevelopment, bringing in tow all of what this entails—lack of proper stages of modernization, weak public spheres, lack of technological innovations, and so on. This is the Latinamericanism of the technocrats and think tank apparatchiks.

The other focus is a Latinamericanism of Third Worldism, or a form of First World romanticization and exoticization of the Latin American. This form of viewing Latin America is the negative picture of the Latinamericanism of Latin America as underdevelopment. This second form of Latin Americanism romanticizes Latin America and explains the fetishizing of the Latin American novel. This "Third-Worldist Latinamericanism" allows agents in the United States to vicariously live a romantic, colonial, premodern past. This Latinamericanism is about ersatz tradition. The interaction between these two types of Latinamericanisms gave rise to the collapse of the epistemological and aesthetic, in which the place of the former is taken by the latter, with respect to Latin America that Román de la Campa points out in his book *Latinamericanism*. Jean Franco also studies it in her recent work *The Decline and Fall of the Lettered City*.[17]

After 1959, the Cuban revolution, and 1969, the Medellín bishops' meeting that essentially made official the ecclesial Christian base communities and liberation theology, a third type of Latinamericanism emerged, which I call "critical Latinamericanism." This is the Latinamericanism that sets Latin American in opposition to the United States, but now in terms of an anti-imperialist and anti-capitalist stand that is accompanied with a thorough critique of the epistemological regimes that have permitted the theorization of Latin America up to then. This is the Latinamericanism that we find in the works of Fals Borda, Darcy Ribeiro, Leopoldo Zea, Agusto Salazar Bondy, Gustavo Gutierrez, and Enrique Dussel. This is a Latin America developed in Latin America to explain the Latin American situation to Latin Americans and the United States. In many ways, this Latinamericanism also emerged to counter the ideological effects of the Latinamericanism developed by the epistemological apparatus of the Cold War establishment of the United States from the 1950s to 1970s.

In contrast to the area studies Latinamericanism that emerged shortly after the two world wars, critical Latinamericanism is one of a historical agent situated in Latin America, thought of as *Latin* America but also as an underdeveloped periphery. This type of Latinamericanism interjects a new global dimension to the question of the relationship between the United States and the world-system.

To this Latinamericanism also belongs the attempt to acculturate Marxism and all forms of critical theory. As the nations behind the so-called Iron Curtain sought to develop socialisms with a human face, Latin Americans also sought to develop "Marxisms" with an Indian face. It is no exaggeration to say that this "historical materialism" with an Indian and indigent face was articulated by liberation theology.[18]

Finally, a fourth type of Latinamericanism has begun to develop over the past two decades. It is linked to the aftermath of the Latino diaspora in the United States and the emergence of a critical consciousness in U.S. Latino populations as they were expressed in the Chicano and Puerto Rican movements of the 1960s. This is a transnational, diasporic, postcultural, and post–Latin American type of Latinamericanism that brings together the critical Latinamericanism produced in Latin America since the 1960s, and the homegrown (U.S.) epistemological and social critique that identity movements develop simultaneously but separately. Thus this Latino Latinamericanism has two foci and loci of enunciation and enactment and operates at various levels of criticism: it is critical of the West but also of the way Occidentalism was deployed in order to normalize and regiment the internal sociality of the West in the Americas.[19] It is about Latin America in the mind of the United States, and Latin America in the mind of Latinos and Latin Americans in Latin America. It is a Latinamericanism that seeks to document and analyze the emergence of a post–pax Americana American imaginary, an imaginary beyond the imperial dreams of a nineteenth- and twentieth-century United States and "Latinized" Latin America.[20]

Most importantly, this type of Latinamericanism seeks to unmake the emperor's map, regardless of whether it is the map of a new European Union asserting its claims over the "West," or the United States offering itself as the "future health of the West."[21] The thinkers that give expression to this type of thought are trans-American intellectuals like Juan Flores, Roberto Fernández Retamar, Román de la Campa, Subcomandante Marcos, Lewis Gordon, José Saldivar, Walter Mignolo, and Santiago Castro-Gómez. The importance of this emergent Latinamericanism is its ability to combine a dual critique of Orientalism, insofar as Latin America itself has been orientalized, and of Occidentalism, insofar as Latin America has been the expiatory sacrifice to the homogenization of America as the West.

This analysis of four types of Latinamericanism would be incomplete without a brief discussion of what could be called Latin American neoliberalism, or globalism with a human face.[22] Economist Hernando de Soto, former President Fernando Henrique Cardoso of Brazil, and the current president of Peru, Alejandro Toledo, have put forward this type of globalism with a human face. Reversing decades of economic nationalism and attempts to modernize stagnant economies through military coups in the last two decades of the twentieth century, Brazil, Argentina, Peru, and Mexico have been experimenting with neoliberal globalization, opening their jealously guarded national markets to foreign (mostly U.S.) investment. Cardoso and de Soto are the theorists of this fin de siècle economic modernization. Both locate the failure of economic growth in Latin America in the lack of a thorough globalization of national capital and the strategic use of floating transnational capital to spur economic growth.[23]

Yet the devastated Argentine economy,[24] growing poverty in Mexico, the near collapse and IMF bailout of the Brazilian economy, as well as the recurring economic backsliding of most of the other Latin American countries, seriously call into question the feasibility of a Latin American neoliberalism, or globalism with a human face. On the contrary, the Harvard and Stanford school of economics–type classroom experimentation that has characterized Cardoso's and Carlos Menem's economic policies has spelled disaster for the Latin American people. Unsurprisingly, since neoliberal globalization entails privatization, which in Latin America is but another euphemism for the export of national capital, during the last decade the Gini coefficients (the ratio of income differential and ownership of national wealth between the richest and poorest within a country) in Latin America have grown to be some of the largest in the world.[25] By the same token, it should not come as a surprise that the recent electoral changes in Latin America could be taken as signs that neoliberal globalism in Latin America has come under serious attack. Luis Inácio Lula da Silva's 2002 electoral triumph in Brazil signals growing skepticism and disenchantment with programs that have plunged Brazil into destabilizing debt.[26]

Analogously, and notwithstanding his neoliberal rhetoric, Alejandro Toledo's electoral win against Alberto Fujimori can be attributed to a resurgence of grassroots populism. Hugo Chavez, Lula, and Toledo represent popular leaders who are calling for a new form of economic development that does not entail selling off the national patrimony. In the end, however, this type of globalism, which is not a critique but an attempt to acculturate it to Latin America, is perhaps less an episode in this narrative and more a chapter in the history of capitalism in its latest stage of neoliberal globalism.

The Economic Life of Culture(s) and Knowledge(s) in the Age of Globalizations

The critical Latinamericanisms identified in this chapter have virtues that make them more appropriate for us (if not more useful), subjects located somewhere on the geopolitical and epistemological matrix of the West as it is imagined by the United States. Let me briefly highlight two virtues that are, as I suggest in the subheading above, about the "economic life" of both culture(s) and knowledge(s) in the age of globalizations.

The first virtue that Latinamericanism exhibits has to do with what is called "transdisciplinarity." As Roland Robertson has pointed out, globalization cuts across many disciplines, for example, sociology, political theory, economics, international relations, anthropology, and many more.[27] Globalization, as an object of study, overlaps and overflows some of these disciplinary boundaries; similarly, it vitiates the social realities around which these disciplines coalesce and crystallize. As the Gulbenkian report pointed out, the disciplines that were housed in the different faculties and departments of the post–World War II university, with its roots in nineteenth-century romanticism, are in crisis because their social signifiers and objects of study have been, if not overtaken and corroded, at least rendered secondary and even superfluous.[28] If, as John Urry put it, sociology has lost "society" and must rethink its object of study,[29] and the social and human sciences have lost their "world," the ground of their certitude, as Immanuel Wallerstein has been arguing, then new conceptual matrixes must be developed in order to deal with a new social cartography.[30]

This is what transdisciplinarity names: the way in which globalization *transcends* the limits and applicability of nineteenth- and twentieth-century conceptual matrixes, and the way in which those disciplines and conceptual matrixes become anachronistic and obsolete. Latinamericanism, both critical and postnational, has been laboring in this abject region of knowledge. The works of some of the figures mentioned above cut across disciplines in ways never before thought possible: Renaissance studies, semiotics, anthropology, American studies, literary studies, history of ideas, philosophy, political economy, and so on.

For this reason, it is safest to say that Latinamericanism is less a circumscribed set of texts and objects of study, and more a particular methodological orientation that always takes Latin America as both its point of departure and litmus test. As a transdisciplinary approach par excellence, Latinamericanism is about how knowledge is produced out of, or at the vortex, where the global meets the local, and the local projects into the global. Since this Latinamericanism has to do with the emergence of unique post–pax Americana imaginaries, it is also about the way in which local agents in the United States exemplify the global meeting the local qua the gigantic flows of people.

The second virtue of the critical Latinamericanisms that I have been profiling has to do with the dialectic between what we could call the globalization of antiglobalism and the antiglobalization of globalism. During the Cold War years, Latin Americans, as well as Latinos, used the discourses of globalization, as well as its networks and infrastructures. For example, the Nicaraguans' failed attempts to use the World Court against the United States (Nicaragua did persuade the World Court to censor the United States and demand that it pay reparations to Nicaragua, to no avail); the uses of what arguably was one of the first institutions of globalization—the Roman Catholic Church—for socially emancipatory goals; and more recently the use of the Internet and cyber technologies by local ethnic and racial minorities to destabilize local governments and make transnational claims.

Zapatistas in the Lacandonian jungle of southern Mexico have made effective use of globalization's infrastructures.[31] They have been followed by indigenous groups in Peru and Ecuador, who are making direct claims on their cultural inheritances by bypassing their regional and national governments. Other forms in which the Latinamericanisms under attention attend to this dialectic is illustrated by their focus on the uses of globalization to project a local imaginary that appeals, seduces, and excites a global imaginary by promising tradition and the exotic—the spice of culture—in terms of literature, music, and tourism. Yet, at the same time, Latinamericanists have been very careful to document and analyze the ways in which the crises of Latin America over the past half decade in particular, are illustrative of what I call the antiglobalization of globalism. NAFTA is perhaps the most illustrative example. The antiglobalization of globalism is another name of asymmetrical globalization, or what is now commonly called globalization from above, in which some globalize without allowing themselves to be globalized.

To summarize, the West has never been (solely and entirely) Western, although it is being westernized, and globalization has never been global, although it is being globalized. In this age of globalizations, the United States is pushing a particular agenda implying that it has assumed the mantle of the civilizational mission of the West. In this way, globalization is another name for McDonaldization and Disneyfication. Four different forms of Latinamericanism have emerged to counter these subterranean but determining relationships among empire, civilizational mission, globalization, and the alterization and homogenization of others and oneself.

Notes

The title of this chapter makes a reverential bow to two thinkers, first, to Jorge Luis Borges and his fascinating vignette or quasi-story that appears in his collection *A Universal History of Infamy* (1935; New York: Dutton, 1979), 142, and, second, to Franz Hinkelammert, who wrote a book in Spanish with the title *El mapa del Emperador: Determinismo, Caos, Sujeto* (The emperor's map: Determinism, chaos, subject) (San Jose, Costa Rica: Editorial Dei, 1996). Hinkelammert is a profoundly original and important Latin American thinker who has been writing about economy philosophically and theologically for the past thirty years.

1. Terry Eagleton, *Ideology: An Introduction* (London: Verso, 1991), 222–23.
2. For incisive analysis of these terms and their variegated uses, see Manfred B. Steger, *Globalism: The New Market Ideology* (Lanham, Md.: Rowman & Littlefield, 2002); Ulrich Beck, *What Is Globalization?* (Cambridge: Polity, 2000).
3. See Walter Mignolo, "Latin American Social Thought and Latino/as American Studies," *APA Newsletter on Hispanic/Latino Issues in Philosophy,*

Spring 2001, 105–12; Walter Mignolo, *Global Designs, Local Histories* (Princeton: Princeton University Press, 2000); and Walter Mignolo, "Are Subaltern Studies Postmodern or Postcolonial? The Politics and Sensibilities of Geo-Cultural Locations," *Subaltern Studies in the Americas* 19, no. 46 (1994 [1996]): 45–71. Special issue of *Dispositio/n*, ed. José Rabasa, Javier Sanjínes, and Robert Carr.

4. For a discussion of my use of chronotope and an extensive bibliography, see Eduardo Mendieta, "Chronotopology: Critique of Spatio-Temporal Regimes," in *New Critical Theory: Essays on Liberation*, ed. Jeffrey Paris and William Wilkerson (Lanham, Md.: Rowman & Littlefield, 2001), 175–97.

5. Edward W. Said, *Orientalism* (New York: Vintage, 1979).

6. Note, for instance, the way Huntington's thesis has become the point of reference de rigueur for White House and pax Americana intellectuals. See Samuel P. Huntington, *The Clash of Civilizations and the Remaking of the World Order* (New York: Simon & Schuster, 1996).

7. Arturo Ardao, *América Latina y la latinidad* (México: Universidad Nacional Autónoma de México, 1993).

8. This first type of Latinamericanism should be more properly demarcated by two dates: first, the pronouncement of the Monroe Doctrine in 1823 and, second, its institutionalization in 1948 with the founding of the Organization of American States. This type of Kulturkampf Latinamericanism, furthermore, should be seen as being internally punctuated by the 1910 Mexican revolution. This revolution, which in Paz's words gave rise to modern Mexico and from which spring the romantic and historicist intellectual currents that have fueled most intellectual Latinamericanism, also registered in the U.S. imaginary, as was documented by John Reed's committed revolutionary journalism. See Robert A. Rosenstone's biography *Romantic Revolutionary: A Biography of John Reed* (New York: Knopf, 1975), especially chap. 10, "Mexico." See also Christopher P. Wilson, "Plotting the Border: John Reed, Pancho Villa, and Insurgent Mexico," in *Cultures of United States Imperialism*, ed. Amy Kaplan and Donald E. Pease (Durham, N.C.: Duke University Press, 1993): 340–61. Yet the revolutionary romanticism that the Mexican revolution inspired in the left-leaning sectors of U.S. society was transferred to Russia and later to the Spanish anarchists.

9. José Enrique Rodo, *Ariel* (Austin: University of Texas Press, 1988).

10. José Martí, *Nuestra America* (Caracas, Venezuela: Biblioteca Ayacucho, 1977).

11. A very valid, nay necessary, question that this sentence raises is "which Europe?" At the risk of overextending my analysis in this chapter, I claim that there is no one Europe, just as there is no one Latin America. Europe is an ideal, an idea, and an ideology. There have been many Europes, and their histories have either been erased or relegated to the dustbin of history, or they

have become salient and orienting. One may talk about the Europe of the six-teenth century, with Spain as its colonial and imperial center, or the seventeenth-century Europe of the Netherlands, and so on. The history of Europe can be written as the history of the succession of different imperial and colonial powers, with their respective series of civilizing missions. See Anthony Pagden, ed., *The Idea of Europe: From Antiquity to the European Union* (Cambridge: Cambridge University Press, 2002). A classical study on this issue is Denys Hay, *Europe: The Emergence of an Idea* (Edinburgh: Edinburgh University Press, 1957).

12. Domingo Sarmiento, *Life in the Argentine Republic in the Days of the Tyrants: or Civilization and Barbarism* (New York: Hafner Library Classics, 1868).

13. Pedro Henriquez Ureña, *La Utopia de America* (Caracas, Venezuela: Biblioteca Ayacucho, 1978), 8–11.

14. Leopold von Ranke, *History of the Latin and Teutonic Nations (1494 to 1514)* (1824; London: George Bell, 1909).

15. See Noam Chomsky et al., *The Cold War and the University: Toward an Intellectual History of the Postwar Years* (New York: New Press, 1997), esp. 195–231, Immanuel Wallerstein's contribution.

16. Carl E. Pletsch, "The Three Worlds, of the Division of Social Scientific Labor, circa 1950–1975," *Comparative Studies in Society and History* 23, no. 4 (1981): 565–90.

17. Román de la Campa, *Latinamericanism* (Minneapolis: University of Minnesota Press, 1999); Jean Franco, *The Decline and Fall of the Lettered City* (Cambridge: Harvard University Press, 2002).

18. For work that develops this line of analysis, see David Batstone, Eduardo Mendieta, Lois Ann Lorentzen, and Dwight N. Hopkins, eds., *Liberation Theologies, Postmodernity, and the Americas* (New York: Routledge, 1997).

19. For my use of "occidentalism," see Fernando Coronil, "Beyond Occidentalism: Toward Nonimperial Geohistorical Categories," *Cultural Anthropology* 11, no. 1 (1996): 52–87.

20. The U.S. counterpart and ideal dialogue partner to this fourth type of Latinamericanism is what has been called the "New Americanists." They form a critical wing of American studies that seeks to redirect and restructure the way we study the cultures of the United States by deconstructing three types of absences, as Amy Kaplan elaborates them: "the absence of culture from the history of U.S. imperialism, the absence of empire from the study of American culture; and the absence of the United States from the postcolonial study of imperialism." Amy Kaplan, "Left Alone with America," in *Cultures of United States Imperialism*, ed. Amy Kaplan and Donald E. Pease (Durham, N.C.: Duke University Press, 1993), 3–21; quote at 11. This entire book should be read as the manifesto of the New Americanists.

21. Huntington, *Clash of Civilizations*, 304.

22. The reader should also consult the special issue of Richard L. Harris, ed., *Latin American Perspectives on Globalization and Globalism in Latin America: Contending Perspectives*, November 2002.

23. See Hernando de Soto, *The Other Path: The Invisible Revolution in the Third World* (New York: Harper & Row, 1989); and de Soto, *The Mystery of Capital: Why Capitalism Triumphs in the West and Fails Everywhere Else* (New York: Basic, 2000). For Cardoso's views, see Geisa Maria Rocha, "Neo-dependency in Brazil," *New Left Review*, July-August 2002, 5–33. See also Theotônio dos Santos, "The Theoretical Foundations of the Cardoso Government: A New Stage of the Dependency-Theory Debate," *Latin American Perspectives*, November 1998, 53–70.

24. See David Rock, "Racking Argentina," *New Left Review*, September–October 2002, 55–86.

25. Rocha, "Neo-dependency in Brazil," 30–31.

26. On Lula's electoral win, see Kenneth Maxwell, "Brazil: Lula's Prospects," *New York Review of Books*, December 5, 2002, 27–30.

27. Roland Robertson, "Globalization Theory 2000+: Major Problematics," in *Handbook of Social Theory*, ed. George Ritzer and Barry Smart (London: Sage, 2001), 458–71.

28. Immanuel Wallerstein et al., *Open the Social Sciences. Report of the Gulbenkian Commission on the Restructuring of the Social Sciences* (Stanford: Stanford University Press, 1996).

29. John Urry, *Sociology beyond Societies: Mobilities for the Twenty-First Century* (London: Routledge, 1999).

30. See Immanuel Wallerstein, *The End of the World As We Know It: Social Science for the Twenty-First Century* (Minneapolis: University of Minnesota Press, 1999); and part 2 of his collected essays, Immanuel Wallerstein, *The Essential Wallerstein* (New York: New Press, 2000).

31. For a fascinating reading of the Zapatistas's theoretical breakthrough, see Walter Mignolo, "The Zapatistas's Theoretical Revolution: Its Historical, Ethical, and Political Consequences," *Review* 25, no. 3 (2002): 245–75.

GLOBALIZATION IN HAWAI'I: THE PROMISE OF GLOBALISM AND THE REALITY OF CAPITALISM

Ibrahim G. Aoudé

This chapter argues that the dominant globalization discourse in Hawai'i is rooted in the fundamentalist language of the "free market." Neoliberal ideas purport to deliver the islands from the economic crisis they have been reeling under for more than a decade. This ahistorical neoliberal discourse has been assembled and organized in an ideological system that Manfred Steger has referred to as "globalism."[1] In Hawai'i, globalists took to new heights the doctrine of neoliberalism by repackaging the old slogan "economic diversification"—a continuing theme in Hawaiian economic and political debates since the days of Governor Jack Burns in the early 1960s. Among other things, contemporary neoliberal voices claim that the "New Economy" has left Hawai'i behind and that public and private forces will have to act quickly on their ideas of "diversification" before the islands' economic cracks reach disastrous proportions.

Hawaiian globalists say little about how the islands arrived at this unprecedented economic crisis. Yet proposals to "fix" the problems are the old "stuff" of classical economics. Resurrected from the ideological graveyard of 1980s Thatcher-Reagan supply-side economics (with its battery of promises that include reducing taxes mostly for corporations, economic deregulation, downsizing government, and so on), the presumed remedies amount to little more than old ideological wine poured into the new rhetorical bottle of "globalization."

This chapter examines the promise of globalism against the reality of contemporary capitalism in Hawai'i, ultimately revealing the highly problematic foundation of the globalist discourse. Rejecting the neoliberal claims made by globalists in the Hawaiian context, I advance my own antiglobalist narrative— one that is anchored in a careful examination of actual economic and social conditions in Hawai'i. Thus I hope to contribute to the creation of a critical theory of globalization that casts its skeptical analysis over the entire globe. However, before sketching the contours of the globalist discourse in Hawai'i from the 1970s to the terrorist attacks of 9/11, I offer a brief general assessment of the role of ideology in sustaining and developing the forces of capitalist globalization.

Globalism: Chasing an Elusive Free Market Nirvana

At a first glance, the grand narrative of capitalist globalization appears rather enticing. Like the mythical Sirens, however, globalists lure their victims to certain disaster. The grand narrative of the globalists culminates in a crescendo of celebrating the virtues of the unfettered "free market"—the realization of full "liberty" through nongovernment intervention in the economy. Any serious restrictions on the "free market" would result in the loss of "liberty."[2] In this manner, it is alleged, the freedom to choose is vastly enhanced, and rapid economic growth, the sine qua non of modernity, becomes both a necessary and sufficient condition to attain an illusive free market nirvana.[3]

The central neoliberal tenets are rooted in classical political economy expressed by Adam Smith and David Ricardo in eighteenth- and nineteenth-century Britain. These tenets were meant to be universal, that is, they apply to humankind without regard to the history of place or culture. Disguised in the rational language of the Scottish enlightenment, these tenets nonetheless are more akin to the components of ancient Greek legends and myths: an invisible hand provides prosperity for all, supply and demand magically find their equilibrium without human interference, and markets are rooted in an eternal *nomos*—the unchanging law of nature.

Unfortunately, the necessary hard-nosed analysis of the workings of social power under free market conditions remains just as invisible as the hand that maintains the supply-demand equilibrium in this fantastic world. The neoliberal myth requires persistent ideological support in order to repel criticisms rooted in material conditions incongruent with the free market vision. Indeed, Steger posits that globalism, despite its roots in the Enlightenment language of progress and modernization, differs from earlier market ideologies in that globalists work hard to imbue globalization—the buzzword of our time—with neoliberal meanings.[4] Functioning as a powerful material force, globalism reinforces the social process of capitalist globalization, which in turn feeds the ideological narrative.

But just as globalization—the social process—contains nuanced features, so does globalism, the market ideology. Hence, one can safely identify subtle nuances—or subnarratives—within this grand narrative of contemporary neoliberalism.[5] Identifying five central claims of globalism, Steger argues that the object of these claims is to convince the public that globalization is (1) primarily economic in character and (2) "good" in a normative sense because it produces wealth in accordance with the natural order of things. According to globalists, full economic liberalization and global market integration are the inevitable and irreversible telos of the globalization process. As Steger observes, this claim of inevitability has a profoundly depoliticizing effect, rendering human agency powerless in the face of globalization. Further, it is claimed that globalization, as a supposed natural phenomenon, is leaderless (i.e., it just rolls forward by the grace of nature); it is beneficial to all of humanity because it generates wealth for all and promotes liberal democracy around the world.[6]

The globalization scholar Abbas Ali notes that "one of the most important trends leading to world integration in recent years is liberalization."[7] In his view, economic liberalization lies at the heart of various public policies designed to speed up globalization. Ali develops a set of assumptions on which rests a "theoretical proposal" about global firms. It states that corporations seek to sustain their competitiveness by establishing a set of worldwide relationships and alliances with competitors, suppliers, customers, politicians, and social and environmental actors. Such involvements, along with advanced information technology and the worldwide appeal of the virtues of civil society, facilitate free movement of trade, capital, and eventually people across the globe, thereby strengthening world interdependence and elevating people's consciousness of the unity and vitality of our planet.[8] Interestingly, Ali assumes that "no inherent contradictions [exist] between global integration and increasing awareness of social, ethnic, and religious identity among many segments of the world's populations. Globalization has cultural, political, and business dimensions."[9] Thus Ali, a globalist, is essentially in agreement with the five claims of globalism presented by Steger, a critical globalization theorist.

While it is true that one of the main goals of globalists is to strive for the global integration of markets through economic liberalization, it is equally true that the history of globalization cannot be written accurately without a sophisticated analysis of power and domination. The globalists' portrayal of this process as natural, innocuous, and inevitable suggests that, theoretically, the economic opportunities open to U.S. individuals and firms are equivalent to those available to individuals in Nicaragua or Ecuador. In practice, however, it is obvious that the countries of the global north led by the United States are both architects and supervisors of powerful international financial organizations such as the International Monetary Fund (IMF), the World Bank, and the World Trade Organization (WTO). For the global south, trade liberalization usually means accepting the dictates of transnational corporations, optimistically pegging national currencies to the dollar, reducing corporate taxes, and lifting social and environmental regulations. The message from the north is that if the south does not agree to open up its market to global enterprises, it will have to bear the costs of economic isolation. Remain isolated or accept your neoliberal destiny.

Having discussed, however briefly, the role of globalist ideology in sustaining and developing the forces of capitalist globalization, this chapter now shifts its focus to an analysis of globalism in Hawai'i.

"Diversification": A Slogan for All Seasons

It is important to note that both the Democratic and Republican parties participate in the globalist discourse. Indeed, all the main gubernatorial candidates in the 2002 elections in Hawai'i displayed their globalist loyalties. Major business as well as some academic elites have been important players in this ideological promotion. On November 5, 2002, Linda Lingle, the former Republican mayor of Maui, was elected governor of Hawai'i. Her platform and plan of action promised "A New Beginning" for Hawai'i. She promised to build a strong economy by supporting tourism, diversifying agriculture, building a high-tech sector, improving public education, and strengthening the private sector.[10] Lingle did not invent this neoliberal discourse, and her program hardly differs from that of her predecessor, Democrat Benjamin Cayetano. The neoliberal narrative in Hawai'i closely resembles the generic neoliberal discourse that pervades most countries in the Northern Hemisphere. However, Hawaiian globalism can be distinguished from the dominant globalization discourse in one crucial respect: its consistent reiteration of the rather nebulous concept of "diversification." Hence it is of vital importance to briefly consider the history of the uniquely Hawaiian "diversification discourse of globalization."

During most of the 1950s and early 1960s, Hawai'i's economy was primarily based on agriculture—mainly sugar and pineapple. In the ensuing decades, the ruling Democratic party was instrumental in passing enabling legislation directed at the "modernization" of the islands—modernization that relied chiefly on what was touted as the necessary "diversification" of the economy, meaning the strengthening of tourism, real estate development and the service industry. Land use laws such as the New Zealand bill and the Pittsburgh bill were critical to the development of hotels and resorts by relying on the "highest and best use" concept.[11]

Hawai'i's project of modernization—and thus its desired economic "diver-

246

sification"—relied on two main pillars: (1) the "1954 revolution," which swept Democrats into power, and (2) the need of U.S. multinational corporations and individual entrepreneurs, such as Henry Kaiser, to extend their activities into the Pacific.[12] Moreover, the structural transformations that occurred in the global economy since the 1970s created new economic opportunities that manifested themselves locally in the expansion of tourism, thus taking advantage of the division of labor existing in the Pacific rim by enhancing the economic diversification of services. Sheraton, for instance, bought hotels from Matson Navigation. Other hotel chains, such as Hilton, Inter-Continental, Holiday Inn, Hyatt, and others followed in the same period.[13] Consequently, the employment structure in the islands changed dramatically, ultimately reflecting the uneven development that resulted from heavy dependency on tourism and real estate.[14]

However, it was not until the 1980s—during Democratic Governor George Ariyoshi's last term in office (1982–1986) and throughout the eight years of Democratic Governor John Waihe'e (1986–1994)—that the diversification discourse emphasized high technology.[15] More clarity about the concrete goals of high-tech diversification was achieved when Waihe'e announced that his administration would pursue projects reflecting Hawai'i's "comparative advantage," such as geothermal energy. However, in their much cited study of the feasibility of high-tech development in the islands, Herbig and Kramer concluded that it would take between thirty and forty years to achieve.[16]

Contemporary Globalism in Hawai'i

When Benjamin Cayetano became governor in 1995, he realized that efforts to create a high-tech sector strong enough to absorb the economic blows resulting from declining tourism were essentially delusional. His administration's economic strategy was to redouble its efforts to revive areas of traditional economic strength, especially tourism. For example, he decided to embark on the controversial construction of an expensive Honolulu Convention Center that would capitalize on the "conventions market."[17] During Cayetano's first term in office the discursive marker "New Economy" became a ubiquitous term. While connected to the old "diversification" slogan, Cayetano's version of the New Economy relied, ironically, on vilified Keynesian policies of "kick-starting" the economy through "big-ticket developments" such as the convention center and many other public construction projects.

At the same time, the Cayetano administration successfully sponsored legislation based on unmistakably neoliberal premises. Cutting government expenditures and lowering corporate taxes in order to attract external investment, however, failed to achieve robust economic growth. Even to casual observers of

Hawai'i's political economy, the dominant globalist discourse appeared to crash on the rocks of anemic economic growth, increasing poverty, unemployment, and the high cost of living.[18]

Promising to make government efficient, Cayetano instituted civil service reform during his second term in office.[19] "Reform" meant a limit on hiring, little or no wage and salary increases for civil servants, and significant cuts in benefits. Cayetano's neoliberal reforms came after he had emasculated government through severe budget cuts in all state departments, including a significant reduction of expenditures on education. Cayetano supported huge corporate tax cuts and initiated "reforms" in worker's compensation laws that favored business. He assembled the Economic Revitalization Task Force (ERTF) made up of businesspeople and individuals sympathetic to business interests.[20] The ERTF offered the sympathetic governor a number of recommendations, including a 50 percent cut in corporate taxes, more state subsidies for the tourism industry, further reductions of worker's compensation, and increasing privatization efforts.[21]

Cayetano justified a swift implementation of these measures by emphasizing Hawai'i's "urgent need" to emerge as a "tough competitor" in the global economy. He also blamed dissenters for not being creative enough to adapt to the winds of the changing global economy. Yet Cayetano never seems to have reflected on the systemic difficulties of taking advantage of conditions conducive to the cutthroat requirements of the New Economy. As Li'ana Petranek argues, the hard truth about Hawai'i's economy is not that people are not creative enough to create new economic opportunities. Rather, there are systemic problems related to capitalist reproductive dynamics—profit and accumulation requirements—that lie at the heart of the problem. Most importantly, Petranek points to a connection between global crisis management and inadequate economic and social policies in Hawai'i. Her conclusion is that it is incumbent on capable analysts to figure out why economic crisis persists and how to remedy the situation.[22]

John Witeck, too, advances his critique of globalism by examining the state's neoliberal public policies. Demonstrating why these policies failed to lift the local economy, Witeck offers a detailed examination of specific policies such as Cayetano's civil service reform. He also ties those failed policies to the stagnant tourism/real estate development model that guided economic development since 1959. Ultimately, however, Witeck finds hope in the recent resurgence of labor struggles and proposes the creation of a democratic, anticapitalist social movement to counter the onslaught of neoliberal globalization.[23]

However, following the 9/11 attacks, the dominant voices of neoliberalism became even louder as the Hawaiian economy suffered a severe setback after a brief period of moderate growth not exceeding 2.5 percent.[24] Those traumatic events go a long way in explaining why, in spite of the popular 2002 teachers' strikes on the islands, large parts of the public are still susceptible to the simplistic ideological slogans of globalism. Fortunately, however, the globalist discourse has not gone entirely unchallenged in Hawai'i. The resistance to neoliberal globalization discourse occurred largely in the form of labor strikes and the struggles of indigenous Hawaiians. Next I wish to examine the main features of this counterdiscourse.

The Counterdiscourse

The 1994 Zapatista insurgency in Chiapas, Mexico, represents a significant marker of the global rebellion against capitalist globalization. The Zapatista rebellion constitutes at once an indigenous struggle and a global fight against the effects of globalization on the world's poor people.[25] Anticapitalist forces around the globe gave support to this insurgency. The insurgency galvanized significant sectors of the American progressive movement and doubled national efforts to work against the North American Free Trade Agreement (NAFTA). These renewed efforts bore fruit at the tumultuous 1999 meeting of the WTO in Seattle. Several indigenous Hawaiian activists were present at the Seattle demonstrations. Less than two years later, the May 2001 meeting of the Asian Development Bank (ADB) in Honolulu gave the final impetus to a gathering of Hawaiian antiglobalist forces on the islands to stage rallies and marches against neoliberal ADB policies in various Asian countries.[26]

The indigenous Hawaiian movement was on the defensive during most of the early neoliberal phase in the 1980s and early 1990s. Starting in 1996, formally elected representatives of native Hawaiians pondered a more comprehensive strategy for self-determination.[27] As a result of the participation of some elements of the Native Hawaiian movement in the anti-ADB demonstrations, some prominent indigenous voices joined forces with existing antiglobalization groups on the islands. Although the theoretical core of the native Hawaiian movement has always been anticolonial, it has not been consistently anticapitalist. Indeed, many Native Hawaiian activists seek to resolve major indigenous grievances within the U.S. capitalist framework.[28] While it might be possible to achieve several worthwhile goals (such as access to special revenues and more Hawaiian control over ceded lands) within this particular framework, the danger is that such agreements might derail the overall struggle for self-determination. Several prominent Native Hawaiian activists such as Kekuni Blaisdell have raised this very point in rejecting proposed federal legislation that seeks to "protect" Native Hawaiian rights.[29] While there are significant differences of opinion on the virtues of the proposed legislation, there is near unanimity in the recognition that the local antiglobalist discourse is deeply rooted in the peculiarities of the Hawaiian experience.

In my view, it is indispensable for the growing alliance of antiglobalist forces in Hawai'i to utilize a political economy framework to advance an adequate critique of neoliberal globalization on the islands. Spurious globalist claims can more easily be debunked when judged against the harsh reality of contemporary "turbo-capitalism."[30] In this vein, local critic Jim Brewer consistently emphasizes that nothing short of "full democracy" is needed to tackle the state's economic and political ills. "Full democracy," for Brewer, centers on the real participation and the systemic inclusion of the entire citizenry in decision-making processes in both the economic and political spheres. Essential to Brewer's concept of "full democracy" is the integral relationship between "global village democracy and Hawaiian sovereignty."[31]

The successful articulation of the antiglobalist discourse in Hawai'i requires the employment of a consistent anticapitalist language critical of the "free market" and its pernicious neoliberal agenda of privatization, deregulation, and generous tax giveaways to powerful corporations. Essential elements of this counterdiscourse include equality, democracy, and the realization that the indigenous Hawaiian movement deserves a special place at the core of the larger antiglobalist movement.

If this agenda is to be pursued successfully, a crucial question naturally arises: what shape should coalition-building efforts take in order to facilitate the development of a comprehensive antiglobalist, anticapitalist movement? Unfortunately, there is strong opposition within the native Hawaiian movement to coalition building in general, not to mention the creation of lasting political alliances. While many non–Native Hawaiian citizens have participated in protests, rallies, and other actions in support of indigenous rights, their actions nonetheless lacked a conscious effort to build solid coalitions and a social movement capable of taking on organized capitalist interests in the state.[32] At the same time, in practical terms, some fruitful cooperation did occur between the environmental movement and sections of the Hawaiian movement in the 1980s, when both camps combined their efforts to protect rainforests from geothermal energy projects on the island of Hawai'i.

Conclusion: Toward a Fourth Stage of Social Struggle in Hawai'i

What emerges from my analysis thus far is the imperative of intensifying social struggles against globalization and its free market ideologists. Elsewhere, I have delineated three stages of social struggles in contemporary Hawai'i.[33] It has now become necessary to introduce the fourth stage of social struggle: the fight against capitalist globalization and its supportive globalist discourse.

In the wake of the 9/11 attacks, both the local and the national economies have entered a protracted period of stagnation. In tourist-dependent Hawai'i, the economy deteriorated literally overnight. The events of 9/11 quickly thwarted ongoing efforts of the Native Hawaiian movement to stop the U.S. military from using Makua valley on the island of Oahu for target practice. In addition, 9/11 also put on the back burner the so-called Akaka bill—federal legislation designed to "solve" the plight of Native Hawaiians by having the federal government recognize them as a Native American tribe and, therefore, prevent legal challenges to Native Hawaiian rights.[34] Introduced by U.S. Senator Daniel Akaka, the bill failed twice to pass Congress.

One intended consequence of the bill's passage would be to significantly quiet off-island investors' concerns regarding political stability and property rights in Hawai'i. To many globalists, "proper" regulation of Hawaiian land rights would remove a major obstacle to foreign investment. The Native Hawaiian movement is at a critical juncture in this fourth stage of social struggles. Would the passage of the Akaka bill indicate a fatal cooptation of the Native Hawaiian movement? Or would it signal the beginning of the movement's integration into the larger anticapitalist globalization movement, which, in the current war with Iraq, has essentially developed into a global peace movement? Shrouded in the mists of the future, the answer to these crucial questions will determine for a long time to come the character of the antiglobalist movement in Hawai'i.

Notes

1. Manfred B. Steger, *Globalism: The New Market Ideology* (Lanham, Md.: Rowman & Littlefield, 2002), x.

2. For an influential twentieth-century expression of this argument, see Milton Friedman, *Capitalism and Freedom* (Chicago: University of Chicago Press, 1962).

3. See Steger, *Globalism*, 9–12, for a lucid discussion of neoliberalism and the "free market."

4. Steger, *Globalism*, 13.

5. See Abbas J. Ali, *Globalization of Business: Practice and Theory* (New York: Hawthorn, 2000), 53–62. Ali discusses the "Typology of the Current Discourse" in which he deals with "factor-driven discourse," "motive-driven discourse," and "consequence-driven discourse."

6. Steger, *Globalism*, 43–80.

7. Ali, *Globalization of Business*, 23.

8. Ali, *Globalization of Business*, 18.

9. Ali, *Globalization of Business*, 19.

10. Linda Lingle, *A New Beginning for Hawai'i* (Honolulu: Linda Lingle Campaign Committee, 2002).

11. George Cooper and Gavan Daws, *Land and Power in Hawai'i: The Democratic Years* (Honolulu: University of Hawai'i Press, 1990), 37.

12. Noel Kent, *Hawai'i: Islands under the Influence* (Honolulu: University of Hawai'i Press, 1993), 122–39.

13. Kent, *Hawai'i*, 164–85.

14. Ibrahim G. Aoudé, "Political Economy," in *Multicultural Hawai'i: The Fabric of a Multiethnic Society*, ed. Michael Haas (New York: Garland, 1998), 269.

15. Kent Keith, then director of the Department of Planning and Economic Development (DPED), the precursor to DBED&T, was at the helm promoting high technology.

16. Paul A. Herbig and Hugh E. Kramer, "The Potential for High Tech in Hawai'i," *Social Process in Hawai'i* 35 (1994): 56–70.

17. Benjamin Cayetano, *Restoring Hawai'i's Economic Momentum* (Honolulu: Department of Business, Economic Development, and Tourism-DBED&T, State of Hawai'i, 1996).

18. Ibrahim G. Aoudé, "Hawai'i: The Housing Crisis and the State's Development Strategy," *Social Process in Hawai'i* 35, (1994): 71–84. See also Aoudé, *Social Process in Hawai'i* 40 (2001).

19. See Li'ana M. Petranek, "Will the Task Masters of the New Economy Please Stand Up!" *Social Process in Hawai'i* 40 (2001): 1.

20. For a discussion on the ERTF, see, for example, John Witeck, "Public Policy in Hawai'i: Globalism's Neoliberal Embrace," *Social Process in Hawai'i* 40 (2001): 36–68.

21. Witeck, "Public Policy in Hawai'i," 56.

22. Petranek, "Will the Task Masters."

23. Witeck, "Public Policy in Hawai'i."

24. First Hawaiian Bank, *Economic Forecast* (Honolulu: First Hawaiian Bank, 1999–2000): 3.

25. Juana Ponce de Leon, ed., *Our Weapon: Selected Writings of Subcommandante Insurgente Marcos* (New York: Seven Stories, 2002), xxv.

26. Marion Kelly, "Occupation/Colonization/Globalization: You Name It, We've Got It; Hawai'i Has It All" (paper presented at the tenth Pacific Science Inter-Congress, Guam, June 2001).

27. Ibrahim G. Aoudé, "Hawai'i: Strategic Considerations for Social Struggles," *Social Process in Hawai'i* 39 (1999): 284–300. For a discussion of the dangers of the Native Hawaiian vote, see, for example, Marion Kelly, "The State of Hawai'i Responds to the Hawaiian Sovereignty Movement: OHA, HSAC, HSEC and the Native Hawaiian Vote," unpublished paper, July 1996, 1–17.

28. For a discussion of the native Hawaiian movement's strategy and tactics, see Aoudé, "Strategic Considerations." See also Ibrahim G. Aoudé, *Indigenous Rights* (Honolulu: Department of Ethnic Studies, University of Hawai'i, 2001). A sixty-minute film.

29. See, for example, the Pro Kanaka Maoli Independence Group, "Some Questions and Answers about Akaka's Federal Recognition Bill: From the Point

of View of Those Who Believe in an Independent Hawaiian Nation," undated pamphlet.

30. See Edward Luttwak, *Turbo-capitalism: Winners and Losers in the Global Economy* (New York: HarperCollins, 1999).

31. Jim Brewer, "Hawai'i: From Globalization to Full Democracy," *Social Process in Hawai'i* 40 (2001): 85.

32. Aoudé, "Strategic Considerations."

33. See Aoudé, "Strategic Considerations," 290–92, where I identify and discuss the following three stages of social struggles in Hawai'i: (1) multiethnic antieviction and antiwar struggles, (2) the struggle for Kanaka Maoli (indigenous Hawaiian) rights, and (3) cooptation and disorientation of the indigenous movement.

34. See, for example, Marion Kelly, "The Akaka Bill Kills All Hope for Hawaiian Independence" (paper presented at the Cultural Diversity in a Globalizing World Conference, Honolulu, Hawai'i, February 2003), 1–7.

SELECTED BIBLIOGRAPHY

Abu-Lughod, Janet. *Before European Hegemony: The World System, A.D. 1250–1350*. New York: Oxford University Press, 1989.

Aina, Tade. *Globalization and Social Policy in Africa: Issues and Research Direction*. Dakar: CODESRIA Working Papers Series, 1997.

Ake, Claude. *Democracy and Development*. Washington, D.C.: Brookings Institution, 1996.

Albrow, Martin. *The Global Age*. Cambridge: Polity Press, 1996.

Ali, Abbas J. *Globalization of Business: Practice and Theory*. New York: Hawthorn, 2000.

Amin, Samir. *Capitalism in the Age of Globalization*. London: Zed, 1997.

———. *Delinking: Towards a Polycentric World*. Translated by Michael Wolfers. London: Zed, 1990.

Bakan, Abigail, and Daiva Stasiulis. *Not One of the Family: Foreign Domestic Workers in Canada*. Toronto: University of Toronto Press, 1997.

Bakhtin, Mikhail M. *The Dialogic Imagination: Four Essays*. Austin: University of Texas Press, 1981.

Bamyeh, Mohammed A. *The Ends of Globalization*. Minneapolis: University of Minnesota Press, 2000.

———. *The Social Origins of Islam*. Minneapolis: University of Minnesota Press, 1999.

Basu, Amrita, ed. *Women's Movements in Global Perspective*. New Delhi: Kali for Women, 1999.

Batstone, David, Eduardo Mendieta, Lois Ann Lorentzen, and Dwight N. Hopkins, eds. *Liberation Theologies, Postmodernity, and the Americas*. New York: Routledge, 1997.

Beck, Ulrich. *What Is Globalization?* Cambridge: Polity, 2000.

———. *World Risk Society*. Cambridge: Polity, 1999.

Black, Jeremy. *Maps and History: Constructing Images of the Past.* New Haven: Yale University Press, 1997.

Booth, Ken, and Tim Dunne, eds. *Worlds in Collision: Terror and the Future of Global Order.* New York: Palgrave, 2002.

Bourdieu, Pierre. *Acts of Resistance: Against the Tyranny of the Market.* New York: New Press, 1998.

Briggs, Asa, and Peter Burke. *A Social History of the Media: From Gutenberg to the Internet.* Cambridge: Polity, 2002.

Calhoun, Craig, Paul Price, and Ashley Timmer, eds. *Understanding September 11.* New York: Free Press, 2002.

Carver, Terrell. *The Postmodern Marx.* Manchester: Manchester University Press, 1998.

Castells, Manuel. *The Rise of the Network Society.* Vol. 1 of *The Information Age: Economy, Society, and Culture.* Malden, Mass.: Blackwell, 1997.

Chan, Anita. *China's Workers under Assault: The Exploitation of Labor in a Globalizing Economy.* Armonk, N.Y.: Sharpe, 2001.

Constable, Nicole. *Maid to Order in Hong Kong.* Ithaca, N.Y.: Cornell University Press, 1997.

Darier, Eric. *Discourses of the Environment.* Oxford: Blackwell, 1999.

De Soto, Hernando. *The Mystery of Capital: Why Capitalism Triumphs in the West and Fails Everywhere Else.* New York: Basic, 2000.

———. *The Other Path: The Invisible Revolution in the Third World.* New York: Harper & Row, 1989.

Deal, Terrence E., and Allan A. Kennedy. *Corporate Cultures: The Rites and Rituals of Corporate Life.* New York: Perseus, 2000.

Der Derian, James. *Virtuous War: Mapping the Military-Industrial-Media-Entertainment Network.* Boulder: Westview, 2001.

Diamond, Jared. *Guns, Germs, and Steel: The Fate of Human Societies.* New York: Norton, 1997.

Eickelman, Dale F., and Jon W. Anderson. *New Media in the Muslim World: The Emerging Public Sphere.* Bloomington: Indiana University Press, 1999.

Enloe, Cynthia. *The Morning After: Sexual Politics at the End of the Cold War.* Berkeley: University of California Press, 1993.

Esack, Farid. *Qur'an, Liberation, and Pluralism: An Islamic Perspective of Interreligious Solidarity against Oppression.* Oxford: Oneworld, 1997.

Fairfield-Sonn, James W. *Corporate Culture and the Quality Organization.* Westport, Conn.: Quorum, 2001.

Faist, Thomas. *The Volume and Dynamics of International Migration and Transnational Social Spaces.* Oxford: Oxford University Press, 2000.

Ferguson, Kathy, and Phyllis Turnbull. *Oh, Say, Can You See? The Semiotics of the Military in Hawai'i.* Minneapolis: University of Minnesota Press, 1999.

Fischer, Frank, and Maarten Hajer. *Living with Nature: Environmental Discourse as Cultural Politics*. Oxford: Oxford University Press, 1999.

Franco, Jean. *The Decline and Fall of the Lettered City*. Cambridge: Harvard University Press, 2002.

Frank, Andre Gunder. *ReORIENT: Global Economy in the Asian Age*. Berkeley: University of California Press, 1998.

Fukuyama, Francis. *The End of History and the Last Man*. New York: Free Press, 1992.

Gibbons, Michael, et al. *The New Production of Knowledge: The Dynamics of Science and Research in Contemporary Societies*. London: Sage, 1994.

Giddens, Anthony. *The Consequences of Modernity*. Cambridge: Polity, 1990.

———. *The Third Way and Its Critics*. Cambridge: Polity, 2000.

Gilpin, Robert. *The Challenge of Global Capitalism: The World Economy in the 21st Century*. Princeton: Princeton University Press, 2000.

Haas, Michael. *Multicultural Hawai'i: The Fabric of a Multiethnic Society*. New York: Garland, 1998.

Halliday, Fred. *Two Hours That Shook the World: September 11, 2001: Causes and Consequences*. London: Saqi, 2002.

Hans-Henrik, H., and G. Sörensen, eds. *Whose World Order: Uneven Globalization and the End of the Cold War*. Boulder: Westview, 1995.

Hardt, Michael, and Antonio Negri. *Empire*. Cambridge: Harvard University Press, 2000.

Harvey, David. *The Condition of Postmodernity*. Oxford: Blackwell, 1989.

Hawken, Paul, Amory Lovins, and L. Hunter Lovins. *Natural Capitalism: Creating the Next Industrial Revolution*. Boston: Little, Brown, 1999.

Hawkesworth, Mary. *Beyond Oppression: Feminist Theory and Political Strategy*. New York: Continuum, 1990.

Held, David, and Anthony McGrew. *Globalization/Anti-Globalization*. Cambridge: Polity, 2002.

Herman, Edward, and Robert McChesney. *The Global Media: The New Missionaries of Corporate Capitalism*. London: Cassell, 1997.

Holton, Robert. *Globalization and the Nation-State*. London: Macmillan, 1998.

Huntington, Samuel P. *The Clash of Civilizations and the Remaking of the World Order*. New York: Simon & Schuster, 1996.

Huyssen, Andreas. *Twilight Memories: Marking Time in a Culture of Amnesia*. New York: Routledge, 1995.

Ishay, Micheline, ed. *The History of Human Rights from Ancient Times to the Era of Globalization*. Berkeley: University of California Press, forthcoming.

———. *The History of Human Rights Reader*. London: Routledge, 1997.

———. *Internationalism and Its Betrayal*. Minneapolis: University of Minnesota Press, 1995.

Jameson, Fredric, and Masao Miyoshi. *The Cultures of Globalization*. Durham, N.C.: Duke University Press, 1998.

Kaldor, Mary. *New and Old Wars: Organized Violence in a Global Era*. Stanford: Stanford University Press, 1999.

Kent, Noel. *Hawai'i: Islands under the Influence*. Honolulu: University of Hawai'i Press, 1993.

Khor, Martin. *Rethinking Globalization: Critical Policy Issues and Policy Choices*. New York: Palgrave/St. Martin's, 2001.

Kirk, Margaret, and Kathryn Sikkink. *Activists beyond Borders: Advocacy Networks in International Politics*. Ithaca, N.Y.: Cornell University Press, 1998.

Lechner, Frank, and John Boli, eds. *The Globalization Reader*. Oxford: Blackwell, 2000.

Linkogle, Stephanie. *Women Resist Globalization: Mobilizing for Livelihoods and Rights*. London: Zed, 2001.

Luttwak, Edward. *Turbo-capitalism: Winners and Losers in the Global Economy*. New York: HarperCollins, 1999.

Mandel, Robert. *Armies without States: The Privatization of Security*. Boulder: Lynne Rienner, 2002.

Marchand, Marianne, and Anne Runyon, eds. *Gender and Global Restructuring*. London: Routledge, 2000.

McClintock, Anne. *Imperial Leather: Race, Gender, and Sexuality in Colonial Context*. New York: Routledge, 1995.

Mignolo, Walter. *Global Designs, Local Histories*. Princeton: Princeton University Press, 2000.

Misra, Kalpana. *From Post-Maoism to Post-Marxism: The Erosion of Official Ideology in Deng's China*. London: Routledge, 1998.

Mittelman, James H. *Globalization: Critical Reflections*. Boulder: Lynne Rienner, 1996.

———. *The Globalization Syndrome: Transformation and Resistance*. Princeton: Princeton University Press, 2000.

Mittelman, James H., and Norani Othman, eds. *Capturing Globalization*. London: Routledge, 2001.

Nabudere, Dani. *Globalization and the Postcolonial African State*. Harare: SAPES, 2000.

Nederveen Pieterse, Jan. *White on Black: Images of Africa and Blacks in Western Popular Culture*. New Haven: Yale University Press, 1995.

Neuhauser, Peg C., Ray Bender, and Kirk L. Stromberg. *Culture.com: Building Corporate Culture in the Connected Workplace*. Toronto: Wiley Canada, 2000.

Ohmae, Kenichi. *The Borderless World: Power and Strategy in the Interlinked World Economy*. New York: Harper Business, 1990.

———. *The End of the Nation State: The Rise of Regional Economies: How Capi-*

tal, Corporations, Consumers, and Communication Are Reshaping the Global Markets. New York: Free Press, 1995.

Olds, Kris, Peter Dicken, Philip F. Kelly, Lily Kong, and Henry W. C. Yeung, eds. *Globalization and the Asia-Pacific*. London: Routledge, 1999.

Parrenas, Rhacel Salazar. *Servants of Globalization: Women, Migration and Domestic Work*. Stanford: Stanford University Press, 2001.

Phillips, Kevin. *Wealth and Democracy: The Politics of the American Rich*. New York: Broadway Books, 2002.

Prazniak, Roxann, and Arif Dirlik, eds. *Places and Politics in an Age of Globalization*. Lanham, Md.: Rowman & Littlefield, 2001.

Robertson, Roland. *Globalization*. London: Sage, 1992.

Rosenberg, Justin. *The Follies of Globalisation Theory: Polemical Essays*. London: Verso, 2000.

Rupert, Mark. *Ideologies of Globalization: Contending Visions of a New World Order*. London: Routledge, 2000.

Said, Edward W. *Orientalism*. New York: Vintage, 1979.

Sandilands, Catriona. *The Good-Natured Feminist: Ecofeminism and the Quest for Democracy*. Minneapolis: University of Minnesota Press, 1999.

Sassen, Saskia. *The Global City: New York, London, Tokyo*. Princeton: Princeton University Press, 1991.

————, ed. *Global Networks, Linked Cities*. New York: Routledge, 2002.

Scholte, Jan A. *Globalization: A Critical Introduction*. London: Macmillan, 2000.

Scott, John. *Corporate Business and Capitalist Class*. Oxford: Oxford University Press, 1997.

Sen, Amartya. *Development as Freedom*. New York: Anchor, 1999.

Sklair, Leslie. *Globalization: Capitalism and Its Alternatives*. Oxford: Oxford University Press, 2002.

————. *The Transnational Capitalist Class*. Oxford: Blackwell, 2001.

Smith, Peter, and Luis Guarnizo, eds. *Transnationalism from Below*. Brunswick, N.J.: Transaction, 1998.

Steger, Manfred B. *Globalism: The New Market Ideology*. Lanham, Md.: Rowman & Littlefield, 2002.

————. *Globalization: A Very Short Introduction*. Oxford: Oxford University Press, 2003.

Stiglitz, Joseph E. *Globalization and Its Discontents*. New York: Norton, 2002.

Strange, Susan. *The Retreat of the State*. Cambridge: Cambridge University Press, 1996.

Tabb, William K. *The Amoral Elephant: Globalization and the Struggle for Social Justice in the Twenty-First Century*. New York: Monthly Review Press, 2001.

Tarazi Fawaz, Leila, and C. A. Bayly, eds. *Modernity and Culture: From the Mediterranean to the Indian Ocean*. New York: Columbia University Press, 2002.

Terdiman, Richard. *Discourse/Counter-Discourse*. Ithaca, N.Y.: Cornell University Press, 1985.

Thrift, Nigel. *Spatial Formations*. London: Sage, 1996.

Wallerstein, Immanuel. *The Capitalist World Economy*. Cambridge: Cambridge University Press, 1979.

Waters, Malcolm. *Globalization*. 2d ed. London: Routledge, 2001.

Wills, John. *1688: A Global History*. New York: Norton, 2001.

Yergin, Daniel, and Joseph Stanislaw. *The Commanding Heights: The Battle between Government and the Marketplace That Is Remaking the Modern World*. New York: Simon & Schuster, 1998.

INDEX

261

ABOUT THE CONTRIBUTORS

Ibrahim G. Aoudé is professor of ethnic studies at the University of Hawai'i, Manoa, teaching courses on ethnic identity, social movements, political economy of Hawai'i and the Pacific, and Middle Eastern politics. He publishes in two research areas: Hawai'i's political economy and Middle Eastern politics. The author of several articles about Hawai'i's political economy and social movements, he edited three volumes of *Social Process in Hawai'i*. Aoudé is a coeditor and book review editor of *Arab Studies Quarterly*, an international journal about Arab affairs.

Mohammed A. Bamyeh is Hubert Humphrey Professor of International Studies at Macalester College. He has taught at Georgetown University, New York University, SUNY, Buffalo, and the University of Massachusetts. His major publications include *The Ends of Globalization* (2000) and *The Social Origins of Islam* (1999).

Terrell Carver is professor of political theory at the University of Bristol, United Kingdom. He has published extensively on Marx and Engels, most recently *The Postmodern Marx* (1998). He is on the editorial board of the Marx-Engels *Gesamtausgabe*, headquartered in Berlin. With Manfred B. Steger, he coedits the *Globalization* series (Rowman & Littlefield).

Arif Dirlik is Knight Professor of Social Science and professor of history and anthropology at the University of Oregon. Among his most recent book-length publications is *Postmodernity's Histories: The Past as Legacy and Project* (2000).

Kathy E. Ferguson is professor of political science and women's studies at the University of Hawai'i, Manoa, and director of the women's studies program. She

273

and Phyllis Turnbull are the authors of *Oh, Say, Can You See? The Semiotics of the Military in Hawai'i* (1999), and she is writing a book about Emma Goldman.

Mary Hawkesworth is professor of political science and women's studies and senior scholar at the Center for American Women and Politics at Rutgers University. Her teaching and research interests include feminist theory, women and politics, contemporary political philosophy, philosophy of science, and social policy. Most recently she edited *The Encyclopedia of Government and Politics* (2d rev. ed., 2003) and coedited *Gender, Globalization, and Democratization* (2001). Her articles have appeared in the leading journals of feminist scholarship, including *Signs, Hypatia, Women and Politics,* and *Journal of Women's History.*

Fumio Iida is professor of political theory at Kobe University. He is the author of many books and articles comparing liberal traditions in Japan and the West, including "Liberalism and Its Civilizing Moral Effects" and "Liberalism in a Communal Society," which appeared in *Kobe University Law Review.*

Micheline Ishay has authored or edited several books, including *Internationalism and Its Betrayal, The Nationalism Reader, The Human Rights Reader,* and *Human Rights: From Ancient Times to the Era of Globalization.* She is director of the human rights program at the Graduate School of International Studies at the University of Denver, Colorado.

Paul James is currently an editor of *Arena Journal* and professor of globalism and cultural diversity at RMIT, Melbourne, where he is director of the Globalism Institute. He has received a number of awards, including the Japan-Australia Foundation Fellowship, an Australian Research Council Fellowship, and the Crisp Medal by the Australasian Political Studies Association for the best Australian book in the field of political studies. He is author or editor of seven books, including *Nation Formation* (1996), *Work of the Future: Global Perspectives* (1997), and *Tour of Duty: Winning Hearts and Minds in East Timor* (with photographs by Matthew Sleeth, 2002).

Kang Liu is professor of Chinese cultural studies at Duke University. He is the author of several books, including *Bakhtin's Cultural Theory* (1995), *Demonizing China* (1997), *Aesthetics and Marxism* (2000), and *Globalization and Cultural Trends in China* (2003).

Timothy W. Luke is University Distinguished Professor of Political Science at Virginia Tech. His areas of specialization include environmental politics and cultural studies as well as comparative politics, international political economy, and modern critical social and political theory. His most recent books include

274

Museums as Politics: Power Plays at the Exhibition (2002); *Capitalism, Democracy, and Ecology: Departing from Marx* (1999); *The Politics of Cyberspace* (coedited with Chris Toulouse, 1998), and *Ecocritique: Contesting the Politics of Nature, Economy, and Culture* (1997).

Zine Magubane is assistant professor of sociology and African studies at the University of Illinois, Urbana. She is author of *Bringing the Empire Home: Race, Class, and Gender in Britain and Colonial South Africa* (2003) and editor of *Postmodernism, Postcolonialism, and African Studies* (2003).

Eduardo Mendieta is associate professor of philosophy at Stony Brook University. In addition to editing and translating Enrique Dussel's *The Underside of Modernity* (1996), he is the editor of *Beyond Philosophy* (2003); *Latin American Philosophy: Issues, Currents, Debates* (2003); and coeditor of *Thinking from the Underside of History* (2000) and *Identities: Race, Class, Gender, and Nationality* (2003). He is presently writing a manuscript entitled *Global Fragments: Latinamericanisms, Globalizations, and Critical Theory.*

James H. Mittelman is professor in the School of International Service at American University, Washington, D.C. He is the author of, among other books, *The Globalization Syndrome: Transformation and Resistance* (2000). His edited and coedited books include *Globalization: Critical Reflections* (1996) and *Capturing Globalization* (2001).

Mark Rupert is professor of political science at Syracuse University's Maxwell School of Citizenship and Public Affairs, and teaches in the areas of international relations and political economy. His research focuses on the intersection of the U.S. political economy with global power structures. He is the author of *Producing Hegemony: The Politics of Mass Production and American Global Power* (1995), *Ideologies of Globalization: Contending Visions of a New World Order* (2000), and coeditor (with Hazel Smith) of *Historical Materialism and Globalization* (2002).

Leslie Sklair is professor of sociology and director of the doctoral program in sociology at the London School of Economics and Political Science. He was visiting professor in the graduate faculty at the New School in spring 2002. He is author of *The Transnational Capitalist Class* (2001). His *Sociology of the Global System* (2d ed., 1995) has been translated into Japanese, Portuguese, Persian, and Spanish. A new version was published by Oxford University Press in 2002 under the title *Globalization: Capitalism and Its Alternatives.* He is on the executive committee of the Global Studies Association, and on the editorial boards of the journals *Global Networks* and *Review of International Political Economy.*

Alvin Y. So teaches in the division of social science of the Hong Kong University of Science and Technology. Previously he taught at the University of Hawai'i for fourteen years. His research interests are social class and development in Hong Kong, China, and East Asia. His recent books include *Hong Kong's Embattled Democracy* (1999); *Asia's Environmental Movements* (coeditor, 1999); *China's Developmental Miracle* (editor, 2002); and *War and State Terrorism* (coeditor, 2003).

Manfred B. Steger is professor of politics and government at Illinois State University and a research fellow at the Globalization Research Center of the University of Hawai'i, Manoa. His academic fields of expertise include theories and ideologies of globalization, political and social theories of nonviolence, comparative political and social theory, and international politics. His most recent publications include *Globalization: A Very Short Introduction* (2003) and *Globalism: The New Market Ideology* (2002). *Globalism* won the 2003 Michael Harrington Book Award of the Caucus for a New Political Science, an organized section of the American Political Science Association. With Terrell Carver, he coedits the series *Globalization* (Rowman & Littlefield).

Richard Terdiman teaches in the literature and history of consciousness departments at the University of California, Santa Cruz, where he specializes in literary and cultural theory. His published books include *Discourse/Counter-Discourse* (1990) and *Present Past: Modernity and the Memory Crisis* (1993). His book *Body and Story*, on the tension between language and materiality, will soon be in press, and *Taking Time* is in progress.

Phyllis Turnbull is professor emerita of political science at the University of Hawai'i, Manoa, where her work focuses primarily on the discursive and spatial dimensions of postcolonialism and the military. She is also the coauthor of *Oh, Say, Can You See? The Semiotics of the Military in Hawai'i* (1999).

Paul Tiyambe Zeleza is professor of history and African studies at Penn State University. He is the author of scores of essays and more than a dozen books, including most recently *Rethinking Africa's Globalization* and *The Routledge Encyclopedia of Twentieth-Century African History*. He won the 1994 Noma Award for his book *A Modern Economic History of Africa* and the 1998 Special Commendation of the Noma Award for *Manufacturing African Studies and Crises*.